بسم الله الرحمن الرحيم

The DIWAN
of Sidi Muhammad
IBN AL-HABIB

MAY ALLAH BE PLEASED WITH HIM

Revised Edition

TRANSLATED BY
ABDURRAHMAN FITZGERALD
& MOHAMED FOUAD ARESMOUK

The Quilliam Press

NEW AND REVISED EDITION PUBLISHED BY
THE QUILLIAM PRESS LTD.,
14 ST PAUL'S ROAD, CAMBRIDGE CB1 2EF

First Printing by Editorial Qasida 2015

www.quilliampress.com

ISBN PAPERBACK: 978-1-872038-27-8
ISBN HARDBACK: 978-1-872038-28-5

PRINTED IN THE UNITED KINGDOM BY CPI BOOKS

Contents

TRANSLITERATION KEY
viii

BIOGRAPHY OF THE SHAYKH
1

THE SHAYKH'S INTRODUCTION
41

THE WIRD OF MUḤAMMAD IBN AL ḤABĪB
51

THE QAṢĀ'ID

1. Yaqūlu ʿubaydu-Llāhi • *The Meanings and Merits of the Noble Wird*
89

2. Fa in Shi•ta • *If You Would Ascend the Path of Lovers*
99

3. Sharibnā mina-l-anwār • *We Drank From the Lights*
116

4. Saqānī Ḥibbī • *My Beloved Gave Me to Drink*
127

5. Yaqūlu ʿabdu Rabbihi • *The Tenets of Unity*
135

6. Yaqūlu afqarul-Warā • *Burāq of the Way*
143

7. Al-Ḥamdu li-Llāhi wa Ṣalla-Llāhu • *The Extraordinary Gifts of the Path*
156

8. Tajarrad ʿani-l-Aghyāri • *On the Merits of the Supreme Name*
171

9. Laka-l-Ḥamd • *Praise*
177

10. A Yā man Yurid Qurban • *Oh You Who Wish for Nearness*
183

11. Tafakkar Jamīla-ṣ-Ṣunʿi • *Reflection*
191

12. Qad Kasānā Dhikru-l-Ḥabībi • *The Robe of Nearness*
196

13. Naḥnu fī Rawḍāti • *In the Meadow of the Messenger*
202

14. Qad Badā • *My Beloved's Face Appeared*
206

15. Muḥammadun Mansha•u • *Muḥammad is the Source of Light and Shade*
210

16. Astaghfiru-Llāh • *Asking Forgiveness*
219

17. Al-Wahm • *Illusion*
225

18. Yā man Yurid • *Seeing the Divine*
228

19. Sa•altu Qalbī • *I asked my Heart*
233

20. Salāmun ʿala-l-Ikhwāni • *Counsel*
237

21. Yā Ṭāliba-l-Fanā' fi-Llāh • *O You Who Seek Effacement in Allah*
241

22. Rūḥī Tuḥaddithunī • *My Spirit Speaks to Me*
247

23. A Shamsun Badā • *Unveiling*
250

24. Fa in Shi•ta Taṭhīran • *Purification*
254

25. Tazawwad Akhī li-l-Mawt • *Make Provision, My Brother, For Death*
256

26. Ahīmu waḥdī • *I am Alone, Ecstatically in Love*
259

27. Kam Laka Min • *How Many Blessings*
261

28. Salāmun ʿalā Ahli-l-Ḥimā • *Greetings to the People of Protection*
263

SUPPLICATIONS AFTER THE FIVE PRAYERS
266

DHIKR OF FAJR
277

AL-ṢALĀT AL-MASHĪSHIYYA
278

Transliteration Key

The transliteration convention used throughout this book represents the Arabic script as follows:

Consonants:

ء	•		د	d		ض	ḍ		ك	k
ب	b		ذ	dh		ط	ṭ		ل	l
ت	t		ر	r		ظ	ẓ		م	m
ث	th		ز	z		ع	ʿ		ن	n
ج	j		س	s		غ	gh		هـ	h
ح	ḥ		ش	sh		ف	f		و	w
خ	kh		ص	ṣ		ق	q		ي	y

Short vowels:	ـَ	a	ـُ	u	ـِ	i
Long vowels:	ـَا	ā	ـُو	ū	ـِي	ī
Diphthongs:	ـَو	aw	ـَي	ay		

The symbol • is also used to indicate a syllable break where the transcribed letters might be misread, as in *aṣ•ḥab,* so that the *sh* is not read as in the English word "ship"

ﷺ An invocation of God's blessings and peace upon the Prophet Muḥammad: "May God's blessings and peace be upon him."

ؓ "May God be pleased with him," often said after the names of saintly people.
ؑ "Upon whom be peace", often said after a Prophet's name other than Muḥammad.

An underlined letter or group of letters e.g. a or la indicates a *madda* or extended vowel.

In the Name of Allah, Merciful and Compassionate.
May Allah send blessings and salutations
to our master Muḥammad and to his Family and Companions.

A Biography of Sīdī Muḥammad ibn al-Ḥabīb
May Allah sanctify his soul[1]

PRAISE BE TO ALLAH, the Generous, the Gracious, the Helper, and may blessings and salutations be upon our protector Muḥammad, the ornament of existence and splendor of the worlds, and upon the good and pure people of his family, and his blessed companions, and may Allah's contentment be upon those who love them and follow in their footsteps with excellence and virtue until the Day of Resurrection.

TO PROCEED:

This brief biography... is meant to be a treasury for lovers to aid them in knowing about the life of someone by whose brilliant light souls were illuminated and by the purity of whose inner mysteries hearts were guided, the spiritual axis and unique Muḥammadan entity (*al-fard al-Muḥammadī*), our teacher and model, Sīdī Muḥammad ibn al-Ḥabīb al-Amghārī al-Idrīsī al-Ḥasanī, may Allah sanctify his soul and benefit us by his blessing... [In setting this down in writing] we turn to Allah, the Compassionate Giver of all gifts, and ask that He make it a benefit for anyone who reads it, or hears it, or publishes it, or learns from its teachings, or corrects any unintentional errors it may contain, and that He make of it a blessed provision and pure and goodly treasury for the journey of anyone who reads it with respect and love for this saintly person...

ORIGIN AND UPBRINGING

He is the realized scholar and teacher, the isthmus between the revealed law and spiritual truth, the unique Muḥammadan entity, the nurturer of hearts and souls, the guide to the path of happiness and salvation, Shaykh Sīdī Muḥammad ibn Sīdī ibn al-Ḥabīb, ibn Sīdī al-Ṣiddīq, al-Amghārī al-Idrīsī al-Ḥasanī, born and raised in Fes, resident of Meknes, Mālikī in his rite, and Shādhilī in his path.

His lineage is through the saint, Mūlay Abū ʿAbdallāh, Sīdī Muḥammad bin ʿAbdallāh al-Sharīf al-Ḥasanī al-Idrīsī, who is known as *Amghār*, from the Amghārī of ʿAyn al-Fiṭr, referred to in the Berber tongue as *Tīṭnafiṭr* and known today as *Tīṭ*. The Amghārī are Idrīsī nobles (*shurafā'*) descended from Mūlay ʿAbdallāh, son of Mūlay Idrīs, may Allah be pleased with them both.

Amghār is a Berber word meaning "master" or "elder" (*shaykh*), first used as a title of honor to refer to their forefather, the perfect spiritual axis and gnostic, Abū ʿAbdallāh, Sīdī Muḥammad Amghār buried in Zemmour, who is also called *Amghāra l-Kabīr* or *al-Akbar* ("the great shaykh" or "the greatest shaykh").

The Amghār is a blessed and noble family which has produced scholars and imams, and has played a major role in the spreading of knowledge and piety in Morocco. Ibn Qunfudh al-Qustanṭīnī says of them in his book, *Uns al-Faqīr*, "This is the largest lineage in Morocco in terms of the number of saintly people who have arisen from it. They pass (sanctity) down from generation to generation the way ordinary people pass down wealth."

One of the forefathers of Sīdī Muḥammad ibn al-Ḥabīb migrated to Tafilalt, to the citadel (*qaṣr*) of the sons of Sīdī Yūsuf of Rīsānī, then his father, Sīdī al-Ḥabīb ibn Sīdī al-Ṣiddīq, may Allah be merciful to him, traveled from there to Fes where he took up residence.

It was in the shelter of this goodly, noble, and blessed family that our Shaykh... was born in 1288/1871 according to the most reliable sources we have and was nurtured by his parents in refined character and virtue, surrounded by their care and kindness, he being their only child.

HIS MEMORIZATION OF THE NOBLE QUR'ĀN

In 1876, at the age of around five, he was placed in the Quranic school (*al-kuttāb*) of the Abū al-Ru'ūs Bridge in the Sharābilīn Quarter of Fes, where he memorized a considerable portion of Allah's Book in a very short time, first with the saintly and pious *faqīh*, Sīdī Ibn al-Hāshimī al-Sanhājī and later, in the Qur'ān school of Qaṣbat al-Nawwār, with the *faqīh* Sīdī Aḥmad al-Filālī (may Allah be merciful to them both).

(The Shaykh) mentions in his autobiography that once, one of Allah's saints visited that school and began speaking to Sīdī Aḥmad, and then he looked at the students with the eye of prescience and what Allah Most High inspired in him, and saw what each of them was to become in life, saying to them, "This one will be a butcher, and this one will be a tailor, and this one... ," seeing what each would become in the future, until he came to our Shaykh ﷺ and said, "And this one is going to be a scholar, one who practices what he knows, pious, an invoker (of Allah), a shaykh and a guide." And what that saint saw came to pass, may all praise be to Allah.

He also had as a teacher in Quranic memorization, Sīdī Muḥammad ibn al-Ḥasan, a great-grandson of the exalted saint, Sīdī ʿAbd al-Salām ibn Mashīsh ﷺ. This teacher worked as a tailor and our Shaykh (still a boy) would help him in his tailoring by holding the threads of braided trim as he sewed it onto clothes. Then he would return to his *lūḥa* where the Quranic verses he was memorizing were written.

It has been related that when (our Shaykh's) father learned that his son was helping in tailor work, he became quite angry and went to the shop thinking that his son was working instead of memorizing, but the teacher received him with kindness and respect and assured him that his son Muḥammad was going to complete his memorization in a very short time, Allah willing. He also said that his son was destined to have, by Allah's will, an important role, and that there would come forth, by his hand, many saintly people and notable scholars. Upon hearing this, Sīdī Muḥammad's father's anger subsided, his heart was calmed, and he left the school praising Allah Most High for the blessing of a righteous son. Indeed, by the time two years had passed, Sīdī Muḥammad ibn al-Ḥabīb had completed the third cycle of memorization[2] and then began helping his master in the teaching of children.

Following this, his master asked him, as was the usual practice, to begin studying and memorizing "the mothers of the books"(*ummahāt al-kutub*), the foundational texts in grammar, *fiqh*, morphology, etc., in which he became completly immersed, both memorizing and understanding them, and thus did he complete his basic religious education, until the day when his teacher called for him and said, "May Allah bless you my son, you have mastered what I had hoped to impart to you and we have completed what I can give you. You now need to turn towards the Qarawīyīn to continue your studies, and may Allah help you."

HIS STUDIES AT THE QARAWĪYĪN

Our Shaykh, may Allah sanctify his soul, was accepted in to the Qarawīyīn University and began to drink deeply from oceans of knowledge, frequenting the greatest of scholars, people known for their achievements, precision, and piety. Concerning them, he wrote:

> I studied the formal religious sciences with Shaykh al-Islām Aḥmad ibn al-Khayyāṭ, with the affirmed teacher Sīdī Abū Bakr Bennānī, with the *faqīh* ʿAbd al-Salām al-Hawārī, with the head of the council of scholars and realized sufi, Sīdī Aḥmad ibn al-Jaylālī, with the blessed noble Sīdī Muḥammad al-Qādirī, with the eloquent scholar, Sīdī Khalīl al-Tilimsānī, with the blessed noble Muḥammad ibn Jaʿfar al-Kettānī, with Sīdī al-Tuhāmī Gannūn, with the head of the *shurafā'* and specialist in the science of *ḥadīth*, Mūlay ʿAbdallāh al-Badrānī, and with the safeguard of his students' welfare, Sīdī Muḥammad al-Īrārī...[3]

When he had completed his studies at the Qarawīyīn, Sīdī Muḥammad ibn al-Ḥabīb was given by each of his shaykhs written permission (*ijāza*) to teach the knowledge and skills (he had acquired), and thus became qualified as a teacher in his own right at the Qarawīyīn.

HIS TEACHING AT THE QARAWĪYĪN UNIVERSITY

Our Shaykh, may Allah sanctify his soul, first volunteered to give lessons at the Qaṣbat al-Nawwār in Fes, and then at the Qarawīyīn, where he had a well-known chair. His lessons were divided between *fiqh* and *tafsīr*, and among his favorite books from which to teach about the virtues and perfections of Muḥammad ﷺ was Qāḍī ʿAyyāḍ's *al-Shifāʾ*.

It is related concerning him at this time that he would get to the Qarawīyīn each morning riding a mule and that on the way there, he would recite five *aḥzāb* of the Qurʾān.[4] Then, after completing his work there, he would ride back home, and complete the recitation of another five *aḥzāb*. In this way, he would complete a recitation of the entire Qurʾān every six days.

In the mosque of Qaṣbat al-Nawwār he would teach *al-Murshid al-Muʿīn* of Sīdī ibn ʿĀshir, *al-Mukhtaṣar* of Sīdī Khalīl, *al-Muwaṭṭaʾ* of Imām Mālik, the Book of *ʿAqīda* by al-Sunūsī, as well as lessons on *tafsīr*.

Among those who attended his lessons were such people as (the independence leader) ʿAlāl al-Fāsī, the leader Muḥammad al-Mukhtār al-Sūsī, the *faqīh* Sīdī Muḥammad al-Ghāzī, the judge, Sīdī Muḥammad ibn Qaddūr, the *faqīh* Sīdī ʿAbd al-Qādir al-Ṣiqillī, the judge, Mūlay Idrīs ibn ʿAlī, the *faqīh*, Sīdī al-Ṣiddīq al-Fāsī, Ibn ʿAbdallāh, head of the Madrasa al-Makhfīya, and others who benefitted from him and learned through him, may Allah be merciful to them all.[5]

HIS STRIVING IN THE WAY OF ALLAH

Morocco, like other Muslim countries, suffered from the woes of oppressive colonialism and the people of that land had no other alternative than to mount both political and military resistance. In this struggle, the scholars and saints of Morocco played a role by encouraging the people towards *jihad*, and among them was our Shaykh ﵁ who in the course of giving lessons in the Qarawīyīn would seek to lift people's aspirations and call them to resistance.

So that his actions might match his words, he himself resolved to join the ranks of the *mujāhidīn*, except that he was not skilled in riding a horse, nor in the techniques of battle, and so he bought a horse and arms, and paid a cavalry man to teach him how to ride, how to fight in a battle, and how to swim. When he completed that training, he bade farewell to his mother, students, and friends, and became enlisted as a fighter in the people's army of resistance that had been raised by the Darqāwī zāwiya in the Middle Atlas.

His absence grew so long that it was rumored in the city of Fes that he had been martyred, and his mother became grief-stricken at the thought of his loss since he was her only child. But eventually, he returned safe and sound after having experienced the field of battle. He made his best efforts with his brother combatants, having met such great men as Sīdī ʿAlī Muhāwash, Shaykh of the Amhīwāsh zāwiya, who was a follower of the Darqāwī Ṭarīqa and who exercised spiritual authority over the tribes of the Atlas to the borders of Tafilalt. Upon his return, happiness returned to his mother and to all the people of Fes.[6]

MEETING WITH THE SPIRITUAL MASTERS OF HIS AGE, MAY ALLAH BE PLEASED WITH THEM

To mention all the scholars and gnostics that our Shaykh met during his life would far surpass the pages allotted to this brief biography, for his life was long and all of it full of visits and meetings for Allah. So here we will mention only a few of those he met for the sake of blessing:

SĪDĪ MĀ' AL-ʿAYNAYN

Our master met Sīdī Mā' al-ʿAynayn[7] in Fes, and there came to be a great love between them. Shaykh Mā' al-ʿAynayn authorized him (to teach) all the books he had written in *ḥadīth*, *fiqh*, and Sufism, and (to recite) all his litanies. Sīdī Muḥammad ibn al-Ḥabīb said, "A great breeze of the spirit (*nafḥat*)[8] came to me from Shaykh Mā' al-ʿAynayn. He gave me permission in all his *aḥzāb*,[9] invocations of Allah's Names, and litanies, both to recite and to transmit to whosoever sought them."[10] And when Sīdī Mā' al-ʿAynayn passed away in 1910, our Shaykh 🕮 frequented his successor and heir, Sīdī Aḥmad al-Shams for ten years, and there was also a powerful love between them. Sīdī Muḥammad ibn al-Ḥabīb 🕮 said, "I met his successor and the heir to his spiritual secret, Sīdī Aḥmad al-Shams, and there was a great connection between our hearts. He asked me to assist him in commented readings (sard) and I helped him with that for about ten years until he migrated to al-Madīnat al-Munawwara where he passed away."[11]

SĪDĪ ʿABD AL-RAḤMĀN BIN ṢĀLIḤ 🕮

Our Shaykh met the gnostic Sīdī ʿAbd al-Raḥmān bin Ṣāliḥ, and they would speak together concerning the realization of servanthood (al-ʿubūdiyya) for Allah Most High. This Shaykh, may Allah sanctify his soul, would often say, "Spiritual opening comes quickest to those sincere fuqarāʾ who realize in themselves the attributes of servanthood before Allah: ignorance, inability, weakness and neediness. For whoever realizes his ignorance, Allah affirms with beneficial knowledge, and so forth for the other (three) qualities. In short, whoever realizes his own attributes, Allah strengthens with His Attributes."[12]

SĪDĪ MUḤAMMAD AL-GHIYĀTHĪ 🕮

Since his youngest days, our Shaykh 🕮 was beloved among the practicing scholars and goodly friends of Allah, and among those from whose gaze and supplication he benefited was (this saint). He said:

> Among Allah's blessings[13] to me was that I was able to meet a great many gnostics. From some of them, I benefitted by putting into practice what they advised and by imitating them, from some, I learned and recited their litanies, and from some I benefitted just from their looking upon me and making supplication for me. Shaykh Sīdī Muḥammad al-Ghiyāthī was an example of these latter. I met him through an ʿAlawī sharīf named Mūlay ʿAlī who used to give the call to prayer (adhān) in the Qaṣbat al-Nawwār neighborhood

(in Fes), who loved me greatly for the sake of Allah, and who always urged me to visit (Sīdī al-Ghiyāthī). Finally, one day I went there with him, and when we got to the door of his house (Mūlay ʿAlī) knocked lightly and (Sīdī Muḥammad himself) came to the door, opened it, and brought Mūlay ʿAlī alone into his house. Then the *sharīf* told him about me and that I had come to visit him only for the love of Allah, and upon hearing this, he brought me into his house as well. I entered and greeted him and kissed his hand and he began looking at me with such intensity that I had to lower my gaze in humility and awe of his majesty. Then he began asking me about what I was doing, and I told him that I had been busy learning the Qur'ān and that now, praise be to Allah, I had memorized it and was ready to undertake the study of the religious sciences. He made a prayer for my well-being and authorized me to recite the formula *Ḥasbuna-l-Lāhu wa niʿma-l-wakīl*[14] a certain number of times. This saint ﷺ, was one of those who rarely left their houses. He passed away, (may Allah be merciful to him), in 1318 (1900).

SĪDĪ ʿABDALLĀH AL-BADRĀWĪ ﷺ

Our Shaykh met this pious and saintly man because the latter came to have a great interest in him and would always ask concerning him. He used to gesture towards Sīdī al-Ṣiddīq, ﷺ, our Shaykh's uncle, and say to him that his nephew was destined to have a great role to play. Concerning this meeting, our Shaykh wrote:

> And among Allah's blessings to me was my meeting with the noble *faqīh*, scholar and teacher, *ḥāfiẓ*, and shaykh of the assembly in this day, our master ʿAbdallāh al-Badrāwī. The way I came to meet him was that my uncle, Sīdī Ṣiddīq, was among those who regularly sat with him and served him, and the Shaykh would ask after me, saying, "Always watch over your nephew, Sīdī Muḥammad ibn al-Ḥabīb, for he is going to be someone with a great role to play." My uncle then told me I should visit Shaykh al-Badrāwī and so I went to where the Shaykh lived in Derb Biḥḥāj, in the

> Ṭalaʿa neighborhood of Fes. The moment he saw me, he began welcoming me again and again, and then he sat me next to him, and I kissed his hand. He asked me about the studies I was doing at the Qarawīyin, and when I told him, he was very happy with me, made a supplication for my well-being, and invited me to the lessons he was giving in the mornings in which he was teaching the summary of Shaykh al-Khalīl ﵀. This I did and was granted a great faculty for memorization by his blessing. He would recite one *sūra*, and present the various commentaries upon it in depth, without omitting the least detail, and I would memorize it, understand it, and then be able to present it perfectly. Then he asked me to do a reading with him, so we read al-Kharshī and followed it by the *Ḥāshiya* of al-Ṣaʿīdī, then al-Zarqānī's additions, then the *Ḥāshiya* of al-Bennānī, then all of al-Ruhūnī, and each point in it he would explain in detail, with rules, sources, texts, and jurisprudence.

SĪDĪ MUḤAMMAD LAḤLŪ ﵀

Sīdī Muḥammad ibn al-Ḥabīb ﵀ came to love the books of the great sufi masters such as *Iḥyāʾ ʿulūm al-Dīn* (by al-Ghazālī), *al-Ḥikam al-ʿAṭāʾiyya*, *Ṭabaqāt al-Ṣūfiyya* by Sīdī ʿAbd al-Wahhāb al-Shaʿrānī, *al-Waṣāyā* by Sīdī Muḥyiddīn Ibn ʿArabī, and others. His aspiration was always towards Allah Most High and his prayer to Allah was always to bring him into contact with someone who would guide him. He said ﵀:

> I turned to the study of the religious sciences and Allah Most High helped me in that so that I mastered in a short time a great deal of formal knowledge, while in my free time, I would read books of admonition which spoke of the remembrance of death and its calamities. The fear of death, in fact, became so dominant in my heart that I slept only a little of the night and turned totally towards preparing myself for it. Each night I would offer thirteen *rakaʿāt* of superogatory Prayers in which I would recite five *aḥzāb* of the Qurʾān in a measured and reflective style. Upon finishing that, I would turn

> to invocation and supplication and humbling myself before Allah until the time of the dawn Prayer (*ṣubḥ*). For that, I would usually go to the mosque, but sometimes offer it (in my house) with my family, and then occupy myself with the things I had to do.

Thus were his moments (may Allah sanctify his soul) filled with the remembrance of Allah and disciplining his soul in hopes that Allah would favor him with someone who would guide him to the direct knowledge (*maʿrifa*) of his Lord. Allah inspired him to search for someone from among the people of the heart and of gnosis who would take him by the hand and direct his heart to the Station of Excellence (*al-iḥsān*), which comprises both vigilance towards Allah as well as a permanent consciousness of Him. This is what is conveyed in the *ḥadīth Jibrīl*, which is in the collections of both al-Bukhārī and Muslim, when (the angel Gabriel) asked the Prophet ﷺ the meaning of excellence (*al-iḥsān*), and he answered, 'It is that you worship Allah as if you saw Him, and if you do not see Him, yet He sees you.' But without a doubt, no one who yearns to experience (the Divine) will reach this Station except with the help of a guide who knows Allah with direct and experiential knowledge, this being the usual case with the sufis (may Allah be pleased with them).

The first person from whom our Shaykh benefitted at the beginning of the path was the master and gnostic, effaced in the love of the saints, Muḥammad Laḥlū ؓ, who was at that time the head of the tanners' guild of Fes. In the Shaykh's own words:

> The study of formal religious knowledge was beginning to weigh heavily upon me, while worship and devotion to Allah were becoming increasingly easier, and so I asked myself, 'If the purpose of (exoteric) knowledge is practice, and I have already learned the amount of knowledge obligatory upon me (to accomplish that), of what use is it for me to learn more? I am not going to be a *muftī*[15] or a judge,' and a great state of confusion came upon me (about this) such that I turned in my need to Allah and asked Him to send me someone who could take me by the hand and guide me to the right path.

It was in the midst of this period of confusion that one day I was passing through Zuqāq al-Ḥajar in Fes, when my vision happened to fall upon this man (Sīdī Muḥammad Laḥlū) in the road, and I saw upon him a visible light that extended from above his head heavenward. I thought that everyone else could see this light as well, but as I followed him, I saw that no one else perceived it. Then I knew that Allah Most High had allowed me to glimpse (that saint's) special nature so that I could benefit from him, even while He had veiled it from other people, and my heart became set on meeting him.

As it turned out, my uncle, Sīdī al-Ṣiddīq, was a dear brother in Allah to (this person). So I went to him and told him about what Allah had allowed me to see. And he said, "That is a man to whom Allah has granted a spiritual opening, someone who has spent time in the company of the elect of the Way, and who has served them with fervor and sincerity, intention and love, and then attained great goodness and light."

I asked my uncle to introduce me to him so that I could ask him about my state and the confusion I was in. My uncle helped me in this and arranged a meeting for noon the next day at his house in the neighborhood of Sīdī ʿAbd al-Qādir al-Fāsī. When the appointed time came, I went to the house, but did not find the man. I asked my uncle, "Where is he?" and he answered, "He will be here without fail." Then my uncle went out to look for him and found that he had already arrived at the door. When he entered, (I heard him) say to my uncle, "O Sīdī Ṣiddīq, where shall we sit? In the lower part of the house or the upper?" My uncle said, "Let's sit in the upper part," and Sīdī Laḥlū responded, "To get to the upper part there has to be a ladder. Anyone who wants to ascend without a ladder will never succeed!"

This was the first spiritual allusion I heard from him and I knew (from it) that I was involved in an ascent that had to be made correctly, one step at a time, and with the help of someone who had been granted a spiritual opening and light. When he reached

> the room where I was awaiting him, I stood with great courtesy and respect and greeted him, then he sat down near me and turned to me with great attention.

Our master remained a disciple of Sīdī Muḥammad Laḥlū for five years and would sit with him along with five other brethren for the remembrance of Allah[16] and spiritual instruction, and he would always encourage them to reflect deeply upon this verse: *The Day when neither wealth nor children will benefit; only the one who comes to Allah with a heart that is pure* (26:88).

It was also Sīdī Muḥammad Laḥlū's character to revere Allah's saints, to seek excuses for the faults of Allah's servants, to respect scholars and teachers, to respect anyone in whose hand Allah had entrusted the affairs of the Muslims, and to pray for that one's well-being. Our Shaykh benefitted greatly from these luminous states, his character became molded by them, and it was to them that he would beckon and train his own disciples.

RECEIVING THE ṬARĪQA FROM SĪDĪ AL-ᶜARABĪ IBN ᶜABDALLĀH BĀBĀ AL-HAWĀRĪ ﷺ

Upon the passing away of Sīdī Muḥammad al-ᶜArabī al-Madaghrī[17] ﷺ, a number of his disciples whom he had left almost in the position of shaykhs in their own right came forward to give spiritual instruction, praise be to Allah. Among them was Shaykh al-Hawārī's son-in-law, Mūlay al-Ḥasan, and also Sīdī al-Ṣiddīq al-Qaddārī in Tafilalt, Sīdī al-ᶜArabī ibn ᶜAbdallāh Bābā al-Hawārī, Sīdi ᶜAbd al-Mālik, Mūlay Aḥmad al-Sabᶜī, Sīdī Muḥammad bin Aḥmad in Sefrou, Sīdī Brīk in Qaṣbat al-Nawwār, Sīdī Muḥammad al-Ḥājj in the region of Zemmour, Sīdī al-Ṭayyib bin ᶜAbd al-Mālik, Sīdī ᶜAlī al-Makkī Lamhawshī, and Sīdī Muḥammad bin ᶜAlī in Marrakesh.

Mūlay al-Saᶜīd al-Belghīthī ﷺ had agreed with one of the *shurafā'* to travel for the Ḥajj, thereby removing themselves from the disagreement that had arisen among the people of Akka,[18] some of whom did not accept Sīdī al-ᶜArabī al-Hawārī as shaykh. So they sought out Sīdī Muḥammad bin Aḥmad in Sefrou... in hopes that he might intervene for them before the Minister B'ḥmad to grant them tickets on a boat to travel to the Holy Lands for the Ḥajj. When they reached Sīdī Muḥammad, he received them with welcome and then they explained to him what they were seeking. He said ﷺ… "Personally, I don't see you going on Ḥajj, but if you have some money (for it), give it to me to spend on the *fuqarā'*."[19]

That night, Mūlay al-Saʿīd al-Belghīthī saw in a dream that it was as if a breast had come forth from Sīdī Muḥammad bin Aḥmad and he began nursing from it sweet milk. When he woke up and recounted the dream to his companion the *sharīf*, they were both convinced that Sīdī Muḥammad was the authorized (*al-ma'dhūn*) shaykh and that they should renew their affiliation through him. So after the *fajr* prayer, they went to him, fervently kissed his hand, and asked him to take them by their hands to Allah.

He said, "Glory be to Allah, you people of Akka! You're like someone who sees a *gharrāb*,[20] and then leaves him standing there to go to someone who has neither a water bag nor a bell, and says to him, 'Give me some water!' There's the Shaykh, Sīdī al-ʿArabī ibn ʿAbdallāh Bābā al-Hawārī, right near you, saying, 'Here's some water for free! Here's some water for free!'[21] Go to him and renew your pledge with him, and I am your guarantor that tomorrow on the Day of Resurrection, if you are asked, 'Why did you take his hand?' say, 'That's what Muḥammad bin Aḥmad told us to do,' and I will bear witness for you to that before Allah.'"

That evening he said to the two of them, "Sīdī al-Hāshimī, Sīdī al-ʿArabī al-Hawārī's brother who is with us in Sefrou, is intending to travel to the Sahara." So Mūlay al-Saʿīd took that opportunity to send a letter to Sīdī al-Hawārī, saying he would like to renew his allegiance to the Ṭarīqa by his hand, and he gave it to Sīdī al-Hāshimī along with a donation for the zāwiya.[22] A week later, Sīdī al-Hāshimī returned to Sefrou with a letter from Sīdī al-Hawārī in which he said, after the *basmalah* and praise, "Your letter has reached me along with your donation and your request for permission. Certainly you merit having it. I am authorizing you in the recitation (of the *wird*) as we used to recite it with Shaykh Sīdī Muḥammad al-ʿArabī al-Madaghrī, may Allah be merciful to him, and I am authorizing you as well to transmit it to whosoever asks for it, but not to anyone who does not ask for it and persists in asking, for it is more precious to me than the pupils of my eyes."

And so it was that Mūlay al-Saʿīd al-Belghīthī renewed his allegiance through Sīdī al-ʿArabī bin ʿAbdallāh al-Hawārī and also became authorized (*ma'dhūn*) himself to transmit it to whosoever sought it in accordance with its conditions.

By the time the Ḥajj season was drawing near, the minister B'ḥmad had passed away, and so Mūlay Saʿīd and his friend were unable to go, exactly as Sīdī Muḥammad bin Aḥmad had foreseen concerning them. Instead, he went to Fes and his friend, the *sharīf*, returned to the Sahara.

One day, in Fes, Mūlay al-Saʿīd went to the Qarawīyīn Mosque and found Muḥammad Laḥlū ﵁ with a group of *fuqarā'* – among whom was Sīdī Muḥammad ibn al-Ḥabīb ﵁, who was the youngest of them – invoking Allah, and Mūlay al-Saʿīd began sitting with them regularly. They would ask him about the life of Shaykh al-Madaghrī and his states, and (among the things) he told them was that he had been one of Shaykh's scribes and his companion for many years. So they saw goodness in him and wished to take allegiance (to the Ṭarīqa) through him.

Before meeting Mūlay al-Saʿīd, every time Sīdī Muḥammad Laḥlū had wanted to take allegiance with someone, one of his masters would appear to him in a dream vision and keep him from doing so. But when he met Mūlay al-Saʿīd and heard him speak, his state was moved and his yearning strengthened. Mūlay al-Saʿīd ﵁ said, concerning his giving allegiance to Sīdī Laḥlū:

> One day after the ʿ*aṣr* prayer, as I was sitting on the roof of the zāwiya in Fes, I heard a voice approaching and it was Sīdī Muḥammad Laḥlū. He greeted me and said, "I want the *wird*." I said to him, "There are plenty of shaykhs out there! Go to them and take it from them. Go to Sīdī Muḥammad ibn Aḥmad in

Sefrou and ask him, or Sīdī Brīk in the Qaṣbat al-Nawwār, or Sīdī Muḥammad al-Hāj in Zemmour.' And hearing this, he left.

After the *maghrib* prayer, I told the *fuqarā'* about what had happened between me and Sīdī Laḥlū and they said, "By Allah, O Sīdī, nothing has kept us from asking you for the *wird* except our respect for (Sīdī Laḥlū)."

I said to them, "Shaykh al-ʿArabī bin ʿAbdallāh al-Hawārī🕮 directed me never to impart the *wird* to anyone unless he asked for it with persistence. If Sīdī Laḥlū is sincere in what he is seeking, he will come back and ask me again…"

The next day, at the same time and in the same place, Sīdī Laḥlū returned in haste and said to me, "Resolve is strong!" I answered him as I had done the day before, and again he said, "Resolve is strong! You say to me, 'Go to Sefrou, go to Zemmour.' But who can guarantee that if I leave you now, death will not overtake me?" When I heard these words from him, I knew he was sincere, and so I recited with him the beginning of the *wird* and gave him permission to (recite it regularly).

Afterwards, he invited me to eat dinner at his house, and when I came in, he said to some friends who were already sitting there (among whom was Sīdī Muḥammad ibn al-Ḥabīb), "I want to let you know that I have taken the *wird* of Sīdī al-ʿArabī ibn ʿAbdallāh al-Hawārī.[23] I am telling you this so that you do not say that I have betrayed you."They answered, "O Sīdī, (what you have done) is what we have all been hoping for, and nothing has held us back from taking allegiance with Mūlay al-Saʿīd except our respect for you." Then all of them took the *wird* from me (that night) in Sīdī Muḥammad's house.

In the morning, Sīdī Muḥammad came to me and (told me about a dream he had had in which he had seen Shaykh al-Hawārī) and described him to me as precisely as if I were looking at him.[24] I said to him, "And what did you see? What did he say?" And he answered, "I saw that it was as if I had a daughter I had given to him," and then I asked him, "And how does she act with you, Sīdī?"

And he answered, "I found her refined and well-mannered, and when she got bit arrogant, I said to her 'Allah is greater (*Allāh akbar*) and you are very small!'"[25]

When I heard this blessed dream, I said to him, "O Sīdī Muḥammad! That is your own soul which you have presented to Shaykh al-Hawārī and may praise be to Allah that he found it refined and well-mannered."[26]

RENEWING HIS ALLEGIANCE WITH SĪDĪ MUḤAMMAD BIN ʿALĪ 🕮

Our Shaykh continued with fervor and effort in the Darqāwī Ṭarīqa until the time when there appeared in Marrakesh the gnostic Sīdī Muḥammad bin ʿAlī 🕮,[27] and he renewed his allegiance through him and followed his blessed way. He said, recalling this:

When (Sīdī Muḥammad bin ʿAlī) came forward (as shaykh), I wrote him a letter about renewing my allegiance through him after having previously taken the Ṭarīqa through Sīdī al-ʿArabī al-Hawārī,[28] and he wrote me back 🕮 asking me to come to him. So following what he said, I travelled to Marrakesh, and when I entered the zāwiya, he became extremely happy and joyful and said to me, "When you came to me, the whole order came to me!"

Then Sīdī Muḥammad bin ʿAlī gave our Shaykh good tidings of what would come to pass by way of him, saying, "For us, your place in this order is like the place of Ibn ʿAṭāʾAllāh in the Shādhiliyya order. Just as Allah gave new life to the Shādhiliyya through Ibn ʿAṭāʾAllāh, He will give new life to this blessed Ṭarīqa through you, Allah willing."

Our Shaykh remained in the zāwiya of Sīdī Muḥammad bin ʿAlī 🕮 for four years. In the beginning of his stay, whenever food was served to the *fuqarāʾ*, he would take the piece of meat that was before him,[29] break it up, and give it to the others. Sīdī Muḥammad bin ʿAlī watched him do this a number of times, without our Shaykh noticing, and finally, after four days, he called to him and asked, "Why are you giving your whole portion of the meat to the others? Why don't you eat some yourself?" He answered him, "O Sīdī, every time I eat, I sense my lower self wanting to take the biggest piece of meat, and so to oppose its cravings, I don't give it any at all!" Hearing this, Shaykh bin ʿAlī was delighted and said to him, "You have taken it all, my son! You have taken it all!"

HIS APPEARANCE AS A SPIRITUAL MASTER AND HIS CALLING TO THE SUFIC PATH

When Sīdī Muḥammad bin ʿAlī found in our Shaykh the traits of knowledge and piety, he asked him to start giving small talks to the *fuqarā'* about the fundamentals of the religion, and this he did by reading and explaining to them (first) *al-Murshid al-Muʿīn* and then a book on sufism by Sīdī Aḥmad al-Badawī[30] ☙ called *al-Munājāt al-Kubrā*.[31] About this latter work, our Shaykh said:

> This book contains all a seeker needs to reach the Station of Excellence (*maqām al-iḥsān*). Among the things the author ☙ says is that each one of Allah's saints enters through the door which Allah opens for him and I have entered through the door of venerating Allah's creation, and my evidence for this are His words, *Whosoever honors Allah's sacred things, that is good for him in the sight of his Lord* (22:30). So first there arose in my heart veneration for the people of the House, such that whenever I saw one of the *shurafā'*,[32] a sense of veneration would arise in my heart as if I were seeing the Prophet ☙ himself. And then whenever I saw one of the scholars, veneration for him would arise in my heart and his light, which was kindled from the light of the Prophet ☙, would envelop me. Then I came to honor all Muslims inasmuch as they are the humble servants of Allah Most High, and I would see myself as the lowest of them all. And then I came to honor all creation inasmuch as it is something known (*maʿlūm*) in the divine knowledge, the effect of Allah's will, the manifestation of His Power, and the perfect artistry of His Wisdom, may He be glorified and exalted.

Our Master travelled with his teacher, Sīdī Muḥammad bin ʿAlī (may Allah be well pleased with them both), on a number of journeys. He writes about the last of these:

> I continued to travel (with my Shaykh) for about two months and when we got to the land of the Sarāghnā tribe,[33] they welcomed the Shaykh and the brethren with joy. Then he instructed me to return to Fes as his representative (*nā'ib*) in guiding people to Allah, he transmitted to me the Unique Name, and instructed me to be abundant in its invocation following the method that had been transmitted to him by his master, Sīdī Aḥmad al-Badawī. This method consists in (invoking the Name) with the consciousness of what is expressed in the words of Ibn ʿAṭā'Allāh in the *Ḥikam*: "Had it not been for His manifestation in created beings, eyesight would not have perceived them."[34] Without a doubt, there is nothing manifested in creation except what this Name contains of the knowledge of Allah's Essence, Attributes, Names, and the Actions through which the traces of the Names and Attributes appear, and these are what are referred to as "created beings" (*al-mukawwanāt*). As Shaykh Abu'l-Mawāhib al-Shādhilī said, "There is nothing in the Cosmos except what has been preceded by (Divine) Knowledge, specified by Will, manifested by Power, and given order by Wisdom." And in another of his aphorisms, Ibn ʿAṭā'Allāh says, "The Cosmos is all darkness. It is illumined only by the manifestation of Allah in it. Whosever sees the Cosmos and does not contemplate Him in it, or by it, or before it, or after it is in need of light and is veiled from the sun of gnosis by the clouds of created things."[35]
>
> So I invoked the Name abundantly with this consciousness and by its blessing lights came to my heart and I attained a portion of vigilance for Allah and the consciousness of Allah, both of which are contained in the Station of Excellence (*maqām al-iḥsān*): "That you worship Allah as if you saw Him, for if you do not see Him, yet He sees you…" In this same *ḥadīth*, when (the

> Prophet ﷺ was then asked who the questioner was, he replied, "That was Gabriel who came to teach you your *dīn* (religion)." In other words, he defined *dīn* as *islām*, *īmān*, and *iḥsān*. And since the sufic way is based on attaining the knowledge of *iḥsān*, just as there must be a guide to explain the rules and terminology of any science, so must there be a guide for this one. Such is what had impelled me to seek such a guide.

As for what led him to come forward as shaykh ... that began around 1908, when he was 37 years old, the year that his shaykh, Sīdī Muḥammad bin ʿAlī, passed away, may Allah sanctify his soul. At first, our Shaykh hesitated for some time concerning this, preferring to remain hidden and anonymous, until he saw in a vision his forefather, al-Muṣṭafa ﷺ, who commanded him in such a way that he had no other choice but to declare himself (a shaykh) and guide Allah's creatures to the True Sovereign. At that time, which was around the year 1911 when he had reached the age of forty, he made his role known for Allah and by Allah. He himself says of this:

> From the time Shaykh Sīdī Muḥammad bin ʿAlī ؓ passed away (that is, since 1908), the *idhn* (permission) kept repeating itself within me, while I saw myself only as lowly and unworthy of that station. Then there came to me (visions) of the four shaykhs – Sīdī Muḥammad bin ʿAlī, Sīdī al-ʿArabī ibn al-Hawwārī, Sīdī Muḥammad al-ʿArabī (al-Madaghrī), and Sīdī Aḥmad al-Badawī (Zouiten) (may Allah be well-pleased with them) – and all of them commanded me to come forward to people as a shaykh and guide them to the True Sovereign. They said, 'The water you have drunk is the sweetest of waters. Stretch forth your hand to the east and to the west and fear no one.' Then, following this, there came permission from al-Muṣṭafā ﷺ and the instruction to show myself (as shaykh), so I showed myself to people for Allah and by Allah.[36]

And glad tidings came to him (may Allah sanctify his soul) from the presence of the Prophet ﷺ, part of which concerned the sweet waters which he had drunk. Speaking of Allah's blessings to him, he said:

> The Prophet ﷺ spoke to me in (in a vision), saying, 'Know, my boy, that Allah will honor you with fresh, sweet waters.' I said, 'O Messenger of Allah, are these the waters of *islām, īmān,* and *iḥsān?*' He answered ﷺ, 'They are.' I then asked, 'And will I drink these waters by myself or will I drink them along with all those who follow me?' He answered, 'You will drink them, as will all those from my community who follow you.'
>
> And Allah has brought to pass what the Prophet ﷺ promised us, for by Allah, I have drunk from those waters, and everyone who has been sincerely my companion has drunk from them in the shortest time. So give praise to Allah, my dear ones, and thanks for the gift with which your Lord has honored you in your time.[37]

He also said, "The master of our master, Sīdī Muḥammad al-ᶜArabī (al-Madaghrī) ﷺ used to say, 'By Allah, no one comes to me except the one who is accepted (*maqbūl*),' and I say – to make mention of the blessings of my Lord – that by Allah, no one comes to me except the one who is beloved (*maḥbūb*)."[38]

Such is the way with the true and sincere masters: they do not make themselves known to people except for Allah and by Allah, and after clear permission comes to them by way of the greatest of intermediaries, the beloved friend and chosen messenger, our master Muḥammad ﷺ. This is so that the guidance they give people might be Muhammadan and holy, free from any desire to be famous or other egoistic goals, protected from the evils of competition in worldly ambitions, supported by the spring of Divine Providence.

Indeed, love and acceptance beyond description came to pass for him ﷺ in every land where his noble feet walked. Like pouring rain, wherever he went, he brought benefit. Speaking of the blessing and mystery of *idhn* (permission), he said:

> By Allah – and again, by Allah! – we have not passed through a town or village or countryside except that its people saw providential aid and new life flowing to their hearts, this being the mystery of permission (*idhn*). And no *faqīr* has sat with us – may praise be to Allah! – except that he has received knowledge that he had not previously possessed along with a deeper sense of humility. And no aspirant to the Path has sat with us except that his aspiration to seek direct knowledge of Allah was increased. And no shaykh from among the shaykhs of this age has sat with us, except that a "taste" of the divine (*dhawq*) was added to his taste and he gained through us something he had not had. All this is by the mystery and blessing of *idhn*.[39]

OPENING HIS ZĀWIYA IN MEKNES

When he returned from the Ḥajj, he saw that the zāwiya in Fes was no longer big enough for the number of aspirants there were, so he thought about making a new one. To this end, he asked the *faqīh*, Sīdī al-Zerhūnī to search for a house in Meknes that would be big enough for a zāwiya. This *faqīh* came upon a very large house owned by the palace (*al-makhzan*) which had been a pasha's residence, so he spoke to those concerned and they agreed to sell it to him. Thus, our Shaykh was able to purchase this property in around 1936 for a price of 13,000 riyals with money which he had saved from selling a piece of land that had been left to him by his father.

Prior to his moving to Meknes, however, a strange thing happened to him. The first time he ever visited Meknes, he traveled with one of his disciples and they went to the shrine of the saint, Sīdī Saʿīd bin ʿUthmān in hopes of meeting there a person of spiritual states named Sīdī Manṣūr, and so he took along with him a gift for the visit, which is said to have been some article of clothing, and he formulated the intention of asking this saintly person to give him a drink from the spiritual realm (*shurba maʿnawiya*).[39] As soon as he entered the shrine, and before having uttered a word, the saint said to him, "Put the gift over there!" And then he took a glass of tea and offered it to our Shaykh, saying, "Here's the drink you came for!" When our Shaykh drank from this glass of tea, his state became completely transformed and he left the shrine invoking aloud the Name of Majesty. He continued in this state until he reached Lehdim square (in the middle of Meknes) where Sīdī Qāsim al-Hilālī, who had known the Shaykh from the time he had been a companion of Sīdī Muḥammad Laḥlū, saw him, took him by the hand, and led him to his house. After the Shaykh's state had calmed down, Sīdī Qāsim invited him to stay the night and also invited over a *faqīh*, Sīdī al-Zerhūnī (mentioned above), to meet the Shaykh. They began talking about certain matters, some concerning *fiqh* and others concerning sufism, and this *faqīh* became so amazed by the Shaykh that he wound up asking him to take his hand. The Shaykh refused to do so because the *faqīh* was already affiliated with another order for which, in fact, he was a *muqaddam*. But Sīdī al-Zerhūnī persisted in his request, explaining that his other affiliation was only for the sake of blessing (*tabarrukan*), and did not involve practicing a method (*sālikan*) at the hand of a shaykh who instructed and trained disciples. When this was clear to the Shaykh, he accepted him, made an oath of allegience with him, and made him the first *muqaddam* of the Ṭarīqa Ḥabībiyya in Meknes. And he fulfilled what he pledged, for it was through him that the first group of *fuqarā'* formed there. Initially, they met in the mosque of Derb al-Fatayān where the Shaykh would visit them from time to time, and it was on one of these visits that he asked Sīdī al-Zerhūnī (his new *muqaddam*) to find a house he could make into a zāwiya.

This is how the *muqaddam* came to find the right place, as we mentioned above. Since that time, it has been the location of the Ḥabībiyya zāwiya in Meknes, and this was after the Shaykh had spent 26 years in the zāwiya in Fes. The new zāwiya became a place of learning and a center for the purification of souls. Its reputation spread and people journeyed to it from afar, both from inside Morocco and abroad, including seekers from as far as Britain and America.

HIS ROLE IN REVIVING RELIGIOUS KNOWLEDGE IN MEKNES

Our Shaykh found the city of Meknes in great need of a revival of religious knowledge, so he resolved to ask his majesty, King Muḥammad V (may Allah be merciful to him) for help in founding an institute of religious studies there. He first consulted with certain of the high-ranking people of Meknes and they advised him not to get involved, but then he offered the *istikhāra* Prayer, traveled to visit the King, and said to him, "You have founded an institute of learning in Marrakesh, while Meknes is the capital of your forefather,[41] so you should give it priority over any other place." To this the King replied that there was already an institute in Fes close by. The Shaykh said, "Even if it is close, if a student stays there until he has earned a diploma, when he returns to Meknes, what does he do? He can either try to get work as a notary, provided he can find someone to support him in doing so, or else he will be forced to take whatever work comes his way and the knowledge which he had left his home to acquire will be wasted. On the other hand, if he found students with no work but to learn, he could begin by teaching them voluntarily and following that, he would find it easier to get paid work in something relating to the field of knowledge."

(Hearing this), His Majesty the King (may Allah be merciful to him) agreed,[42] and our Shaykh suggested the necessary steps: the creation of teachers' chairs[43] in the Zaytūna mosque in Meknes, the creation of a curriculum, and (eventually) the creation of a system of rotation for both teachers and students.

Thus did our Shaykh ﵀ share in the revival of religious knowledge in his land and begin teaching in the Zaytūna Mosque in Meknes. About this latter, he says recounting the blessings of Allah to him:

> Then I began to teach in the Zaytūna Mosque.[44] I started with lessons in *tafsīr*, which were attended by a large number of students and others, and followed those with lessons from *al-Risāla* of Abū Zayd ﵀. So in one session, I would begin with *tafsīr*, then

follow it by *al-Risāla*. The people of Meknes benefited greatly from these lessons, may praise be to Allah. With the general of public of Meknes, I (also) completed a reading of *al-Murshid* (*al-Muʿīn*), which was attended by certain students as well, and a reading of the *Ḥikam ʿAṭā'iyya* which I had studied extensively with the Shaykh of the assembly, Sīdī Aḥmad ibn al-Khayyāṭ, may Allah reward him with goodness.[45]

HIS CONNECTION WITH SĪDĪ AḤMAD BIN ʿALĪWA[46]

Between Sīdī Muḥammad ibn al-Ḥabīb and the gnostic, Sīdī Aḥmad bin ʿAlīwa al-Mustaghānimī there was a deep connection and sincere love as shown by their meetings together, communications, and many correspondances.

Part of what we learn from the communications between the two shaykhs is that Sīdī Muḥammad ibn al-Ḥabīb asked Shaykh bin ʿAlīwa to grace him with a commentary on the formula of blessing upon the Prophet (which is part of the Ḥabībī litany) entitled *Kanz al-Ḥaqā'iq*, which Sīdī Muḥammad had received by inspiration from the presence of al-Muṣṭafā. Shaykh bin ʿAlīwa answered his request by dedicating an entire treatise to this, entitled *Dawḥat al-Asrār fī Maʿnā al-Ṣalāti ʿalā al-Nabīyi l-Mukhtār*. In the introduction of this book, (Shaykh bin ʿAlīwa) writes:

> I must acknowledge my debt to the one who was the means by which this book was written, our close friend and brother in Allah, Sīdī Muḥammad ibn al-Ḥabīb ibn Mawlānā al-Ṣiddīq, may Allah make us both among those who honor what they have pledged to Him.
>
> Sīdī, after having been blessed by your goodness and after asking after your well being – may peace and safety encompass you from every direction as is your due – I am honored by your letter and receive it with great esteem as if it were the writing of one who is wise and knowing.[47] Both my vision and thoughts have ranged through (this formula of blessing) and I have found it to be a verdant meadow and a blossom, sufficient evidence of (the

> station of) the one who wrote it, and particularly of the Prophetic vision which encompassed him. It is indeed a grace for which you need to be grateful, so praise be to Allah that there remain in existence people such as you.
>
> As for what you have asked from me concerning it – to clarify the meaning of the formula of blessing that Allah caused to flow from your lips – we have nothing more than you do (and Allah knows best), but in order to respond to what you have asked, to be at your service, and out of our love for the invocation of blessings upon the Prophet ﷺ, even as we recognize how short we fall of this task in every way, we say .....[48]

And here he begins his commentary.

Shaykh Sīdī Muḥammad ibn al-Ḥabīb ﵁ had a great breadth to his spirituality. He was open to all sorts of religious experience and interested in knowing the benefits that Allah, in His generosity, bestows upon His saints by way of openings and gifts. Evidence of this can be found in the letter, quoted below in its entirety, which he sent to Shaykh Sīdī Aḥmad bin ʿAlīwa ﵁. (In this letter) he recounts the conditions which led him to declare himself a shaykh. He also asks Shaykh bin ʿAlīwa for a letter in which he describes what Allah had opened to him concerning the spiritual retreat (*al-khalwa*), as well as the method of invoking the Supreme Name along with permission to do so. He indicates as well that he, too, followed a particular method of invoking the Name which he had received from his shaykh, Sīdī Muḥammad bin ʿAlī ﵁, but that he wished to know about other methods of invocation used by the gnostics as a way of broadening and spreading its goodness and benefit. Here is the complete text of the letter:

> Praise be to Allah Who made the substance of His Prophet something particular that flows to certain individuals of His community in every age, and has singled them out from among all other creatures to know the mysteries of His Essence, the lights of His

Attributes, the manifestations of His Names, and the marvels of His Acts, who then inform others of their spiritual "tastes," perceptions, and ecstasies so that they might bring benefit by way of their teachings, knowledge, words, and thoughts to whosoever is destined to be among the blessed in the presence of the All-Merciful.

And may prayers and blessings be upon our master, Muḥammad, the first of the manifestations from whose light Allah caused to appear all other created beings, and upon his people, companions, and representatives – blessings as numerous as all the words of glorifications uttered by the inhabitants of the heavens and earth.

Among the most distinguished representatives (of the Prophet) ﷺ whom Allah has caused to appear in our time, that by his excellence servants might be guided, is the greatest shaykh, the known example, master of the gnostics and guide of the aspirants, our master and protector Aḥmad bin Sīdī Muṣṭafā bin ʿAlīwa, may Allah prolong your existence among us for the benefit of His servants and make of you a spring of fresh water for those who seek to drink, that both the city-dwellers and country people might benefit. May salutations of peace be upon you and upon those who are connected to you, the highest of greetings and purest of salutations, as bountiful as all that Allah, the Truth, discloses in all the nights and days (of this world).

TO PROCEED:

Your letter, sweetened by glowing lights, perfumed breaths, and by your evident spiritual opening, has reached us. We received it with respect and honor and read it with attention, reflection, and understanding, and we found that it fulfilled its purpose, may Allah be praised, and was an unveiling of subtle mysteries of which we were unaware. May Allah recompense you, for us, with the best of recompense and bestow upon you His complete support and contentment.

You should know, Sīdī – and may Allah be praised – that I met with individuals and masters from the Muḥammadan community and received from them what had been apportioned to me through their hands. Then, when Sīdī Muḥammad bin ʿAlī appeared in Marrakesh, I journeyed to him, he received me with welcome, and he unveiled to me the presence of the Beloved Friend. He imparted to me the Supreme Name along with a particular method of invoking it, and gave me permission to guide the servants of Allah and show them the way to Allah. So I obeyed what he ordered me to do, and attained by his blessing great benefit. When he passed away 🕮, I proceeded slowly until I saw the Prophet 🕮 and he ordered me to guide the servants of Allah and show them the way to Allah, and so I undertook what he ordered me to do, and if anyone came to me seeking guidance, I would remind him of what would bring him nearer to Allah. Then when it was decreed that I should make your acquaintance, and your sanctity was disclosed to me by Allah – in light of acknowledging that to be satisfied with (one's knowledge of) Allah is deprivation[49] and to be satisfied with something other than Allah is misguidance and loss – there arose in my soul the wish, O Sīdī , that you would write for us a letter... concerning the spiritual retreat (al-khalwa) and its correct practice (ādābihā) as well as the correct way to invoke the Unique Name and the benefits of concentrating on it alone to the exclusion of the other Divine Names. I would also ask you to speak of what is disclosed to the spiritual traveller in his spiritual retreat at the beginning, middle, and end, the signs that indicate he has succeeded in his journey, and also the things by which he may be cut off on his journey, and how he may strengthen himself against them, such that someone who reads this letter may have deep insight into this matter. I also ask that you might write for me permission to practice that method. And after this – may Allah bless you – we would love for you to honor us by coming to this blessed region, for its people have a great longing to meet you,[50] and your coming would fulfill my hopes as well as those of Sīdī Muḥammad, Sīdī ʿAbdurraḥmān, and Sīdī Ḥabīb bin Manṣūr, spread divine aid, and increase brotherhood.

> We ask Allah Most High to bring us together soon, and verily, He is the One Who hears and answers our prayers.
>
> The servant of the people of Allah who stands waiting at their doors, Muḥammad ibn al-Ḥabīb ibn al-Ṣiddīq, may Allah keep him in His care.

Along with this, we must mention the fact that our Shaykh visited Sīdī bin ʿAlīwa (may Allah be pleased with them both) in the year 1934 in Mustaghānim towards the end of (Shaykh bin ʿAlīwa's) life, at a time when he was ill, and he permitted him to come to him when he was semiconscious and not allowing anyone else to visit him. They remained together for a considerable time with no-one else present, so no-one knows what (exactly) passed between them during this time, but one of the closest disciples of Sīdī Muḥammad ibn al-Ḥabīb ؓ related that Shaykh ibn ʿAlīwa ؓ complained to him about how much time he had spent responding to those who deny (Sufism) and how that had occupied him from (accomplishing) what was better, to which our Shaykh replied that what he had written (in the defense of Sufism) was a form of striving (*jihād*) for the sake of Allah and a support and aid to the people of Allah. Sīdī bin ʿAlīwa ؓ was pleased (with these words) and said to him, "Sīdī, you have given me good news and brought happiness to my heart, and I would like to convey to you a vision in return that you will be granted a long life." He also described to him (from his vision) the journeys he was to make and his meetings with *fuqarā'* wherever they were, and then said to him, symbolically, "Take hold of the millstone handle after me."[51]

The Shaykh's vision of a long life came true, for Sīdī Muḥammad ibn al-Ḥabīb ؓ was more than a hundred years old when he passed away and he acted upon what Sīdī bin ʿAlīwa (may Allah sanctify his soul) advised him, for he continued to journey even into his old age, visiting his zāwiyas and disciples and those who loved him in every corner of Morocco and Algeria, and continued to give guidance and instruction such that he was on a journey when he met his Lord.[52]

HIS METHOD OF INSTRUCTION

Our Shaykh 🕮 began his mission of calling people to the Way of Allah from his zāwiya in Qaṣbat al-Nawwār in Fes, which was a center where hearts thirsty for spiritual knowledge could drink and where those longing for training and guidance could find it. He himself would oversee the teaching of the religious and linguistic sciences as well as the instruction of those who aspired to the station of *iḥsān*. In addition, he gave lessons in *fiqh* and *tafsīr* in the Qarawīyīn mosque. He said, 🕮, describing his method of instruction and spreading knowledge:

> When that shaykh who had imparted to me knowledge of the station of *iḥsān* – that is, Sīdī Muḥammad bin ʿAlī – passed away, people started coming to me and I undertook the task of reminding them, directing them, and advising them in accordance with their capacity and readiness, without any personal ambition and without any innovation.[53] We would gather with the brethren for invocation and spiritual discourse from the Book of Allah, Mighty and Majestic, at which time I would ask a student with a good voice to recite a portion of the Qur'ān, particularly those verses which encourage the remembrance of Allah and reflection upon the wonders of Allah's creations, such as, *Those who remember Allah standing, sitting, and lying upon their sides, and reflect upon the creation of the heavens and the earth (and say): "Our Lord, You have not created this in vain. Glory be to You! Shield us from the punishment of the Fire." (3:191)* and *O you who believe, remember Allah with much remembrance and glorify Him morning and evening* (33:41-42). Then the spiritual discourse would be directed to those who were present so that each person could receive from it some meaning of the verse.[54]

He would see after the needs of the disciples 🕮, teachers, and the *fuqarāʾ* who had withdrawn from the workaday world. He would not ask anyone who was seeking knowledge from him to become affiliated with his Ṭarīqa, but he would require them to keep (the injunctions) of the pure revealed law. Thus, his good student Muḥammad ʿAyyāṭ

ؓ who was the *muqaddam* in Oran (Algeria) recounted that one night when everyone had stayed up so late in a *ḥaḍra* in the zāwiya that they were late in getting up for the dawn prayer (*al-ṣubḥ*), our Shaykh looked down from the window of the rooftop room (*al-minzah*) of the zāwiya where he lived, made the call to prayer himself, and came downstairs quickly and angrily and woke them up. When one of the them said to him, "Sīdī, a second call to prayer does not need to be loud," our Shaykh replied, "That call is for the women. As for you, you must wake up early. I will never allow any of you to get lax concerning the Prayer, especially given that you are students of knowledge and affiliated with the people of Allah."

The Ḥabībiyya zāwiya was a mosque where the Prayer was offered, a school where various lessons in religious knowledge were given, and a center for spiritual training and the purification of souls, and it followed a particular schedule. Activity began some hours before dawn when the *fuqarā'* would rise for the supererogatory night Prayer (*al-tahajjud*) until the call for the dawn Prayer (*al-ṣubḥ*). Immediately after the call, they would invoke the Supreme Name aloud in a certain way (for a short while). Then the Shaykh ؓ would go forward and lead the Prayer, and after having completed it, the Noble *Wird* would be recited followed by a short lesson. Then those who had work would go to their work, while those who lived in the zāwiya would stay in order to complete the invocations and litanies they had been given.

Every Friday eve (i.e. Thursday night), the Shaykh would lead a gathering for invocation and teaching and would encourage people to attend it. During it, he would urge people to hold fast to the pure religious law and to develop in themselves the Muḥammadan virtues. In respect to this, he would often say, "He who has no comportment (*adab*) has no Ṭarīqa."

He would also enjoin upon people to have the best opinion of Allah (*ḥusn al-ẓann bi'l-Lāh*) and of Allah's creatures, to look upon all the rest of Allah's creation with respect, to love one's brethren in Allah, to gather for the sake of Allah, to keep their pledges, and to be abundant in the invocation of Allah, especially during the last third of the night, saying, "Upon abundant invocation is built the station of vigilance, then of perception. When the servant's heart is illuminated and the sun of gnosis dawns for him, he sees the entire cosmos as a grace from Allah to him – the grace of existence and the grace of sustenance, both of which are inestimably precious – and he comes to love Allah Most High through his nature, his mind, and the divinely-revealed law."

He would ﷺ direct the *muqaddams* to respect the *fuqarā'*, to treat them with goodness, make every effort to give them good advice, to guide them, to ask about their states, and to be gentle and kind towards them just as he would direct the *fuqarā'* to deal with the *muqaddams* with goodness by honoring and loving them, following what they asked of them, and maintaining the best conduct with them. He would also exhort them many times over to stay with the assembly and avoid division.

But anyone who would like to know his method of spiritual training in detail is advised to return to his Noble Dīwān, a treasury of spiritual training, in which he gathered a summation of the science of Sufism that had come to him in this age.

In speaking of the program of training, we must also mention that each year he would celebrate the week of the birthday (*mawlid*) of the beloved and chosen one ﷺ, when *fuqarā'* and beloved ones from inside Morocco and beyond would travel to the zāwiya. This evening of celebration would begin with a short recitation from the Noble Qur'ān, then the chanters would begin their chanting of *qaṣīdas* which would lead to the *fuqarā'* standing for the *ʿimāra*[55] at the end of which they would sit while someone recited some verses from the Book of Allah. After this, the Shaykh ﷺ would present a lesson based on the verses that had been recited and the evening would close with (his) offering a supplication, then donations to the zāwiya would be received from those who were able to give.

Our Shaykh accorded great importance to the *ʿimāra*. He would encourage it and viewed it as something which would shorten the way to a spiritual opening for the aspirant if undertaken according to its conditions. He 🕌 said, speaking of it: "An ʿimāra of a quarter of an hour is equivalent to a spiritual retreat of a week," and also, "If three fuqarāʾ gather in a circle of invocation and do not accomplish the ʿimāra, they have cheated me (ghashshūnī)." Supporting these sayings is what occurred one evening when a feast had been offered[56] to which the fuqarāʾ were invited. At the end of it, they started an ʿimāra and everyone present began moving ecstatically. When it was over, one of those present from the people of unveiling had a vision of himself drinking from a glass of milk. He later told the Shaykh about this and asked him to write down what spiritual inspirations came to him that night. It was then that Allah inspired him to write the Tāʾiyat al-Wusṭā which begins:

> We drank from the lights in the tavern of the Presence
> a wine that removed confusion without doubt ...

In this qaṣīda, he 🕌 affirms the excellence of the ʿimāra and also the necessity of accepting those who perform it, saying:

> Keep company with a folk who have trained their own souls
> and so swim in love's oceans at all of its depths
> And accept it if you see them seized by love
> and dancing at the mention of the Beloved in song.
> For were you to taste the meaning of our words,
> you would be first among them in all their states.
> And you would lower your eyelids on the motes in your vision
> and rend the robes of shyness and reserve.
> And you would say to the chanter, "Make us lovers of His Name!"
> for in that chant and that love is neither fault nor blame.

Then he cautions 🕌 against what could result from disapproving of this practice or from disregarding it, saying that someone in that state (of disapproval) is dominated by his own ego and will not be liberated from it afterwards:

> But the one who has fallen under the power of his ego is kept back from
> (knowing) the mysteries of that Path.

HIS FIRST PILGRIMAGE

Sīdī Muḥammad ibn al-Ḥabīb (may Allah sanctify his soul) set out for the sacred precincts to accomplish the rites of the pilgrimage around the year 1931 (when he was 60 years old) and it was one of the breezes of the spirit that occur throughout life.[57] It was on that Ḥajj that he visited the resting-place of the Prophet (*al-Rawḍat al-Sharīfa*) and chanted in the presence of his forefather, al-Muṣṭafā 鐌, his well-known qaṣīda:

> *We are present in the Meadow of the Messenger,*
> *seeking Allah's contentment and most beautiful acceptance.*

When he had completed the rites of pilgrimage, he traveled to Syria and met with a number of its scholars, including Shaykh Tawfīq al-Ayyūbī and the *muḥaddith* Badr al-Dīn al-Ḥasanī al-Dimashqī (may Allah be well-pleased with them), and it was at this time that the latter gave the shaykh written authorization. He had also intended to meet with one who loved the Messenger of Allah, Yūsuf al-Nabahānī 鐌, but he received word that he had passed away about one month before his arrival.

He also passed through the land of Egypt and contacted there a number of its scholars, such as Shaykh Bakhīt al-Muṭīʿī and Shaykh Muḥammad al-Samālūṭī (may they rest in peace), and there passed between those scholars and our Shaykh a number of talks, as well as assemblies for knowledge and spiritual gatherings, for they found him 鐌 a vast ocean of gnosis and virtue. They were so dazzled by his luminous states that they asked him to stay on with them that they might benefit more from him, but he begged their pardon and permission to leave.

He then resumed the journey back to his land, and on the way he stopped in Algeria. There he met a large number of the learned and pious people, many of whom entered the Ṭarīqa and became the first to spread the *Ṭarīqat al-Ḥabībiyya* throughout that land of Algeria. When he reached the city of Figuig in the southeast of Morocco, a great number of scholars greeted him, led by Shaykh Muḥammad al-

Qāḍī, (may Allah be merciful to him). At that time, they were about to begin a reading with commentary (*sard*) of *Ṣaḥīḥ al-Bukhārī* and they asked him to lead it. In addition to al-Bukhārī, he gave lessons from *al-Murshid al-Muᶜīn*, all of which took nine months to complete. During this time, many of the people of Figuig and its region became affiliated with the Ṭarīqa.

HIS SECOND PILGRIMAGE

His second journey for Ḥajj took place in 1360 (1942) and included much travel around Morocco and Algeria, spreading the sciences of Islam and calling to the way. His students increased as did those who became affiliated with him because of the mysteries, lights, and blessings surrounding him. The number of zāwiyas in Morocco, Algeria, and several other countries was nearly fifty during his life, and later, after his passing, his students from England founded others in South Africa, the United States, Mexico, Spain, and Great Britain.

In 1972, he left Meknes intending to complete his third pilgrimage accompanied by some of his disciples and spouses – may Allah have mercy upon them all – but he was forced to stop in Blida (Algeria) due to poor health, and it was there that he passed away (may Allah be merciful to him) on Monday, the 23rd of Dhu'l-Qiᶜda, 1391, (January 11, 1972) at over a hundred years old. Thus, he was someone to whom the words of Allah Most High may be applied: *Whoever goes forth from his home in the cause of Allah migrating for Allah and His Messenger, and then death overtakes him, His reward becomes due by Allah: And Allah is Oft-forgiving, Most Merciful,* (4:100) and the words (of the Messenger) ﷺ, "One who goes forth in this direction intending to make the Ḥajj or ᶜ*umra* and then dies on the way will be spared from the Exposition and Reckoning (on the Day of Resurrection) and it will be said to him: enter Paradise."[58] It has also been recorded in this context that the Prophet ﷺ said, "For whosoever goes forth from his home intending to perform the Ḥajj and dies before he performs it, Allah (Mighty and Majestic) appoints an angel to take his place in the Ḥajj every year thereafter until the Day of Resurrection." And in another ḥadīth, related by Abū Hurayra ☙, the Prophet ☙ is reported to have said, "For whosoever goes forth for the Ḥajj, or for the ʿumra, or for a battle, and then dies on the way, Allah will write the reward of a combatant, a pilgrim, or one who accomplishes the ʿumra until the Day of Resurrection."[59]

So: Praise be to Allah for the glad tidings and precious blessings our Shaykh was given, and may Allah make his dwelling place the highest garden of Firdaws near his forefather, the beloved and accepted friend of Allah, upon whom be peace and salutations.

He was interred initially in the zāwiya in Blida (in Algeria) that he had inaugurated one week before his passing, and then, twenty-nine days later, in answer to requests from his family and disciples, his body was transported back to Meknes. When the grave was opened for the purpose of moving his pure body, those present were witness to a miraculous thing: there arose from his tomb a pure and perfumed scent which all who were present could smell, and they found his body in the same condition as when it had been interred.

He was buried permanently ☙ in his zāwiya in Meknes in Derb al-Pasha near the Zaytūna mosque. There he was laid to rest after the ʿaṣr prayer, Monday, 14th of Dhi'l-Ḥijja in the place where his tomb is today.

His mysteries and blessings ☙ continue to flow forth from generation to generation by way of his goodly and sincere followers who remained with the guidance of his method, and conveyed it to those who followed them, with trust, love, and sincerity, and without alteration or change.

Concerning his writings, nothing has come down to the present except a long, hand-written letter he wrote to King Muḥammad V (may Allah be merciful to him) and a few handwritten letters that he sent to his students concerning certain of his lessons on the tafsīr of Sūrat al-Aʿrāf that had been tape-recorded. He left as well his Dīwān containing poetry as well as his litanies. In this Dīwān, which has been printed several times in Algeria and Morocco and is entitled Bughyatu al-Murīdīn al-Sā'irīn wa Tuḥfatu al-Sālikīn al-ʿĀrifīn, he gathered what he had received of the science of Sufism in his time. Thus, it can be considered as a compendium of method and doctrine for anyone seeking to realize the stations of *islām*, *īmān*, and *iḥsān*, and was translated into English by some of his English disciples. The late teacher and scholar Muḥammad ibn al-Fāṭimī al-Sullamī, known as Ibn al-Ḥājj, also said, "He has a commentary on the *Ḥafiẓa* of Shaykh Sīdī Muḥammad al-ʿArabī al-Madaghrī ؓ in which he gathered supplications from the Prophet ﷺ and Qur'ānic verses, a portion of the *aḥzāb* of the Shādhiliyya, and a commentary on the *Ṣalāt al-Mashīshiyya*." But we have not found these writings up to the time when this biography was written. We ask Allah Mighty and Majestic that we might still discover and publish them.

May Allah have mercy upon this spiritual axis, sanctify his soul, and ennoble his dwelling place in the highest garden of Firdaws, and may He provide for us and all Muslims the best way to emulate him and all those saintly people of Allah who are the heirs of the Noble Messenger and greatest friend, our beloved Prophet, the coolness of our eyes, our master Muḥammad, may the most excellent of blessings and purest salutations of peace be upon him and upon his family and companions. Amen, amen, amen. *And the conclusion of their supplication shall be, "Praise be to Allah, Lord of the worlds!"* (10:10)

ENDNOTES:

1 This biography is translated and adapted from *Dhukhru'l-Muḥibbi'l-Najīb min Sīrati'l- Shaykh Sayyidī Muḥammad bin al-Ḥabīb*, a biography which appears in the 2020 edition of the Dīwān published by the Ḥabībī zāwiya in Laghouat, Algeria, edited by Dr. al-Akhdar Quideri.

2 The first memorization of the Qur'ān in Morocco traditionally involves reciting it from memory with a teacher. Following that, there can be one or two more recitations with other teachers, each time with greater understanding.

3 In the original text, there follows long list of the books he studied and the teachers with whom he studied them. To make this section more easily accessible to the general reader, we have summarized it in the paragraph that follows:

Among of the works he studied with these scholars are: *al-Ājrūmiyya* and Ibn Mālik's *Alfiyya* (Arabic grammar); Mayyāra's commentary on *al-Murshid al-Muʿīn* (an overview of the fundamentals of Islam); *Mukhtaṣar Khalīl* and *Kitāb al-Zaqāqiyya* (Mālikī jurisprudence); portions of *Ṣaḥīḥ al-Bukhārī, al-Musnad* of Imām Aḥmad, and *Tuḥfa al-Aḥwadhī*, a commentary on the *Sunan* collection of al-Tirmidhī, (*ḥadīth*); *al-Jāmiʿ fī ādāb al-ʿālim wa'l-mutaʿallim* (ethics and comportment); and *al-Ḥikam al-ʿAṭā'iyya* and Ibn Ḥajar's commentary on al-Būṣīrī's *Hamziyya* (Sufism).

4 A *ḥizb (pl. aḥzāb)* of the Qur'ān is equal to a half a *juz'*, which is one thirtieth of the Book. In Morocco, a long-standing tradition has been for people to recite collectively and aloud, one *ḥizb* after the *fajr* prayer and one after the *maghrib* prayer, thus completing one thirtieth of the Qur'ān each day and the entire book, once a month. For the use of this word in respect to litany, see note 9 below.

5 From manuscript copy of a letter sent by the Shaykh to King Mohamed V.

6 From a recorded narration of Sīdī Muḥammad Belkurshī.

7 Shaykh Mā' al-ʿAynayn (d. 1910) was a figure of major importance in the contemporary history of Saharan culture and the successor to his father as the Shaykh of the Ṭarīqa Fāḍiliyya, a branch of the Qādiriyya. He was the author of many works, both in poetry and prose, on the Islamic sciences, including sufism. His tomb is in the town of Tiznīt about 60 miles south of Agadir.

8 See note 58 below

9 In this context, *aḥzāb* (singular, *ḥizb*) means literally, "portions," a daily recitation, often composed by the sufi shaykh, containing Quranic verses,

formulae of praise, formulae of invocation, and supplication. All the litanies left by Imām al-Shādhilī, for example, are referred to by this word. See also note 4 above.

10 Letter sent by the Shaykh to King Mohamed V.

11 Ibid.

12 Ibid.

13 He repeats this phrase with some variation several times when recounting his life as a reminder that he only mentions these things because Allah enjoins this in the verse, *And as for the blessings of your Lord, speak of them!* [93:11].

14 *Allah suffices us and He is the most excellent Protector* [3:173].

15 A *muftī* is a scholar who has completed the long and extensive studies necessary to be qualified to formulate a *fatwā*, or religious ruling, concerning a particular issue that has arisen in a particular time.

16 Those five were the ones Sīdī Saʿīd al-Belghīthī would gather with afterwards and and to whom Sīdī al-ʿArabī ibn ʿAbdallāh Bābā al-Hawārī transmitted the *wird*.

17 He was born in Qaṣr Madaghra in 1215/1801 into a sharifian family and studied at the Qarawīyīn in Fes. After a long time spent seeking knowledge, he returned to Madaghra and to the spread of knowledge and gnosis amongst its people. He was impressed by the Sufi thought of the Darqāwa in Fes and founded near his homeland a Darqāwī zāwiya called Raḥmat Allāh, then another in Tafilalt south of al-Safālāt, the zāwiya Ghūz near Qāṣr Tīnghrās.

18 A small town in the south of Morocco about 25 miles north of Morocco's southeast border with Algeria. Its name is also pronounced "Wakka."

19 The Arabic version specifies here that he meant "disciples," i.e. those who had renounced the world, lived in the zāwiya, and were dependent on charity.

20 A *gharrāb* (also written *guerrab*) is a traditional Moroccan water-carrier. The *gharrāb* carries water in a large goat skin bag with a tap attached to it, along with brass cups, and a bell to let people know where he is.

21 *Mā' al-sabīl* may be understood to mean either "water given for the sake of God" (that is, free), or "water for the path."

22 Traditionally, zāwiyas in Morocco, besides being centers for learning and spiritual instruction and practice, also provided food for the poor, largely supported by individual donations.

23 That is, Sīdī Laḥlū received from Mūlay al-Saʿīd the *wird* of Shaykh al-Hawārī ﷺ.

24 It should be noted that at this time Sīdī Muḥammad Laḥlū had never seen

Shaykh al-Hawārī in person.

25 That is, "Allah is greater than anything else, while you are very small."

26 This story was related by Sīdī Muḥammad ibn Muḥammad Belkurshī, the present *muqaddam* of the zāwiya of Turug, as related to him by his father.

27 Abū ʿAbdallāh Sīdī Muḥammad (pronounced in Morocco *Maḥammad*) bin ʿAlī al-Darʿī al-Farklī ﷺ is generally acknowledged as Shaykh Ibn al-Ḥabīb's principal teacher before he himself took on the role of shaykh. He passed away in 1908 and is buried in the middle of his zāwiya in Marrakesh.

28 That is, by way of Mūlay al-Saʿīd al-Belghītī as mentioned earlier. It should also be pointed out that during this period of time, Shaykh al-Hawārī had passed away.

29 On a communal platter, this meant the portion directly before him.

30 Sīdī Aḥmad al-Badawī al-Fāsī Zouiten was born in Fes in the 18th century and passed away there in the year 1275/1858. During his life, he became one of the principle *muqaddams* appointed by Shaykh al-Darqāwī. See his biography in al-Talīdī's *al-Muṭrib bi mashāhīr awliyā' al-Maghrib*, 4th edition, Rabat, 2003, p. 233.

31 This book is a collection of letters of spiritual advice. It has never been printed.

32 That is, those whose family line can be traced back to the Prophet Muḥammad ﷺ.

33 About 100 kilometers from Marrakesh.

34 *Book of Wisdom*, Danner translation, aphorism no. 138.

35 Ibid, no. 14.

36 Quoted from the introduction of the Dīwān, second edition, 1949, p. 5.

37 Ibid, p. 4.

38 Ibid, p. 4.

39 Ibid, pp. 3-4.

40 That is, he wanted to seek from him a particular blessing.

41 The city of Meknes was built by the third ʿAlawī ruler of Morocco, Mūlay Ismāʿīl (d. 1139/1727).

42 Recounted in his letter to the King, p. 4.

43 *Karāsī ʿilmiyya* means both positions and actual seats in the mosque where a teacher would sit with a circle of students.

44 Located very near the Ḥabībiyya zāwiya in Meknes.

45 Letter to the King, p. 5.

46 Shaykh Aḥmad al-ʿAlāwī, affectionately known in Algeria as Sīdī bin ʿAlīwa (the diminutive of ʿAlawī), was the shaykh of the *Ṭarīqat al-ʿAlāwiyya al-Darqāwiyya al-Shādhiliyya* in Algeria (1869-1934).

47 *Ḥakīm ʿalīm*, "wise, knowing," refers to Allah in the Qur'ān. In this context, they fit into the rhymed prose that Shaykh al-ʿAlawī used throughout the introduction to this book. They could also be understood to mean "a knowledgeble physician."

48 *Dawḥat al-Asrār*, Mustaghānim, al-Maṭbaʿat al-ʿAlawiyya, 3rd edition, 1991, p. 12.

49 A saying of the sufis which means that if we think we have attained "enough" knowledge of Allah – which is, in fact, limitless – it is an indication that our understanding is deficient of just what that knowledge is, while to be satisfied in life with something besides knowing Allah is simply misguidance and loss.

50 It is affirmed in the biography of Sīdī Aḥmad bin ʿAlīwa (may Allah sanctify his soul) that he visited Morocco twice, first in 1342/1924 and then again in 1346/1928, and that he conversed in Fes with a number of the scholars of the Qarawīyīn.

51 The hand-turned mill, once part of every Moroccan kitchen, can still be found in some rural parts of the country.

52 Quoted from the website of the *Ṭarīqat al-Ḥabībiyya*, Marrakesh.

53 He adds this to clarify that his role as shaykh had nothing to do with any personal ambition to be well-known or have some status, nor did it involve introducing ideas or practices that were not part of the tradition.

54 Letter to King Mohamed V, pp. 9-10.

55 The *ʿimāra* or *ḥaḍra* is a form of invocation accompanied by rhymic movement, usually done standing.

56 Recounted by Ḥāj al-Ṭāhir, *muqaddam* of the Ḥabībiyya in Mascara, Algeria.

57 He is referring to the *ḥadīth* found in Ṭabarānī and other collections, "Your Lord has breezes of the spirit (*nafaḥāt*) throughout the days of your life, so be open to them that perchance one of those breezes might touch you and you will never grieve again."

58 Bayhaqī, *Shuʿab al-Īmān*, quoted in *Kanz al-ʿummāl*, 11847 and 11848.

59 *Isʿāf al-Ikhwān al-Rāghibīn*, p. 176.

SHAYKH MUḤAMMAD IBN AL-ḤABĪB'S INTRODUCTION TO HIS DĪWĀN

PRAISE BE TO Allah Who establishes in every age certain people whose role it is to give new life to His way, and so He extends to them the Muḥammadan Lights which give support and aid to all those who love and follow them, be it singly or in pairs.

We praise Allah, the Exalted and Glorified, for the mysteries which He has chosen us to receive and for the teachings, gnosis, and lights which He has poured out upon us,

And we thank Him, the All-Mighty, with a gratitude that encompasses all the many gifts which have come to us and to all the servants of Allah, be they bondsmen or free.

We testify that there is no god but Allah, One, without partner, with the testimony of those who have been brought near and who are effaced in His Oneness.

And we testify that our master Muḥammad is His servant and Messenger, sent as a mercy to all the worlds. May Allah bless him and his People and Companions, who spent freely of themselves and their possessions in order to give life to his way and establish his Sunna, and who were undaunted by the insults of the hypocritical or of those who were veiled from the truth.

TO PROCEED:

Know with certitude, dear brethren of the Darqāwa Shādhiliyya order and all other servants of our Lord who wish to follow the path in any of Allah's lands, that Allah تعالى, has decreed for this blessed Way that in every age there be someone who rectifies any deviations that have entered it and manifests [anew] its mysteries and lights, a Shaykh who combines within him the Inner Truth and the Revealed Law and has been granted permission by Allah, His Messenger, and all the other saints. He is the Muḥammadan entity (*al-fardu al-Muḥammadī*) of whom there can be only one in any given age, such that even if there are many spiritual masters living in his time, they are subordinate to him whether they are aware of it or not.[1]

Many are the pretenders to this role who utter falsehoods and fabrications, seeking wealth and worldly rank, unaware that anyone who claims to be what he is not will be shown up as a liar by trials,[2] for it is by being tested that a person is raised up or brought low. The true masters of the way, however, find their sufficiency in knowing Allah and have no attachments to anything except Allah. If they speak openly of anything, it is only to mention Allah's bounty, for the Most High has said, *And as for the bounty of your Lord – mention it!* [93:11].

So here is the servant – in need of his Lord Who is free of all need – Muḥammad, son of al-Ḥabīb, Amghārī and Ḥasanī in descent, Fāsī in origin and residence, saying as a way to mention Allah's bounty that permission has come to us from Allah and His Messenger and from all the other saints, and that I have been singled out to receive teachings and mysteries not given to any except to that Muḥammadan person. If we wanted to speak of all that Allah has bestowed upon us, we would need volumes, but here we will only mention to the *fuqarā'* the distinction that my master and teacher, Sīdī Muḥammad bin ᶜAlī accorded me. This was after he had been recognized as the new master of the order and I wrote to him ﵁ about renewing my affiliation through him after having been the disciple of the master and gnostic Sīdī al-ᶜArabī b. al-Huwwārī,[3] and he wrote back to me ﵁ requesting that I come to him. So following his request, I set out for Marrakesh, and when I entered upon him ﵁, a boundless happiness and joy came over him and he said, "When you came to me, the whole order came to me!" At another time, in a discourse of good tidings too long to mention here, he said, "For us, in this order, you hold the place of Ibn ᶜAṭā'illāh in the order of the Shādhiliyya. Just as that Way was given new life by Ibn ᶜAṭā'illāh, this blessed Way will be given new life through you, Allah willing."

And his hope for us has come to pass, for by Allah – and again, by Allah! – we have not passed through a town or village or countryside except that its people have borne witness to having received providential aid and new life flowing to their hearts, this being the mystery of permission (*idhn*). And no *faqīr* has sat with us – may praise be to Allah! – except that he has received knowledge that he had not previously possessed along with a deeper sense of humility and lowliness. And no aspirant has sat with us except that his fervor has been strengthened and his aspiration raised. And no shaykh among the masters of this time has come to us except that his direct experience (*dhawq*) of the divine has been increased and he has benefitted by something from us that he did not have before. All of that is by the mystery and blessing of permission, about which Ibn ʿAṭā'illāh said, "Whoever has been given permission to speak out will find that his expression is understood by his listeners and that his symbolic allusion is clear to them."[4] The one given permission to speak out is the one who speaks by Allah and for the sake of Allah. That is why his speech makes the impression it does on hearts so that both people of particular distinction and people who are beloved defer to his authority. The Shaykh of our Shaykh, Sidī Muḥammad al-ʿArabī ﷺ said, "By Allah, no-one comes to me except one whom Allah has accepted." And I say, mentioning the bounty of my Lord, that by Allah, no-one comes to me except one whom Allah loves. The Prophet ﷺ also spoke to me in a dream and said, "Know, my boy, that Allah will honor you with fresh, sweet waters." I said, "O Messenger of Allah, are these the waters of surrender, faith, and excellence?"[5] He answered, "They are." I then asked, "And will I drink these waters by myself or will I drink them along with all those who follow me?" He answered, "You will drink them, as will all those from my community who follow you."

What the Prophet ﷺ promised us Allah has brought to pass, for by Allah, we have drunk of those waters and all who are truly our companions will drink of them in the shortest time. So give praise and thanks to Allah, my dear sirs, for the gift by which your Guardian Lord has honored you in this, your time. Allah Most High says, *None of Our revelations do we abrogate or cause to be forgotten, but that we bring (in its place) one that is better or one that is like it* [2:106]. To mention "the one that is better" before "the one that is like it" alludes to the fact that any perfect saint must have a successor who will appear even if it is after some period of time and that this successor will excel him in knowledge and gnosis as an honor to him. For the outpouring of Allah's blessings is shown in increase, even as our Shaykh, Sīdī Aḥmad al-Badawī ﷺ said,

Your outpouring [is shown] in increase
And Your generosity, in continuation.

And I have alluded to this in one of my odes which speaks of the gifts Allah chose me to receive:

The Remembrance of the Beloved enrobed us in beauty
and in splendor, honor, and joy.
Coming near, we put aside all reserve and formality
and proudly proclaimed the One we love.

This is a well-known ode in twenty couplets, included in this blessed collection, and one who reads it will find what I am referring to. When Shaykh Sīdī Muḥammad ibn ᶜAlī ﷺ passed away and permission passed to me, I saw myself as lowly and undeserving of that station until four masters came to me (in dreams)—Sīdī Muḥammad bin ᶜAlī ﷺ, Sīdī al-ᶜArabī bin al-Huwwārī ﷺ, Sīdī Muḥammad al-ᶜArabī ﷺ, and Sīdī Aḥmad al-Badawī ﷺ—and told me to go out to people and guide them to the True Sovereign. They also said to me, "The water you drank from us is the freshest and sweetest there is. Stretch forth your hand to the east and the west and fear no one." Then there came to me permission from Muṣṭafā ﷺ, and after that I had no choice but to go out to people as a teacher. So—by Allah and for Allah—I did so, and I said as Ibn ᶜAṭā'illāh had said in the words of the *Ḥikam*: "My God! You have commanded me to return to created things, so return me to them with the raiment of lights and guidance of inner vision, so that I may return from them to You just as I entered Your Presence from them with my innermost being protected from looking at them and my fervor raised above dependence upon them. *Verily You have Power over all things.*"[6]

Know too that it is an obligation for anyone who seeks the Presence of Allah to take as his teacher a living master. The evidence for this comes from the words of Allah Most High, *O you who believe, fear Allah and be with those who are utterly sincere* [9:199]. "To be *with*" someone means physical companionship, not just companionship in spirit. Also, the Most High says, *And follow the way of the one who turns to Me* [31:15]. In this latter verse, Allah Most High commands the son[7] to follow the father of souls rather than the father of physical forms, because the father of the soul fosters the spiritual dimension, while the father of the body fosters the sensory dimension, and what a vast difference there is between someone whose aspiration is towards the sensory and someone whose aspiration is towards the spiritual. Moreover, the Prophet ﷺ said, "A person's religion will be that of his dearest friend, so let each of you look carefully at whom he takes as his dearest friend".[8] In the community of Muḥammad ﷺ, from the earliest times until now, there has been agreement that the first thing required of an aspirant, as soon as he becomes aware of his heedlessness towards Allah, is to depend upon a shaykh who can counsel and guide him, who knows the faults and pretentions of the ego and also their remedies, and who himself has completed the training of his own ego and its desires. This teacher can then give the aspirant insight into his own faults and bring him out of a state of being engrossed in the sensual. And for the one who has no shaykh to direct him to the path of guidance, the devil will surely direct to the path of ruin.

The word "aspirant" (*murīd*) is derived from "will" (*al-irāda*) and is related to sincerity (*ikhlāṣ*). The true meaning of *murīd* is someone who has turned away from his own wants towards what Allah wants for him, and what Allah wants for him is worship, as

He has said: *I did not create jinn and men except to worship Me* [51:56].
An aspirant alone, dominated by his ego and the devil, is too weak
to gain mastery over himself. When he places himself under the
instructions and care of a shaykh, it is the shaykh's aspiration,
which operates through the permission of Allah, and his words,
which deeply impress the soul, that help him to obey and worship
Allah. So it becomes an obligation for an aspirant to become
attached to the shaykh of his time to whom he is best disposed.

Thus did Sīdī ʿAbd al-Wāḥid ibn ʿĀshir say (in *al-Murshid al-
Muʿīn*):

> *He makes his companion a master with deep knowledge*
> *who can warn him away from the roads to ruin.*
> *Whenever he sees him, he is reminded of Allah.*
> *Thus is the servant brought to his Lord.*

If you refer to what the commentators have said about these lines,
any questions you might have about this will be answered. Ibn
ʿAṭāʾillāh 🙏 says in his *Ḥikam*, "Do not keep company with anyone whose state does not inspire you, and whose speech does not
lead you to Allah."[9]

Both of these—inspiration and direction—result from companionship. If someone does not find these qualities in his companion, then he should leave him for the sake of Allah and search
for someone who has them. In this search, he will succeed to the
degree of his sincerity and strength of his resolve, and Allah is the
One Whose help we seek.

Explaining the attributes of the teaching Shaykh, I said in one
of my poems ending in *tā'*:

> *The invocation of the shahāda dispels all whisperings*
> *when imparted by a master who knows the Real.*
> *And the signs of [such a one] are: a light that shines outwardly,*
> *a secret that shows from within, and high aspiration.*
> *Just to see him uplifts you before a single word is uttered,*
> *and should speech come forth from him, it comes forth enrobed,*

By which I mean by the mysteries which run straight to the heart
of the one who aspires to the True God, without partner.
Detachment from what people have is the mainstay of his journey;
his work is solely the vision of the Friend,
And his speech is by permission of the Best of this people,
upon whom the greatest of the saintly depend.
If you've found such a one as we have mentioned,
then go ahead and give yourself without hesitation.
And do not consider other than what I have written,
for therein is sufficiency and therein every joy.

And to quote al-Junayd ﵁:

Purify yourself with the water of the Unseen if you have the Secret.
And if not, then with earth or stone.
Then place before you as imam the one you were facing
and pray the midday prayer at the start of the afternoon.
This is the prayer of those who deeply know their Lord
And if you are among them, then moisten the dry land with the ocean.

Al-Junayd ﵁ is telling the aspirant to purify himself with the water of the Unseen. This implies that there are two sorts of purifications. One is the physical act done with the water of this physical world and concerns the entire body in the case of the greater impurity. In these verses, however, the poet does not mean this action. Rather, he is speaking of the second sort of purification—spiritual purification—which is to cleanse the heart of any maladies that veil it from the presence of the Knower of the Unseen. This latter sort of purification is done only with spiritual water: the water of religious teachings, experiential knowledge, and the mysteries which flow from the realm of the Unseen into the heart of a gnostic master who has purified himself of faults. This is the water which the master pours out for the aspirant and through which his heart may be cleansed of otherness and filled with inner knowledge and mysteries.

However, this may only happen if the aspirant himself is someone who possesses the Secret, that is to say, who has an inner vision which leads him to the one who will take him by the hand, the master who is given help from the Unseen realm, as we have mentioned. If the aspirant is not such a one, then he should accomplish purification "with earth or stone," which here signifies outward deeds and formal knowledge, until Allah opens the way for him to the Secret and insight.

And when he says, "Then place before you as imam the one whom you were facing," he is alluding to the fact that the aspirant must then place before him a shaykh, one whose knowledge is by Allah, whom he will follow in offering the Prayer of the Spirit, which means [bringing about in the soul] a profound consciousness of the Worshipped Sovereign, just as one who is following an imam in the canonical Prayer must follow him in the bowing and prostration of that worship.

His words, "the one you were facing," allude to the fact that an aspirant will only follow the master he had already known in the World of Souls (*ᶜālam al-arwāḥ*). This is based on the saying of the Prophet ﷺ, "[Before the creation of the world] souls were grouped according to their similarities. Those who knew one another [there] are drawn to one other [here], and those who did not are not."[10] So the meaning here could be, "Place before you as imam in this physical world the one you were facing in the World of Souls, because from the encounter and knowledge you had of one another that world, there will be an attraction and harmony in this world."

Then he says, "Pray the midday prayer (*al-ẓuhr*) at the start of the afternoon (*al-ᶜaṣr*)." This means offer the Prayer of *al-ẓuhr* that is a manifestation (*ẓuhūr*) of your desire towards your Lord. This prayer, as we have said, is [the birth within the soul of] a deep and on-going consciousness of the presence of the Worshipped Sovereign. To offer this prayer "at the start of the afternoon (*ᶜaṣr*)" signifies that you will do so with a shaykh who is of your time (*muʿāṣaratik*) and make your will subordinate to his.

What is meant [in these lines], then, is not the midday and late afternoon prayers comprised of bowing and prostrating, for it is well-known that the midday prayer is supposed to be offered at the beginning its time and not at the beginning of the late afternoon. This is what has led us to the meaning we have mentioned, so understand it that you might be guided—and may Allah guide us and guide all creation. Amen!

Thus, by his words, "This is the prayer of those who deeply know their Lord," he means of those [in whose souls is born] a profound consciousness of the Worshipped Sovereign, and it is the prayer of *Those who are constant in their prayer* [70:23] because this consciousness is continuous, constant, and uninterrupted.[11]

Then he says, "If you are among them, then moisten the dry land with the ocean", which is to say that if you are one of the gnostics —those who are not veiled by creation from Allah, nor by Allah from creation—then moisten, that is sprinkle, the dry land of the Revealed Law (*sharīʿatika*) with water from the ocean of Inner Spiritual Truth (*ḥaqīqatika*). That is, be among those who combine them both in themselves, for as our imam, Mālik ﷺ, said, "He who follows the Law but does not realize the inner truth is immoral, and he who realizes the inner truth but does not follow the Law is heretical, but he who combines them is a person of true realization," that is, a person who realizes both states of servanthood: the servanthood of obligation and the servanthood of gnosis.

Endnotes

1. The Shaykh uses this term in the same way as the term *al-quṭb*, the "spiritual pole or axis" is usually used.
2. This echoes the Arabic saying, *Kullu muddaᶜin mumtaḥanun*, "Every pretender is tested."
3. Sīdī al-Huwwārī ﵁ had passed away and the Shaykh intended to take new allegiance.
4. *The Book of Wisdom* 184.
5. *Islām, Īmān,* and *Iḥsān* – devotional actions, faith, and an inner realization of the Divine Presence – are the triad which, according to famous ḥadīth Jibrīl, make up the religion. See pages 7 and 8 above.
6. *The Book of Wisdom* (*Munājāt,* 21).
7. This verse is from Sūra Luqmān and occurs in the context of Luqmān's advice to his son.
8. Aḥmad ibn Ḥanbal, *Musnad,* 16:7685, Bayhaqī, *Shuᶜab al-Īmān,* 9118, and others.
9. *The Book of Wisdom,* 43.
10. A ḥadīth found in Bukhārī and Muslim.
11. In the Quranic phrase, *ᶜalā ṣalātihim dā·imūn,* usually translated "constant in their prayer," the noun "prayer" is singular and so may refer to the five daily prayers and or to a state of constancy in a single prayer. Ibn ᶜAjība, in his spiritual allusion on these verses, says that this speaks of the "prayer of hearts," about which someone asked a shaykh, "Does the heart have a prayer?" and he responded, "Yes, and when it prostrates, it never raises its head again." *Al-Baḥr al-Madīd,* 70:23.

Transcription and Translation of

The Noble Wird

OF SĪDĪ MUḤAMMAD IBN AL-ḤABĪB

MAY ALLĀH BE PLEASED WITH HIM

This note precedes the original edition of the litany in Arabic

This is our Noble *Wird*. For one who wishes it and seeks it, it is a means to all goodness and a shield against all evil. One who wishes to recite it regularly should do so with permission from the Shaykh or from a *muqaddam* to whom the Shaykh has given permission to convey this litany. May Allāh unite in the servant the *sharīʿa* and the *ḥaqīqa*.

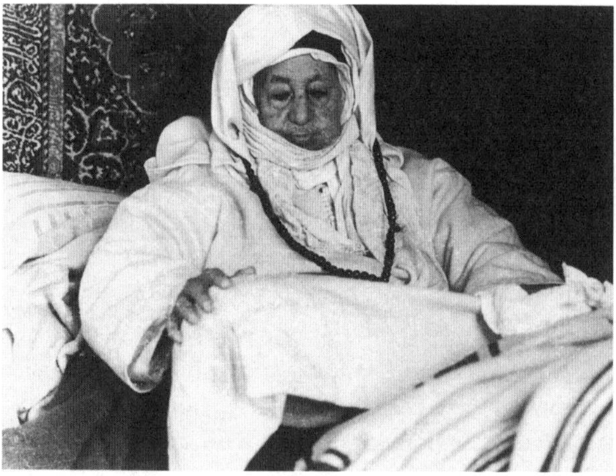

اللّٰهُمَّ صَلِّ على سَيِّدِنا مُحَمَّدٍ عَبْدِكَ وَرَسُولِكَ النَّبِيِّ الأُمِّيِّ وَعَلَىٰ آلِهِ وصَحْبِهِ وَسَلِّمْ تَسْلِيماً ، عَدَدَ خَلْقِكَ وَرِضَا نَفْسِكَ وَزِنَةَ عَرْشِكَ وَمِدَادَ كَلِمَاتِكَ . أَعُوذُ بِاللهِ السَّمِيعِ العَلِيمِ مِنَ الشَّيطَانِ الرَّجِيمِ. بِسْمِ اللهِ الرَّحْمٰنِ الرَّحِيمِ ، وَلاَ حَوْلَ وَلاَ قُوَّةَ إِلاَّ بِاللهِ العَلِيِّ العَظِيمِ .

Allāhumma ṣalli ʿalā Sayyidinā Muḥammadin, ʿabdika wa rasūlika-n-nabiyyi ʿl-ummīyī, wa ʿalā ālihi wa ṣaḥbihi wa sallim taslīmā, ʿadada khalqika, wa riḍā nafsika, wa zinata ʿarshika, wa midāda kalimātik. Aʿūdhu bi-Llāhi-s-Samīʿi-l-ʿAlīm mina-sh-shayṭāni-r-rajīm, bismi-Llāhi-r-Raḥmāni-r-Raḥīm, wa lā ḥawla wa lā quwwata illā bi-Llāhi-l-ʿAlīyi-l-ʿAẓīm

O Allah, send blessings to our master Muḥammad, Your servant and Messenger, the unlettered prophet, and to his Family and Companions, and greetings upon greetings of peace, (as limitless as) Your creation, Your contentment, the weight of Your Throne, and the ink of Your words. I seek refuge in Allah, the Hearer and Knower, from the devil, accursed. In the Name of Allah, the Merciful and the Compassionate: There is no power nor strength but in Allah, the Sublime and the All-Mighty.[§]

§ In beginning his litany with blessings upon the Prophet ﷺ, seeking refuge (*al-istiʿādha*), the *basmala*, and the *ḥawqala*, Sīdī Muḥammad ibn al-Ḥabīb followed the practice of Sidi Aḥmad al-Badawī Zouiten (note 30 of the biography) as well as of his successor, Sīdī Muḥammad al-ʿArabī al-Madaghrī (note 17 of the biography).

أَسْتَغْفِرُ اللهَ (3)

Astaghfiru-Llāh

I seek forgiveness of Allah

اللّٰهُمَّ صَلِّ عَلَى سَيِّدِنَا مُحَمَّدٍ عَبْدِكَ وَرَسُولِكَ النَّبِيِّ الأُمِّيِّ وَعَلَىٰ آلِهِ وَصَحْبِهِ وَسَلِّمْ (3)

Allāhumma ṣalli ʿalā Sayyidinā Muḥammadin, ʿabdika wa rasūlika-n-nabiyyi-l-ummiyyi, wa ʿalā ālihi wa ṣaḥbihi wa sallim (3)

O Allah, send blessings to our master Muḥammad, Your servant and Messenger, the unlettered Prophet, and to his Family and Companions, and greetings of peace

لَآ إِلٰهَ إِلاَّ اللهُ وَحْدَهُ لاَ شَرِيكَ لَهُ ٭ لَهُ الْمُلْكُ وَلَهُ الحَمْدُ ٭ وَهُوَ عَلَى كُلِّ شَيْءٍ قَدِيرٌ (3)

Lā ilāha illa-Llāh, waḥdahu lā sharīka lah, lahu-l-mulku wa lahu-l-ḥamd, wa huwa ʿalā kulli shay•in qadīr (3)

There is no god but Allah, One, without partner, His is the Sovereignty and His the Praise, and He, over all things, has power. (3)

سُبْحَانَ اللهِ وَالحَمْدُ لِلهِ وَلَا إِلٰهَ إِلَّآ اللهُ وَاللهُ أَكْبَرُ٭ وَلَا حَوْلَ وَلَا قُوَّةَ إِلَّا بِاللهِ العَلِيِّ الْعَظِيمِ (3)

Subḥāna-Llāhi wa-l-ḥamdu li-Llāhi, wa lā ilāha illa-Llāh, wa-Llāhu akbar, wa lā ḥawla wa lā quwwata illā bi-Llāhi-l-ʿAlīyyi-l-ʿAẓīm (3)

Glory be to Allah and Praise, there is no god but Allah, Allah is greater and there is no strength nor power but by Allah, Sublime and All Mighty

سُبْحَانَ اللهِ وَبِحَمْدِهِ سُبْحَانَ اللهِ الْعَظِيمِ (3)

Subḥāna-Llāhi wa bi-ḥamdihi, subḥāna-Llāhi-l-ʿAẓīm (3)

Glory be to Allah and Praise, Glory be to Allah, the All Mighty

الحَمْدُ لِلهِ وَالشُّكْرُ لِلهِ (3)

Al-ḥamdu li-Llāhi, wa-sh-shukru li-Llāh (3)

Praise be to Allah and thanks be to Allah

﴿لَقَدْ جَآءَكُمْ رَسُولٌ مِنْ أَنْفُسِكُمْ عَزِيزٌ عَلَيْهِ مَا عَنِتُّمْ ٭ حَرِيصٌ عَلَيْكُم ٭ بِالْمُؤْمِنِينَ رَؤُوفٌ رَّحِيمٌ﴾

Laqad jā•akum rasūlun min anfusikum, ʿazīzun ʿalayhi mā ʿanittum, ḥarīṣun ʿalaykum, bi-l-mūminīna ra•ūfu-r-raḥīm.

There has come to you a Messenger from among yourselves, distressed if you suffer, anxious for your (welfare), full of compassion and mercy for the faithful. (9:129)

﴿فَإِنْ تَوَلَّوْا فَقُلْ حَسْبِيَ اللهُ ٭ لَآ إِلٰهَ إِلَّا هُوَ ٭ عَلَيْهِ تَوَكَّلْتُ وَهُوَ رَبُّ الْعَرْشِ الْعَظِيمِ﴾ (3)

Fa in tawallaw, fa qul ḥasbiya-Llāhu, lā ilāha illā Hu, ʿalayhi tawakkalt, wa Huwa Rabbu-l-ʿArshi-l-ʿAẓīm (3)

But if they turn away, say, Allah suffices me. There is no god but He. In Him I put my trust, and He is the Lord of the Mighty Throne. (9:130)

﴿بِسْمِ اللهِ الرَّحْمَٰنِ الرَّحِيمِ ۞ قُلْ هُوَ اللهُ أَحَدٌ ۞ اللهُ الصَّمَدُ ۞
لَمْ يَلِدْ وَلَمْ يُولَدْ ۞ وَلَمْ يَكُن لَّهُ كُفُوًا أَحَدٌ﴾ (3)

Bismi-Llāhi-r-Raḥmāni-r-Raḥīm ✶ Qul Huwa-Llāhu Aḥad ✶ Allāhu aṣ-Ṣamad ✶ Lam yalid wa lam yūlad ✶ wa lam yakun lahu kufu•an aḥad (3)

In the Name of Allah, Merciful and Compassionate: Say: He, Allah, is One. Allah, the eternally Besought. He does not beget and He was not begotten. And there is nothing else like Him. (112: 1-4)

تَبَارَكَ اللهُ (3)

Tabāraka-Llāh (3)

Blessed be Allah!

﴿بِسْمِ اللهِ الرَّحْمَٰنِ الرَّحِيمِ ۞ الْحَمْدُ لِلهِ رَبِّ الْعَالَمِينَ الرَّحْمَٰنِ
الرَّحِيمِ ۞ مَلِكِ يَوْمِ الدِينِ ۞ إِيَّاكَ نَعْبُدُ وَ إِيَّاكَ نَسْتَعِينُ ۞ اِهْدِنَا
الصِّرَاطَ الْمُسْتَقِيمَ ۞ صِرَاطَ الَّذِينَ أَنْعَمْتَ عَلَيْهِمْ ، غَيْرِ
الْمَغْضُوبِ عَلَيْهِمْ وَلَا الضَّآلِّينَ﴾ آمين (3)

Bismi-Llāhi-r-Raḥmāni-r-Raḥīm ✶ Al-ḥamdu li-Llāhi Rabbi-l-ᶜĀlamīn ✶ Ar-Raḥmāni-r-Raḥīm ✶ Maliki yawmi-d-dīn ✶ Iyyāka naᶜbudu wa iyyāka nastaᶜīn ✶ Ihdina-ṣ-ṣirāṭa-l-mustaqīm ✶ ṣirāṭa-l-ladhīna anᶜamta ᶜalayhim, ghayri-l-maghḍūbi ᶜalayhim wa la-ḍ-ḍa̱llīn ✶ A̱mīn (3)

Praise be to Allah, Lord of the worlds. The Merciful, the Compassionate. Sovereign of the Day of Judgment. You alone do we worship and You alone do we ask for help. Guide us along the straight path. The path of those whom You have graced, not those who have earned Your wrath nor those who go astray. Amen (1: 1-7)

﴿سُبْحَانَ رَبِّكَ رَبِّ الْعِزَّةِ عَمَّا يَصِفُونَ * وَسَلَامٌ عَلَى الْمُرْسَلِينَ *
وَالْحَمْدُ لِلَّهِ رَبِّ الْعَالَمِينَ﴾

Subḥāna Rabbika Rabbi-l-ʿizzati ʿammā yaṣifūn, wa salāmun ʿala-l-mursalīn, wa-l-ḥamdu li-Llāhi Rabbi-l-ʿālamīn.

Glorified be your Lord, Lord of Honor, above all they attribute to Him, and Peace be upon all the Messengers, and praise be to Allah, Lord of the Worlds (37: 180-182)

اللّٰهُمَّ صَلِّ عَلَى سَيِّدِنَا مُحَمَّدٍ عَبْدِكَ وَنَبِيِّكَ وَرَسُولِكَ النَّبِيِّ الأُمِّيِّ
وَعَلَىٰ آلِهِ وَصَحْبِهِ وَسَلِّمْ تَسْلِيماً * بِقَدْرِ عَظَمَةِ ذَاتِكَ فِي كُلِّ وَقْتٍ
وَحِينٍ (3)

Allāhumma ṣalli ʿalā sayyidinā Muḥammadin, ʿabdika wa nabīyika wa rasūlika-n-nabiyyi-l-umiyyi wa ʿala̱ a̱lihi wa ṣaḥbihi wa sallim taslīmā, bi qadri ʿaẓamati dhātika fī kulli waqtin wa ḥīn (3)

O Allah! Send blessings to our master Muḥammad, Your Servant, Prophet, and Envoy, the Unlettered Prophet, and to his Family and Companions, and send them salutations upon salutations of peace as infinite as the infinitude of Your Essence, at every time and place.

آمين آمين آمين

A̱mīn A̱mīn A̱mīn

﴿سُبْحَانَ رَبِّكَ رَبِّ الْعِزَّةِ عَمَّا يَصِفُونَ * وَسَلَامٌ عَلَى الْمُرْسَلِينَ *
وَالْحَمْدُ لِلَّهِ رَبِّ الْعَالَمِينَ﴾

Subḥāna Rabbika Rabbi-l-ʿizzati ʿammā yaṣifūn, wa salāmun ʿala-l-mursalīn, wa-l-ḥamdu li-Llāhi Rabbi-l-ʿālamīn.

Glorified be your Lord, Lord of Honor, above all they attribute to Him, and peace be upon all the Messengers, and Praise be to Allah, Lord of the Worlds. (37: 180-182)

اللّٰهُمَّ إنِّي أسْأَلُكَ إسْلَامًا صَحِيْحًا يَصْحَبُهُ الاِسْتِسْلَامُ لِأَوَامِرِكَ وَنَوَاهِيكَ ، وإيْمَاناً خَالِصًا رَاسِخًا ثَابِتًا مَحْفُوظًا مِنْ جَمِيعِ الشُّبَهِ وَالمَهَالِكِ ، وإحْسَانًا يَزُجُّ بِنَا فِي حَضَرَاتِ الغُيُوبِ ، ونَتَطَهَّرُ بِهِ مِنْ أنْوَاعِ الغَفَلَاتِ وَسَآئِرِ العُيُوبِ ، وإيقَانًا يَكْشِفُ لَنَا عَنْ حَضَرَاتِ الاَسْمَآءِ وَالصِّفَاتِ، وَيَرحَلُ بِنَآ إِلَى مُشَاهَدَةِ أنْوَارِ تَجَلِّيَاتِ الذَّاتِ ، وعِلْماً نَافِعاً نَفْقَهُ بِهِ كَيْفَ نَتَأَدَّبُ مَعَكَ وَنُنَاجِيكَ فِي الصَّلَوَاتِ ، وَامْلأْ قُلُوبَنَا بِأنْوَارِ مَعْرِفَتِكَ حَتَّى نَشْهَدَ قَيُّومِيَّتَكَ السَّارِيَةَ فِي جَمِيعِ الْمَخْلُوقَاتِ ، وَاجْعَلْنَا مِنْ أَهْلِ دَآئِرَةِ الفَضْلِ الْمَحْبُوبِينَ لَدَيْكَ ، وَمِنَ الرَّاسِخِينَ الْمُتَمَكِّنِينَ فِي التَّوَكُّلِ وَصِدْقِ الإِعْتِمَادِ عَلَيْكَ ،

Allāhumma, innī as•aluka islāman ṣaḥīḥan, yaṣ•ḥabuhu l-istislāmu li awāmirika wa nawāhīk, wa īmānan khāliṣan, rāsikhan, thābitan, maḥfūẓan min jamīʿi-sh-shubahi wa-l-mahālik, wa iḥsānan yazujju binā fī ḥaḍarāti-l-ghuyūb, wa nataṭahharu bihi min anwāʿi-l-ghafalāti wa sā̱•iri-l-ʿuyūb, wa īqānan yakshifu lanā ʿan ḥaḍarāti-l-asmā̱•i wa-ṣ-ṣifāt, wa yarḥalu binā ilā mushāhadati anwāri tajalliyāti-dh-Dhāt, wa ʿilman nāfiʿan, nafqahu bihi kayfa nata•addabu maʿaka wa nunājīka fī-ṣ-ṣalawāt, wa-mla' qulūbanā bi anwāri maʿrifatika ḥattā nash•hada qayyūmīyataka-s-sāriyata fī jamīᶜi-l-makhlūqāt, wa-jᶜalnā min ahli dā̱•irati-l-faḍli-l-maḥbūbīna ladayk, wa mina-r-rāsikhīna-l-mutamakkinīna fi-t-tawakkuli wa ṣidqi-l-iᶜtimādi ᶜalayk

O Allah, I ask You for genuine submission (that) comes with active acceptance of Your commandments and prohibitions, and faith (that is) sincere, deep-rooted, firm, protected from all doubtful things and destructive sins, and excellence by which we plunge into the worlds of the Unseen and are cleansed of the varied forms of heedlessness and all the other faults, and certitude that reveals to us the domains of the Names and Attributes and carries us to directly perceive the Lights of the Essence revealing Itself and beneficial knowledge by which we will know right action in Your Presence and how to speak with You in prayer. Fill our hearts with the Lights of direct knowledge of You that we might perceive Your Immutability flowing through all creation, And make us among the people in the circle of Your grace, beloved in Your Presence, (make us) among those deeply-rooted in faith and firmly established in trust and true dependence upon You.

وَحَقِّقْ رَجَآءَنَا بَالإِجَابَةِ يَا كَرِيمُ يَا وَهَّابُ فِي كُلِّ مَا سَأَلْنَاكَ ، وَلَا تَكِلْنَا يَا مَوْلَانَا فِي جَمِيعِ حَرَكَاتِنَا وَسَكَنَاتِنَآ إِلَىٰٓ أَحَدٍ سِوَاكَ ، فَإِنَّكَ عَوَّدْتَنَّآ إِحْسَانَكَ مِنْ قَبْلِ سُؤَالِنَا وَنَحْنُ فِي بُطُونِ الأُمَّهَاتِ ، وَرَبَّيْتَنَا بِلَطِيفِ رُبُوبِيَّتِكَ تَرْبِيَةً تَقْصُرُ عَنْ إِدْرَاكِهَا الْعُقُولُ الْمُنَوَّرَاتُ

wa ḥaqqiq rajā̱•anā bi-l-ijābati, *yā* Karīmu, *yā* Wahhābu, fī kulli mā sa•alnāk, wa lā takilnā, *yā* Mawlānā, fī jamīᶜi ḥarakātinā wa sakanātinā̱ ilā̱ aḥadin siwāk. Fa innaka ᶜawwadtanā̱ iḥsānaka min qabli su•ālinā, wa naḥnu fī buṭūni-l-ummahāt, wa rabbaytanā bi laṭīfi rubūbīyyatika tarbīyyatan taqṣuru ᶜan idrākihā-l-ᶜuqūlu-l-munawwarāt.

Fulfil our hopes with an answer, O You Who are Infinitely Generous, O Bestower of gifts, to all that we ask of You, and do not place us, O Lord and Protector, in all our movements and rests in the charge of anyone else but You. For truly, You accustomed us to Your Excellence before we (could even) ask for it when we were (still) in our mothers' wombs, and You nurtured us with the gentleness of Your Nurturing in a way that (even the most) illuminated minds cannot fully grasp.

فَنَسْأَلُكَ اللّٰهُمَّ بِنَبِيِّكَ الَّذِي فَضَّلْتَهُ عَلَى سَآئِرِ الأَنْبِيَآءِ
وَالْمُرْسَلِينَ ، وَبِرَسُولِكَ الَّذِي جَعَلْتَ رِسَالَتَهُ عَآمَّةً وَرَحْمَةً
لِلْخَلاَئِقِ أَجْمَعِينَ ، أَنْ تُصَلِّيَ وَتُسَلِّمَ عَلَيْهِ وَعَلَىٰٓ آلِهِ صَلاَةً
وَسَلاَماً نَنَالُ بِهِمَا مَحَبَّتَهُ وَمُتَابَعَتَهُ فِي الأَقْوَالِ وَالأَفْعَالِ
وَالْمُرَاقَبَةِ وَالْمُشَاهَدَةِ وَالآدَابِ وَالأَخْلاَقِ وَالأَحْوَالِ

Fa nas•aluka-Llāhumma bi nabiyyika-l-ladhī faḍḍaltahu ʿalā sā̲•iri-l-anbiyā•i wa-l-mursalīn, wa bi rasūlika-l-ladhī jaʿalta risālatahu ʿā̲mmatan wa raḥmatan li-l-khalā̲•iqi ajmaʿīn, an tuṣallīya wa tusallima ʿalayhi wa ʿalā̲ ā̲lihi ṣalātan wa salāman nanālu bihimā maḥabbatahu wa mutābaʿatahu fī-l-aqwāli, wa-l-afʿāli, wa-l-murāqabati, wa-l-mushāhadati, wa-l-ā̲dābi, wa-l-akhlāqi wa-l-aḥwāl

So we ask You by Your Prophet whom You favored above the rest of the prophets and Messengers, and by Your Messenger whose message You made all-inclusive and as a Mercy for all creatures, that You send blessings and salutations of peace upon him and his folk, blessings and peace by which we might attain his love and be among those who follow him in word and deed, in vigilance and perception, in manners, virtues, and states

وَنَسْأَلُكَ يَا مَوْلَانَا بِجَاهِهِ أَنْ تَهَبَ لَنَا عِلْمًا نَافِعًا يَنْتَفِعُ بِهِ كُلُّ سَامِعٍ ، وَتَخْشَعُ لَهُ الْقُلُوبُ وَتَقْشَعِرُّ مِنْهُ الْجُلُودُ وَتَجْرِي لَهُ الْمَدَامِعُ ، إِنَّكَ أَنْتَ الْقَادِرُ الْمُرِيدُ الْعَالِمُ الْحَيُّ الْوَاسِعُ

wa nas·aluka, yā Mawlānā, bi jāhihi an tahaba lanā ʿilman nāfiʿan yantafiʿu bihi kullu sāmiʿ, wa takhshaʿu lahu-l-qulūbu wa taqshaʿirru minhu-l-julūdu, wa tajrī lahu-l-madāmiʿ, innaka Anta-l-Qādiru-l-Murīdu-l-ʿĀlimu-l-Ḥayyu-l-Wāsiʿ.§

and we ask You, our Guardian Lord, by his honor, to endow us with beneficial knowledge by which those who hear may benefit, and by which hearts may grow humble, and skin may tingle, and tears may flow. You are the One Who is Able, the One Who Wills, the One Who Knows, the Living, the All-Encompassing.

﴿سُبْحَانَ رَبِّكَ رَبِّ الْعِزَّةِ عَمَّا يَصِفُونَ ⋆ وَسَلَامٌ عَلَى الْمُرْسَلِينَ ⋆ وَالْحَمْدُ لِلَّهِ رَبِّ الْعَالَمِينَ﴾

Subḥāna Rabbika Rabbi-l-ʿizzati ʿammā yaṣifūn, wa salāmun ʿala-l-mursalīn, wa-l-ḥamdu li-Llāhi Rabbi-l-ʿālamīn.

Glorified be your Lord, Lord of Honor, above all they attribute to Him, and Peace be upon all the Messengers, and Praise be to Allah, Lord of the Worlds. (37: 180-182)

§ This supplication is called *al-wāridāt al-rabbāniyya fī al-daʿawāt al-jāmiʿa*. Sīdī Ḥamūd bin al-Bashīr al-Nāṣirī al-Blīdī, the Algerian scholar and disciple who wrote a commentary on this prayer, said, "I heard from (the Shaykh) ﵁ that this supplication came to his heart by inspiration, phrase by phrase, one night in the time before the Fajr prayer, complete from its beginning to its end."

اللّٰهُمَّ صَلِّ وَسَلِّمْ بِأَنْوَاعِ كَمَالَاتِكَ فِي جَمِيعِ تَجَلِّيَاتِكَ عَلَى سَيِّدِنَا
وَمَوْلَانَا مُحَمَّدٍ، أَوَّلِ الْأَنْوَارِ الْفَآئِضَةِ مِنْ بُحُورِ عَظَمَةِ الذَّاتِ ،
الْمُتَحَقِّقِ فِي عَالَمَيِ الْبُطُونِ وَالظُّهُورِ بِمَعَانِي الْأَسْمَآءِ وَالصِّفَاتِ ،
فَهُوَ أَوَّلُ حَامِدٍ وَمُتَعَبِّدٍ بِأَنْوَاعِ الْعِبَادَاتِ وَالْقُرُبَاتِ ، وَالْمُمِدُّ فِي عَالَمَيِ
الْأَرْوَاحِ وَالْأَشْبَاحِ لِجَمِيعِ الْمَوْجُودَاتِ ، وَعَلَىٰ آلِهِ وَأَصْحَابِهِ صَلَاةً
تَكْشِفُ لَنَا النِّقَابَ عَنْ وَجْهِهِ الْكَرِيمِ فِي الْمَرَائِي وَالْيَقَظَاتِ ، وَتُعَرِّفُنَا
بِكَ وَبِهِ فِي جَمِيعِ الْمَرَاتِبِ وَالْحَضَرَاتِ ، [وَالْطُفْ بِنَا يَا مَوْلَانَا بِجَاهِهِ
فِي الْحَرَكَاتِ وَالسَّكَنَاتِ وَاللَّحَظَاتِ وَالْخَطَرَاتِ] (3)

Allāhumma ṣalli wa sallim bi anwāʿi kamālātika fī jamīʿi tajalliyyātika ʿalā sayyidnā wa mawlānā Muḥammadin, awwali-l-anwāri-l-fā̱•iḍati min buḥūri ʿaẓamati-dh-Dhāt, al-mutaḥaqqiqi fī ʿālamayi-l-buṭūni wa-ẓ-ẓuhūri, bi maʿāni-l-asmā̱•i wa-ṣ-ṣifāt. Fa huwa awwalu ḥāmidin wa mutaʿabbidin bi anwāʿi-l-ʿibādāti wa-l-qurubāt, wa-l-mumiddu fī ʿālamayi-l-arwāḥi wa-l-ashbāḥi li jamīʿi-l-mawjūdāt, wa ʿalā̱ ā̱lihi wa aṣ•ḥābihi ṣalātan takshifu lanā-n-niqāba ʿan wajhihi-l-karīmi fī-l-marā̱•ī wa-l-yaqaẓāt, wa tuʿarrifunā bika wa bihi fī jamīʿi-l-marātibi wa-l-ḥaḍarāt. [Wa-lṭuf binā, yā Mawlānā, bi-jāhihi fī-l-ḥarakāti, wa-s-sakanāti, wa-l-laḥaẓāti, wa-l-khaṭarāt] (3)

---

§ The Shaykh ﵁ called this formula of invoking blessings upon the Prophet ﷺ *Kanz al-Ḥaqā'iq fī al-ṣalāti ʿalā ashrafi-l-khalā'iq* (The Treasure of Inner Truths in Blessing the Noblest of Creation). It was concerning this formula of blessing, which he received by inspiration from the presence of the Prophet ﷺ, that the Shaykh ﵁ asked Shaykh al-ʿAlawī (or ibn ʿAlīwa as he was affectionately known) to write the commentary, referred to on page 24 of the biography.

O Allah, send blessings and salutations through all Your Perfections and unveilings to our master and guardian Muḥammad, first of the Lights overflowing from the seas of the Majesty of the Essence, the one who realizes, in both the Inward and Outward domains, the Meanings of the Names and Qualities. He is the first of those to praise and worship through (all) the modes of worship and means of approach, the one who helps all that exists in the two worlds of spirit and form, and (send blessings) to his Family and Companions, (blessings) which unveil to us his noble face, both in dream visions and (while) awake. And bestow upon us a direct knowledge of You and of him at every level (of the way) and every realm of your Presence. And we ask You, O our Guardian and Protector, by his honor, that Your Infinite Kindness (be ever with us) in (our) movements and rests, (our) glances, and thoughts.

﴿سُبْحَانَ رَبِّكَ رَبِّ الْعِزَّةِ عَمَّا يَصِفُونَ * وَسَلَامٌ عَلَى الْمُرْسَلِينَ * وَالْحَمْدُ لِلَّهِ رَبِّ الْعَالَمِينَ﴾

Subḥāna Rabbika Rabbi-l-ʿizzati ʿammā yaṣifūn, wa salāmun ʿala-l-mursalīn, wa-l-ḥamdu li-Llāhi Rabbi-l-ʿālamīn.

Glorified be your Lord, Lord of Honor, above all they attribute to Him, and Peace be upon all the Messengers, and Praise be to Allah, Lord of the Worlds. (37: 180-182)

أَعُوذُ بِاللهِ مِنَ الشَّيْطَانِ الرَّجِيمِ ﴿الَّذِينَ قَالَ لَهُمُ النَّاسُ إِنَّ النَّاسَ قَدْ جَمَعُوا۟ لَكُمْ فَاخْشَوْهُمْ فَزَادَهُمْ إِيمَاناً ۚ وَقَالُوا۟:﴾

Aʿūdhu bi-Llāhi mina-sh-shaytāni-r-rajīm: Al-ladhīna qāla lahumu-n-nāsu: Inna-n-nāsa qad jamaʿū lakum fa-khshawhum, fa zādahumū īmāna(n), wa qālū:

I take refuge in Allah from the devil accursed. Those to whom people say, "The people have gathered against you! Fear them!" And they are increased in faith and say,

﴿حَسْبُنَا اللهُ وَنِعْمَ الْوَكِيلُ﴾ (10)

ḥasbuna-Llāhu wa niʿma-l-Wakīl (10)

Allah suffices us, the most excellent one to trust. (3:173)

﴿فَانْقَلَبُوا بِنِعْمَةٍ مِّنَ اللهِ وَفَضْلٍ لَّمْ يَمْسَسْهُمْ سُوٓءٌ﴾ (3)

Fa-nqalabū bi niʿmatin mina-Llāhi wa faḍlin,
lam yamsas-hum sū (3)

And they returned with bounty and favor from Allah and no harm touched them. (3:174)

﴿وَاتَّبَعُوا۟ رِضْوَانَ اللهِ ۚ وَاللهُ ذُو فَضْلٍ عَظِيمٍ﴾ (3)

Wa-ttabaʿū riḍwāna-Llāh. Wa-Llāhu dhū faḍlin ʿaẓīm (3)

And they followed the good pleasure of Allah. And Allah is the Possessor of Infinite Bounty. (3:174)

﴿وَإِنْ يُرِيدُوٓا۟ أَنْ يَّخْدَعُوكَ فَإِنَّ حَسْبَكَ اللهُ * هُوَ الَّذِيٓ أَيَّدَكَ
بِنَصْرِهِۦ وَبِالْمُومِنِينَ وَأَلَّفَ بَيْنَ قُلُوبِهِمْ * لَوْ أَنْفَقْتَ مَا فِي الْاَرْضِ
جَمِيعاً مَّآ أَلَّفْتَ بَيْنَ قُلُوبِهِمْ وَلَٰكِنَّ اللهَ أَلَّفَ بَيْنَهُمْ * إِنَّهُ عَزِيزٌ
حَكِيمٌ * يَٓا أَيُّهَا النَّبِيٓءُ حَسْبُكَ اللهُ * وَمَنِ اتَّبَعَكَ مِنَ الْمُومِنِينَ﴾

(3)

Wa in yurīdū̲ a(y)-yakhdaᶜūka, fa inna ḥasbaka-Llāh. Huwa-l-ladhī̲ ayyadaka bi naṣrihi wa bi-l-mūminīna, wa allafa bayna qulūbihim. Law anfaqta mā fi-l-arḍi jamīᶜan, mā̲ allafta bayna qulūbihim, wa lākinna-Llāha allafa baynahum, innahu ᶜAzīzun Ḥakīm. Yā ayyuha-n-nabiyyu̲, ḥasbuka-Llāhu wa mani-t-tabaᶜaka mina-l-mūminīn. (3)

And if they would deceive you, Allah is surely sufficient for you. He is the One Who supported you with His victory and with the faithful, and put harmony between their hearts. If you had spent all that was on the earth, you could not have put harmony between their hearts, but Allah put harmony between them. Truly, He is Precious and Wise. O Prophet! Allah is sufficient for you and for those of the faithful who follow you.

(8:63-65)

أَلَا يَا لَطِيفُ يا لَطِيفُ لَكَ اللُّطْفُ فَأَنْتَ اللَّطِيفُ مِنْكَ يَشْمَلُنَا اللُّطْفُ

A lā, yā Laṭīfu, yā Laṭīfu, laka l-luṭfu
fa Anta-l-Laṭīfu, minka yashmaluna-l-luṭfu

O Laṭīf, O Laṭīf! Is not Kindness Yours?
For You are al-Laṭīf and Your Kindness envelops us

لَطِيفُ لَطِيفُ إِنَّنِي مُتَوَسِّلٌ بِلُطْفِكَ فَالْطُفْ بِي وَقَدْ نَزَلَ اللُّطْفُ

Laṭīfu, Laṭīfu, innanī mutawassilun
bi luṭfika fa-lṭuf bī, wa qad nazala-l-luṭfu

Laṭīf, Laṭīf, truly I am one beseeching You by Your Kindness
to grant me your kindness and Your Kindness descends

بِلُطْفِكَ عُذْنَا يَا لَطِيفُ وَهَا نَحْنُ دَخَلْنَا فِي وَسْطِ اللُّطْفِ وَانْسَدَلَ اللُّطْفُ

Bi luṭfika ʿudhnā, yā Laṭīfu, wa hā naḥnu
dakhalnā fī wasṭi-l-luṭfi wa-nsadala-l-luṭfu

In Your Kindness we have taken refuge, O Laṭīf, and here we are entering the center of Your Kindness, and Kindness comes down

نَجَوْنَا بِلُطْفِ اللهِ ذِي اللُّطْفِ إِنَّهُ لَطِيفٌ لَطِيفٌ لُطْفُهُ دَائِماً لُطْفُ

Najawnā bi luṭfi-Llāhi, dhī-l-luṭfi innahu
Laṭīfun Laṭīfun, Luṭfuhu dā•iman Luṭfu

We are saved by the Kindness of Allah, the One Who possesses Kindness, truly He is Laṭīf, Laṭīf, and His Kindness is always Kindness.

أَلَا يا حَفِيظُ يا حَفِيظُ لَكَ الْحِفْظُ فَأَنْتَ الْحَفِيظُ مِنْكَ يَشْمَلُنَا الْحِفْظُ

A lā, yā Ḥafīẓu, yā Ḥafīẓu, laka-l-ḥifẓu
fa Anta-l-Ḥafīẓu, minka yashmalunā-l-Ḥifẓu

Ḥafīẓ, is not Protection Yours? You are al-Ḥafīẓ
and Your Protection envelops us

حَفِيظُ حَفِيظُ إِنَّنَا نَتَوَسَّلُ بِحِفْظِكَ فَاحْفَظْنَا وَ قَدْ نَزَلَ الْحِفْظُ

Ḥafīẓu, Ḥafīẓu, innanā natawāssalu
bi Ḥifẓika fa-ḥfaẓnā wa qad nazala-l-Ḥifẓu

Ḥafīẓ, Ḥafīẓ, surely we are beseeching You by Your Protection,
that You protect us, and Your Protection descends

بِحِفْظِكَ عُذْنَا يا حَفِيظُ وَهَا نَحْنُ دَخَلْنَا فِي وَسْطِ الْحِفْظِ وَانْسَدَلَ الْحِفْظُ

Bi Ḥifẓika ʿudhnā yā Ḥafīẓu wa hā naḥnu
dakhalnā fī wasṭi-l-ḥifẓi wa-nsadala-l-Ḥifẓu

In Your Infinite Protection have we taken refuge, O Ḥafīẓ, and here we are:
We have entered the center of Your Protection, and Your Infinite
Protection comes down

نَجَوْنَا بِحِفْظِ اللهِ ذِي الْحِفْظِ إِنَّهُ حَفِيظٌ حَفِيظٌ حِفْظُهُ دَائِماً حِفْظُ

Najawnā bi ḥifẓi-Llāhi, dhī-l-ḥifẓi innahu
Ḥafīẓun Ḥafīẓun, Ḥifẓuhu dā•iman ḥifẓu

We are saved by Allah's Infinite Protection, the One
Who possesses Protection, truly He is Ḥafīẓ, Ḥafīẓ, and His Protection
is always protection.

بِجَاهِ إِمَامِ الْمُرْسَلِينَ مُحَمَّدٍ فَلَوْلَاهُ عَينُ الحِفْظِ مَا نَزَلَ الحِفْظُ

Bi jāhi imāmi-l-mursalīna Muḥammadin
fa law lāhu ʿaynu-l-ḥifẓi, mā nazala-l-ḥifẓu

By the honor of the Imam of the Messengers, Muḥammad,
Were he not the spring of Protection, Protection would not descend.

عَلَيهِ صَلاةُ اللهِ مَا قَالَ مُنْشِدٌ أَلَا يا حَفِيظُ يا حَفِيظُ لَكَ الْحِفْظُ

ʿAlayhi ṣalātu-Llāhi mā qāla munshidun
alā, yā Ḥafīẓu, yā Ḥafīẓu, laka-l-Ḥifẓu

Upon him be blessings as long as those who chant his blessings say:
O Ḥafīẓ, O Ḥafīẓ, is not Infinite Protection Yours?

لَآ إِلٰهَ الاَّ اللهُ (١٠)

Lā ilāha illa-Llāh (10)

لَآ إِلٰهَ الاَّ اللهُ، سَيِّدُنَا مُحَمَّدٌ رَسُولُ اللهِ ، صَلَّى اللهُ عَلَيْهِ وسَلَّمَ وعَلَىٰ آلِهِ

Lā ilāha illa-Llāh, Sayyidunā Muḥammadu-r-Rasūlu-Llāh,
ṣalla-Llāhu ʿalayhi wa sallama wa ʿalā ālih(i)

There is no god but Allah. Our master Muḥammad is the Messenger of Allah, may Allah bless him and send to him and to his Family salutations of peace,

ثَبِّتْنَا يَا رَبِّ بِقَوْلِهَا ، وَانْفَعْنَا يَا مَوْلَانَا بِذِكْرِهَا ، وَأَدْخِلْنَا فِي مَيْدَانِ حِصْنِهَا، واجْعَلْنَا مِنْ أَفْرَادِ أَهْلِهَا ، وَعِنْدَ الْمَوتِ نَاطِقِينَ بِهَا عَالِمِينَ بِهَا ، واحْشُرْنَا فِي زُمْرَةِ سَيِّدِنَا وَمَوْلَانَا مُحَمَّدٍ ، صَلَّى اللهُ عَلَيهِ وَسَلَّمَ وَعَلَىٰ آلِهِ وأَصْحَابِه وَعَلَىٰ جَمِيعِ عِبَادِ اللهِ الْمُومِنِينَ

آمين آمين آمين

Thabbitnā yā Rabbi bi qawlihā, wa-nfaʿnā yā Mawlānā bi dhikrihā, wa-'adkhilnā fī maydāni ḥiṣnihā, wa-jʿalnā min afrādi ahlihā, wa ʿinda-l-mawti nāṭiqīnā bihā, ʿālimīnā bihā, wa-ḥshurnā fī zumrati sayyidinā wa mawlānā Muḥammadin ṣalla-Llāhu ʿalayhi wa sallama wa ʿalā̱ ā̱lihi wa aṣ‧ḥābihi wa ʿalā jamīʿi ʿibādi-Llāhi-l-mūminīn. A̱mīn A̱mīn A̱mīn

Make us steadfast, O Lord, by saying it, And benefit us, O Guardian Lord, by its mention and remembrance, and bring us inside the domain of its citadel, and make us among its people, and at the moment of death, one of those who pronounce it and know it, and resurrect us among the ranks of our master and guardian, Muḥammad, may Allah bless him and his Family, and Companions, and all the faithful servants of Allah.

[وَسَلامٌ عَلَى الأَنْبِيَاءِ وَالْمُرْسَلِينَ] (3)

وَعَلَىٰ جَمِيعِ عِبَادِ اللهِ الصَّالِحِينَ ، وَآخِرُ دَعْوَانَا أَنِ الْحَمْدُ لِلهِ رَبِّ الْعَالَمِينَ

[wa salāmun ʿala-l-anbiyā̱‧i wa-l-mursalīn] (3) wa ʿalā jamīʿi ʿibādi-Llāhi-ṣ-ṣāliḥīn, wa ākhiru daʿwānā̱ ani-l-ḥamdu li-Llāhi Rabbi-l-ʿālamīn,

And salutations of peace be upon (all) the Prophets and Messengers and upon all right-acting servants of Allah. And our final supplication is: praise be to Allah, Lord of the Worlds.

وَلَا حَوْلَ وَلَا قُوَّةَ إِلَّا بِاللهِ الْعَلِيِّ الْعَظِيمِ ، وَمَا تَوْفِيقِي إِلَّا بِاللهِ ، عَلَيْهِ تَوَكَّلْتُ وَإِلَيْهِ أُنِيبُ .الْحَمْدُ لِلهِ عَلَىٰ نِعْمَةِ الإِسْلَامِ وَكَفَى بِهَا نِعْمَةً

wa lā ḥawla wa lā quwwata illā bi-Llāhi-l-ʿAlīyyi-l-ʿAẓīm. Wa mā tawfīqīya illā bi-Llāh, ʿalayhi tawakkaltu wa ilayhi unīb, wa-l-ḥamdu li-Llāhi ʿalā niʿmati-l-islāmi wa kafā bihā niʿma

And there is no strength nor power but in Allah, the Sublime and Mighty; And I have no success except in Allah. In Him do I put my trust, and to Him do I return. And praise be to Allah for the blessing of Islam, sufficient it is as a blessing!

يَآ أَوَّلُ يَآ آخِرُ يَا ظَاهِرُ يَا بَاطِنُ اِسْمَعْ نِدَآئِي بِمَا سَمِعْتَ بِهِ
نِدَآءَ عَبْدِكَ سَيِّدِنَا زَكَرِيَّآءَ عَلَيهِ السَّلَامُ ، وَانْصُرْنِي بِكَ لَكَ ،
وَأَيِّدْنِي بِكَ لَكَ ، وَاجْمَعْ بَينِي وَبَينَكَ ، وَحُلْ بَيْنِي وَبَيْنَ غَيرِكَ

Yā Awwalu, Yā Ākhiru, Ya Ẓāhiru, Ya Bāṭin ismaʿ nidā•ī bimā samiʿta bihi nidā•a ʿabdika sayyidinā Zakarīyyā ʿalayhi s-salām, wa-nṣurnī bika lak, wa ayyidnī bika lak, wa-jmaʿ baynī wa baynak, wa ḥul baynī wa bayna ghayrik[§]

O You who are the First! You who are the Last! You who are the Outward! You who are the Inward! hear my call as You heard the call of Your servant, our master Zakariya, upon whom be peace. And help me by You for You. And support me by You for You. And unite me with You, and come between me and all else but You.

اللهُ

ALLĀH (10)

§ This supplication, including the invocations of the Name Allah, is from the end of the *Ṣalāt Mashīshīya*. Scriptually, it is related to the third verse of Sūrat al-Ḥadīd: *He is the First and the Last and the Outward and the Inward and He is the Knower of all things* [57:3] and to a ḥadīth in the collection of Muslim and elsewhere that states that upon retiring to his bed at night, the Prophet ﷺ would say, "*You are the First, and there is nothing before You, and You are the Last, and there is nothing after You, and You are the Outward, and there is nothing above You, and You are the Inward and there is nothing beneath you. Fulfill for us our dīn and suffice us from poverty.*"

بِسْمِ اللهِ الرَّحْمَٰنِ الرَّحِيمِ ، اللّٰهُمَّ إِنِّيَ أَسْأَلُكَ بِسِرِّ الذَّاتِ ، وَبِذَاتِ السِّرِّ ، هُوَ أَنْتَ وَأَنْتَ هُوَ ، اِحْتَجَبْتُ بِنُورِ اللهِ ، وَبِنُورِ عَرْشِ اللهِ ، وَبِكُلِّ اِسْمِ اللهِ مِنْ عَدُوِّي وعَدُوِّ اللهِ ، بِمِائَةِ أَلْفِ لَا حَوْلَ وَلَا قُوَّةَ إِلاَّ بِاللهِ ، خَتَمْتُ عَلَى نَفْسِي وَعَلَى دِينِي وَعَلَى كُلِّ شَيْءٍ أَعْطَانِيهِ رَبِّي بِخَاتَمِ اللهِ الْمَنِيعِ ، الَّذِي خَتَمَ بِهِ أَقْطَارَ السَّمَوَاتِ وَالارْضِ

Bismi-Llāhi-r-Raḥmāni-r-Raḥīm. Allāhumma inniya as•aluka bi sirri-dh-Dhāt, wa bi dhāti-s-Sirr. Huwa Anta wa Anta Hu(wa). Iḥtajabtu bi nūri-Llāh, wa bi nūri ʿarshi-Llāh, wa bi kulli ismi-Llāh, min ʿadūwwī wa ʿadūwwi-Llāhi, bi mi•ati alfi Lā ḥawla wa lā quwwata illā bi-Llāh, khatamtu ʿalā nafsī, wa ʿalā dīnī, wa ʿalā kulli shay•in aʿṭānīhi Rabbī bi khātami-Llāhi-l-manīʿ, al-ladhī khatama bihi aqṭāra-s-samāwāti wa-l-arḍ

O Allah, I ask You by the innermost secret of Your Essence and by the essence of Your innermost secret, You are It and It is You. I have veiled myself with the Light of Allah, and with the Light of Allah's Throne, and with each of Allah's Names, from my adversary, and the adversary of Allah, through a hundred thousand: "There is no strength nor power but in Allah" and I seal (it) closed upon myself, and my religion, and everything that my Lord has given me, by the seal of Allah, the Invulnerable, Who has thereby sealed closed the heavens and earth.

وحَسْبُنَا اللهُ وَنِعْمَ الْوَكِيلُ ، نِعْمَ الْمَولَى وَنِعْمَ النَّصِيرُ ، وَصَلَّى
اللهُ عَلَىٰ سَيِّدِنَا ومَوْلانَا مُحَمَّدٍ وَعَلَىٰ آلِهِ وَأَصْحَابِهِ أَجْمَعِينَ ،
وَسَلَّمَ تَسْلِيماً كَثِيراً ، والحَمْدُ لِلهِ رَبِّ العَالَمِينَ .

Wa ḥasbuna-Llāhu wa niᶜma-l-Wakīl, niᶜma-l-Mawlā, wa niᶜma-n-Naṣīr, wa ṣalla-Llāhu ᶜalā sayyidnā wa mawlānā Muḥammadin wa ᶜala̱ a̱lihi wa aṣ•ḥābihi ajmaᶜīn, wa sallama taslīmān kathīrā, wa-l-ḥamdu li-Llāhi Rabbi-l-ᶜālamīn.

And Allah is sufficient for us, the most excellent on whom to depend, the most excellent guardian, and most excellent ally. And may Allah bless our master and guardian Muḥammad and his Family and Companions all together. And greet them with salutations of peace in abundance, and thanks be to Allah, Lord of the Worlds.

يَا وَدُودُ(3) يَا ذَا الْعَرْشِ الْمَجِيدِ(3) يَا مُبْدِىءُ يَا مُعِيدُ(3)
يَا فَعَّالاً لِمَا يُرِيدُ(3) أَسْأَلُكَ بِنُورِ وَجهِكَ الَّذِي مَلأَ أَرْكَانَ
عَرْشِكَ(3) وَأَسْأَلُكَ بِالقُدْرَةِ الَّتِي قَدَرْتَ بِهَا عَلَى خَلْقِكَ(3)
وَبِرَحْمَتِكَ الَّتِي وَسِعَتْ كُلَّ شَيْءٍ (3) لآ إِلَهَ إِلآَّ أَنْتَ يَا مُغِيثُ
أَغِثْنَا (3)

Yā Wadūd (3), Yā Dha-l-ᶜarshi-l-majīd (3), Yā Mubdi•u yā Muᶜīd (3), Yā Faᶜᶜālan limā yurīd (3) as•aluka bi Nūri Wajhika-l-ladhī mala•a arkāna ᶜarshik (3), wa as•aluka bi l-Qudrati-l-latī qadarta bihā ᶜalā khalqik (3) wa bi Raḥmatika-l-latī wasiᶜat kulla shay (3) La̱ ilāha illa̱ Anta, Ya Mughīthu, aghithnā (3)

O You Who Loves, You of the Glorious Throne, You Who begins creation and starts it anew, You Who accomplishes what He wills, I ask You by the Light of Your Face which fills the pillars of the Throne, and I ask You by the Power with which You determine Your creation and by Your Mercy which envelops all things. There is no god but You, O You who sends relief, send us relief!

﴿سُبْحَانَ رَبِّكَ رَبِّ الْعِزَّةِ عَمَّا يَصِفُونَ ۞ وَسَلَامٌ عَلَى الْمُرْسَلِينَ ۞ وَالْحَمْدُ لِلَّهِ رَبِّ الْعَالَمِينَ﴾

Subḥāna Rabbika Rabbi-l-ʿizzati ʿammā yaṣifūn, wa salāmun ʿala-l-mursalīn, wa-l-ḥamdu li-Llāhi Rabbi-l-ʿālamīn.

Glorified be your Lord, Lord of Honor, above all they attribute to Him, and Peace be upon all the Messengers, and Praise be to Allah, Lord of the Worlds

﴿اللَّهُ لَطِيفٌ بِعِبَادِهِ ۞ يَرْزُقُ مَن يَشَآءُ ۞ وَهُوَ الْقَوِيُّ الْعَزِيزُ﴾ (3)

Allāhu Laṭīfun bi ʿibādihi, yarzuqu ma(n)y yashā', wa Huwa ʿl-Qawīyyu-l-ʿAzīz (9)

Allah is the Infinitely Kind to His servants. He provides for whomsoever he wills and He is the Strong, the Precious. (42:17)

MORNING RECITATION ONLY

لَآ إِلٰهَ إِلاَّ اللهُ واللهُ أَكْبَرُ، وسُبْحَانَ اللهِ وَبِحَمْدِهِ وَأَسْتَغْفِرُ اللهَ، وَلاَ حَوْلَ وَلاَ قُوَّةَ إِلاَّ بِاللهِ، هُوَ الاَوَّلُ وَالآخِرُ وَالظَّاهِرُ وَالبَاطِنُ، بِيَدِهِ الخَيْرُ، يُحْيِي وَيُمِيتُ، وهُوَ عَلَى كُلِّ شَيْءٍ قَدِيرٌ. (10)

Lā̱ ilāha illā-Llāh, wa-Llāhu akbar, wa subḥāna-Llāhi wa bi ḥamdihi, wa-'astaghfiru-Llāh, wa lā ḥawla wa lā quwwata illā bi-Llāh, Huwa-l-Awwalu wa-l-Ākhiru wa-ẓ-Ẓāhiru, wa-l-Bāṭin, bi Yadihi-l-khayr, yuḥyī wa yumīt, wa Huwa ʿalā kulli shay·in qadīr (10)

There is no god but Allah and Allah is greater. Glory be to Allah and thanks, and I seek forgiveness from Allah. There is no strength nor power but in Allah. He is the First and the Last, the Outward and the Inward, in His hand is all good. He gives life and gives death, and He, over all things, has Power.

وَصَلَّى اللهُ عَلَى سَيِّدِنَا وَمَوْلَانَا مُحَمَّدٍ وَعَلَىٰ آلِهِ وَصَحْبِهِ وَسَلَّمَ تَسْلِيماً ،
عَدَدَ خَلْقِكَ ، وَرِضَا نَفْسِكَ ، وَزِنَةَ عَرْشِكَ ، وَمِدَادَ كَلِمَاتِكَ

Wa ṣalla-Llāhu ʿalā sayyidinā wa mawlānā Muḥammadin, wa ʿalā̱ ā̱lihi wa ṣaḥbihi wa sallama taslīmā ʿadada khalqika, wa riḍā nafsika, wa zinata ʿarshika, wa midāda kalimātik.

And may Allah bless our master and guardian Muḥammad, and his Family and Companions and send them salutations of peace in abundance, as (limitless as) Your creation, Your contentment, the weight of Your Throne, and the ink of Your words.

﴿سُبْحَانَ رَبِّكَ رَبِّ الْعِزَّةِ عَمَّا يَصِفُونَ * وَسَلَامٌ عَلَى الْمُرْسَلِينَ *
وَالْحَمْدُ لِلَّهِ رَبِّ الْعَالَمِينَ﴾

Subḥāna Rabbika Rabbi-l-ʿizzati ʿammā yaṣifūn, wa salāmun ʿala-l-mursalīn, wa-l-ḥamdu li-Llāhi Rabbi-l-ʿālamīn.

Glorified be your Lord, Lord of Honor, above all they attribute to Him, and Peace be upon all the Messengers, and Praise be to Allah, Lord of the Worlds.

سُبْحَانَ اللهِ والْحَمْدُ لِلهِ ، وَلآ إِلَهَ إِلَّا اللهُ وَاللهُ أَكْبَرُ ، وَلَا حَوْلَ وَلَا قُوَّةَ إِلَّا بِاللهِ الْعَلِيِّ الْعَظِيمِ ، عَدَدَ مَا عَلِمَ ، وَ زِنَةَ مَا عَلِمَ ، وَمِلْءَ مَا عَلِمَ (3)

Subḥāna-Llāh, wa-l-ḥamdu li-Llāhi, wa la̱ ilāha illa-Llāh, wa-Llāhu akbar, wa lā ḥawla wa lā quwwata illā bi-Llāhi-l-ʿAliyyi-l-ʿAẓīm, ʿadada mā ʿalima, wa zinata mā ʿalima, wa mil•a mā ʿalim (3)

Glory be to Allah, Praise be to Allah, there is no god but Allah, Allah is greater. There is no strength nor power but in Allah the Sublime, the All Mighty. (Glorification and praise) as limitless as all He knows, and as weighty as all He knows, and as full as all He knows.

END OF MORNING RECITATION

﴿سُبْحَانَ رَبِّكَ رَبِّ الْعِزَّةِ عَمَّا يَصِفُونَ ٭ وَسَلَامٌ عَلَى الْمُرْسَلِينَ ٭ وَالْحَمْدُ لِلهِ رَبِّ الْعَالَمِينَ﴾

Subḥāna Rabbika Rabbi-l-ʿizzati ʿammā yaṣifūn, wa salāmun ʿala-l-mursalīn, wa-l-ḥamdu li-Llāhi Rabbi-l-ʿālamīn.

Glorified be your Lord, Lord of Honor, above all they attribute to Him, and Peace be upon all the Messengers, and Praise be to Allah, Lord of the Worlds.

CLOSING SUPPLICATIONS

اللّٰهُمَّ افْتَحْ بَصَآئِرَنَا لِمُرَاقَبَتِكَ وَمُشَاهَدَتِكَ بِجُودِكَ وَفَضْلِكَ ، وَنَوِّرْ سَرَآئِرَنَا لِتَجَلِّيَاتِ أَسْمَآءِكَ وَصِفَاتِكَ بِحِلْمِكَ وَكَرَمِكَ ، وَأَفْنِنَا عَنْ وُجُودِنَا الْمَجَازِي فِي وُجُودِكَ الْحَقِيقِي بِطَوْلِكَ وَمَنِّكَ ، وَأَبْقِنَا بِكَ لَا بِنَا مُحَافِظِينَ عَلَى شَرِيعَتِكَ وَسُنَّةِ نَبِيِّكَ، إِنَّكَ عَلَى كُلِّ شَيْءٍ قَدِيرٌ ، وَبِالإِجَابَةِ جَدِيرٌ ، بِسِرِّ وَبَرَكَةِ

Allāhumma-ftaḥ baṣā•iranā li murāqabatika wa-mushāhadatika, bi jūdika wa faḍlik, wa nawwir sarā•iranā li tajalliyāti asmā̱•ika wa ṣifātika bi ḥilmika wa karamik, wa-'afninā ʿan wujūdinā-l-majāzī fī Wujūdika-l-ḥaqīqī bi ṭawlika wa mannik, wa-'abqinā bika, lā binā, muḥāfaẓīna ʿalā sharīʿatika wa sunnati Nabiyyik, innaka ʿalā kulli shay•in qadīr, wa bi-l-ijābati jadīr, bi-sirri wa barakāti.

O Allah, open our inner vision to Your Vigilance and Perception by Your excellence and grace, and illuminate our innermost being to the unveilings of Your Names and Attributes by Your Gentleness and Generosity, and efface us from our figurative beings in Your true being by Your Forbearance and Favor, and sustain us by way of You, not by way of ourselves, in Your Revealed Law and the way of Your Prophet. Verily You, over all things, have power and are the most reliable to answer (prayers). By the secret and blessing of

﴿بِسْمِ اللهِ الرَّحْمَٰنِ الرَّحِيمِ ٭ الْحَمْدُ لِلهِ رَبِّ الْعَالَمِينَ الرَّحْمَٰنِ الرَّحِيمِ ٭ مَلِكِ يَومِ الدِّينِ ٭ إِيَّاكَ نَعبُدُ وَ إِيَّاكَ نَسْتَعِينُ ٭ اِهْدِنَا الصِّرَاطَ الْمُسْتَقِيمَ ٭ صِرَاطَ الذِينَ أَنْعَمْتَ عَلَيْهِمْ غَيْرِ الْمَغْضُوبِ عَلَيْهِمْ وَلَا الضَّآلِّينَ﴾ آمين

Bismi-Llāhi-r-Raḥmāni-r-Raḥīm ✶ Al-ḥamdu li-Llāhi Rabbi-l-ʿĀlamīn ✶ Ar-Raḥmāni-r-Raḥīm ✶ Maliki yawmi-d-dīn ✶ Iyyāka naʿbudu wa īyyāka nastaʿīn ✶ Ihdinā-ṣ-ṣirāṭa-l-mustaqīm ✶ ṣirāṭa-l-ladhīna anʿamta ʿalayhim, ghayri-l-maghḍūbi ʿalayhim wa la-ḍ-ḍā̲llīn ✶ A̲mīn

Praise be to Allah, Lord of the worlds, the Merciful, the Compassionate, Sovereign of the Day of Judgment. You alone do we worship and You alone do we ask for help. Guide us along the straight path. The path of those whom You have graced, not those who have earned Your wrath nor those who go astray. Amen

﴿سُبْحَانَ رَبِّكَ رَبِّ الْعِزَّةِ عَمَّا يَصِفُونَ ٭ وَسَلَامٌ عَلَى الْمُرْسَلِينَ ٭ وَالْحَمْدُ لِلهِ رَبِّ الْعَالَمِينَ﴾

Subḥāna Rabbika Rabbi-l-ʿizzati ʿammā yaṣifūn, wa salāmun ʿala-l-mursalīn, wa-l-ḥamdu li-Llāhi Rabbi-l-ʿālamīn.

Glorified be your Lord, Lord of Honor, above all they attribute to Him, and Peace be upon all the Messengers, and Praise be to Allah, Lord of the Worlds.

[Here is the place for a personal prayer, silently or aloud, which should include asking forgiveness for yourself, your parents, your teachers in the way, the present shaykh of the tariqa, and all believers, male and female.]

اللّٰهُمَّ صَلِّ عَلَىٰ سَيِّدِنَا مُحَمَّدٍ وَعَلَىٰ آلِ سَيِّدِنَا مُحَمَّدٍ صَلاةً تُنْجِينَا بِهَا مِنْ جَمِيعِ الأَهْوَالِ وَالآفَاتِ ، وتَقْضِي لَنَا بِهَا جَمِيعَ الحَاجَاتِ ، وَتُطَهِّرُنَا بِهَا مِنْ جَمِيعِ السَّيِّئَاتِ ، وتَرْفَعُنَا بِهَا أَعْلَا الدَّرَجَاتِ ، وتُبَلِّغُنَا بِهَا أَقْصَى الْغَايَاتِ مِنْ جَمِيعِ الْخَيْرَاتِ فِي الْحَيَاةِ وَبَعْدَ الْمَمَاتِ .

Allāhumma ṣalli ʿalā sayyidinā Muḥammadin wa ʿalā a̱li sayyidinā Muḥammadin, ṣalātan tunjīnā bihā min jamīʿi-l-ahwāli wa-l-a̱fāt, wa taqḍī lanā bihā jamīʿa-l-ḥājāt, wa tuṭahhirunā bihā min jamīʿi-s-sayyi•āt, wa tarfaʿunā bihā aʿlā d-darajāt, wa tuballighunā bihā aqṣā-l-ghāyāti min jamīʿi- l-khayrāti fī-l-ḥayāti wa baʿda-l-mamāt.[§]

O Allah, bless our master Muḥammad, and the people of Muḥammad, with a blessing which delivers us from all crises and tribulations, and through which all our needs are fulfilled, and by which we are cleansed of ill deeds and elevated to the highest degree and brought to the utmost of all goodness, both in life and after death.

§ This formula of blessing the Prophet ﷺ, called *al-Ṣalāt al-Munjīya*, the Prayer of Deliverance, is attributed to Shaykh Abū al-Ḥajāj Mūsā al-Dirār (d. 520/1126). Abū Mūsā was a theologian and grammarian from Zaragoza (Saragossa) in north-eastern Spain and author of *Al-Tanbīh wa'l-Irshād fī ʿIlm al-Iʿtiqād*, a long poem on Ashʿarī theology. It has been said that Abū Mūsā was travelling on a ship that was caught in a violent storm which threatened to sink the ship when he had a vision of the Prophet ﷺ who said to him, "Tell the people on board to (repeat this blessing), one thousand times." Abū Mūsā later wrote, "So I told the passengers about what I had seen, and by the time we had recited the blessing about three hundred times, Allah had delivered us from the storm."

اللّٰهُمَّ أَنْزِلْ عَلَيْنَا فِي هَذِهِ السَّاعَةِ مِنْ خَيْرِكَ وبَرَكَاتِك كَمَآ أَنْزَلْتَ
عَلَىٰ أَوْلِيَآئِكَ وَخَصَّصْتَ بِهِ أَحِبَّآئِكَ ، وَ أَذِقْنَا بَرْدَ عَفْوِكَ وَحلاَوَةَ
مَغْفِرَتِكَ ، وَانْشُرْ عَلَيْنَا رَحْمَتَكَ الَّتِي وَسِعَتْ كُلَّ شَيْءٍ ، وَارْزُقْنَا
مِنْكَ مَحَبَّةً وَ قَبُولاً ، وَتَوْبَةً نَصُوحاً ، وَإِجَابَةً وَمَغْفِرَةً وَعَافِيَةً ، تَعُمُّ
الْحَاضِرِينَ وَالْغَآئِبِينَ وَالأَحْيَآءَ وَالْمَيِّتِينَ بِرَحْمَتِكَ
[يَآ أَرْحَمَ الرَّاحِمِينَ] (3) يا رَبَّ الْعَالَمِينَ .

Allāhumma anzil ʿalaynā fī hādhihi-s-sāʿati min khayrika wa barakātika, kamā̲ anzalta ʿalā awliyā•ik, wa khaṣṣaṣta bihi aḥibbā̲•ak, wa adhiqnā barda ʿafwika wa ḥalāwata maghfiratika, wa-nshur ʿalaynā raḥmataka-l-latī wasiʿat kulla shay', wa-rzuqnā minka maḥabbatan wa qabūlā, wa tawbatan naṣūḥā, wa ijābata(n)w wa-maghfirata(n)w wa-ʿāfiya, taʿummu-l-ḥāḍirīna wa-l-ghā̲•ibīn Wa-l-aḥyā̲•a wa-l-mayyitīn, bi raḥmatika, [Yā̲ arḥama-r-Rāḥimīn] Yā Rabba-l-ʿālamīn.

O Allah, send down to us at this time Your goodness and blessings as You send (them) down to Your saints, and choose for Your beloved friends, and give us a taste of the coolness of Your Pardon, and the sweetness of Your Forgiveness, and spread over us Your Mercy which envelops all things, and grant us Your Love and acceptance, sincere repentance, an answer (to our prayers), and forgiveness and well-being that embraces all those who are present, absent, living or dead by Your Mercy, [O Most Merciful of those who are merciful!] (3) *O Lord of the Worlds.*

اللّٰهُمَّ لاَ تُخَيِّبْنَا مِمَّا سَأَلْنَاكَ ، وَلاَ تَحْرِمْنَا مِمَّا رَجَوْنَاكَ
وَاحْفَظْنَا وَاحْفَظْنَا وَاحْفَظْنَا فِي الْمَحْيَا وَالْمَمَاتِ ،
إِنَّكَ مُجِيبُ الدَّعَوَاتِ .

Allāhumma lā tukhayyibnā mimmā sa•alnāk, wa lā taḥrimnā mimmā rajawnāk, wa-ḥfaẓnā, wa-ḥfaẓnā, wa-ḥfaẓnā fī-l-maḥyā wa-l-mamāt, innaka Mujību-d-daʿawāt.

O Allah, do not disappoint us in what we ask of You, and do not forbid us from what we hope from You, and Protect us, protect us, protect us, in life and in death. Truly You are the one who answers prayers.

﴿سُبْحَانَ رَبِّكَ رَبِّ الْعِزَّةِ عَمَّا يَصِفُونَ ٭ وَسَلاَمٌ عَلَى الْمُرْسَلِينَ ٭
وَالْحَمْدُ لِلّٰهِ رَبِّ الْعَالَمِينَ﴾

Subḥāna Rabbika Rabbi-l-ʿizzati ʿammā yaṣifūn, wa salāmun ʿala-l-mursalīn, wa-l-ḥamdu li-Llāhi Rabbi-l-ʿālamīn.

Glorified be your Lord, Lord of Honor, above all they attribute to Him, and Peace be upon all the Messengers, and Praise be to Allah, Lord of the Worlds.

اللّٰهُمَّ إِنِّيَ أَسْتَخِيرُكَ بِعِلْمِكَ ، وَأَسْتَقْدِرُكَ بِقُدْرَتِكَ وَأَسْأَلُكَ مِنْ فَضْلِكَ الْعَظِيمِ الأَعْظَمِ ، فَإِنَّكَ تَقْدِرُ وَلَآ أَقْدِرُ ، وَتَعْلَمُ وَلَآ أَعْلَمُ وَأَنْتَ عَلاَّمُ الْغُيُوبِ .

Allāhumma inniya astakhīruka bi ʿilmik, wa astaqdiruka bi qudratik, wa as•aluka min faḍlika-l-ʿaẓīmi-l-aʿẓam, fa innaka taqdiru wa l̲ā aqdir, wa taʿlamu wa l̲ā aʿlam, wa Anta ʿAllāmu-l-ghuyūb.

O Allah, I truly seek what You choose (for me) in Your Knowledge, and what You Determine (for me) in Your Power, and I ask You for Your Grace, the greatest of (all that is) great. For You are the One Who is able, and I am unable, and You are the One Who Knows, and I do not know, and You are the Knower of all things unseen.

اللّٰهُمَّ إِنْ كُنْتَ تَعْلَمُ أَنَّ هَذَا الأَمْرَ ، وَهُوَ جَمِيعُ حَرَكَاتِي وَسَكَنَاتِي ، الظَّاهِرَةِ وَالبَاطِنَةِ ، مِنْ قَوْلٍ وَفِعْلٍ وَخُلُقٍ وَحَالٍ ، عِبَادَةً وَعَادَةً ، فِي حَقِّي وَفِي حَقِّ غَيْرِي ، [فِي هَذَا الْيَوْمِ وَفِيمَا بَعْدَه] [فِي هَذِهُ اللَّيْلَةِ وَفِيمَا بَعْدَهَا] وَفِي بَقِيَّةِ عُمُرِي خَيْرٌ لِّي فِي دِينِي وَدُنْيَايَ وَمَعَاشِي وَمَعَادِي وَعَاقِبَةِ أَمْرِي وَ عَاجِلِهِ وَآجِلِهِ فَاقْدُرْهُ لِي وَيَسِّرْهُ لِي ، ثُمَّ بَارِكْ لِي فِيهِ

Allāhumma, in kunta taʿlamu anna hadha-al-amr wa huwa jamīʿu ḥarakātī wa sakanātī, aẓ-ẓāhira wa-l-bāṭina, min qawlin, wa fiʿlin, wa khuluqin, wa ḥāl, ʿibādatan wa ʿāda, fī ḥaqqī wa fī ḥaqqi ghayrī, [*fī hādha-l-yawmi wa fī mā baʿdahu*] [*fī hādhihi-l-laylati wa fī mā baʿdahā*] wa fī baqīyyati ʿumurī khayru(n) l-lī fī dīnī, wa dunyāya, wa maʿāshī, wa maʿādī, wa ʿāqibati amrī, wa ʿājilihi wa a̲jili(h), fa-qdurhu lī, wa yassirhu lī, thumma bārik lī fīh

O Allah, if in Your knowledge, You know that this matter which is the totality of my movements and rests, outward and inward, in speech and in deed, in virtue and state, whether worship or everyday actions, in respect to myself or in respect to another, in this day and in what follows it (in this night and in what follows it) and in the remainder of my life is good for me in my religion, my worldly life, and my living, in my appointed destiny and the outcome of my concern, in the long run and in the short run, then put it within my reach and make it easy for me, and bless me therein.

وَإِنْ كُنْتَ تَعْلَمُ أَنَّ هَذَا الأَمْرَ وَهُوَ جَمِيعُ حَرَكَاتِي وَسَكَنَاتِي ، الْظَّاهِرَةِ وَالبَاطِنَةِ ، مِنْ قَوْلٍ وَفِعْلٍ وَخُلُقٍ وَحَالٍ عِبادَةً وَعَادَةً ، في حَقِّي وَ فِي حَقِّ غَيرِي ، [فِي هَذَا الْيَوْمِ وَفِيمَا بَعْدَهُ] [فِي هَذِهِ اللَّيْلَةِ وَفِيمَا بَعْدَهَا] وَفِي بَقِيَّةِ عُمُرِي شَرٌّ لِي فِي دِينِي وَدُنْيَايَ ومَعَاشِي وَمَعَادِي وَعَاقِبَةِأَمْرِي وَ عَاجِلِهِ وَآجِلِهِ ، فَاصْرِفْهُ عَنِّي وَاصْرِفْنِي عَنْهُ ، وَاقْدُرْ لِيَ الْخَيْرَ حَيْثُ كَانَ ، ثُمَّ رَضِّنِي بِهِ إِنَّكَ عَلَى كُلِّ شَيءٍ قَدِيرٌ .

Wa in kunta taʿlamu anna hādha-l-amra wa huwa jamīʿu ḥarakātī wa sakanātī, aẓ-ẓāhira wa-l-bāṭina, min qawlin, wa fiʿlin, wa kẖuluqin, wa ḥāl, ʿibādatan wa ʿāda, fī ḥaqqī wa fī ḥaqqi ghayrī [*fī hādha-l-yawmi wa fī mā baʿdahu*] [*fī hādhihi-l-laylati wa fī mā baʿdahā*] wa fī baqīyyati ʿumurī sharru(n) l-lī fī dīnī, wa dunyāya, wa maʿāshī, wa maʿādī, wa ʿāqibati amrī, wa ʿājilihi wa a̱jili(h) fa-ṣrifhu ʿannī, wa-ṣrifnī ʿanh(u) waqdur līya-l-khayra ḥaythu kān, thumma raḍḍinī bih(i), innaka ʿalā kulli shay·in qadīr.

And if in Your knowledge, You know that this matter which is the totality of my movements and rests, outward and inward, in speech and in deed, in virtue and state, whether in worship or in everyday actions, in respect to myself or in respect to another, in this day and in what follows it (in this night and in what follows it) and in the remainder of my life is bad for me in my religion, my worldly life, and my living, in my appointed destiny and the outcome of my concern, in the long run and in the short run, then keep it away from me and me away from it, and decree for me what is good, whatever it may be, then make me content with it.
Verily You, over all things, have power.

اللّٰهُمَّ اقْسِمْ لَنَا مِنْ خَشْيَتِكَ ما تَحُولُ بِهِ بَيْنَنَا وبَيْنَ مَعَاصِيكَ ، وَمِنْ طَاعَتِكَ مَا تُبَلِّغُنَا بِهِ جَنَّتَكَ ، وَمِنَ الْيَقِينِ مَا تُهَوِّنُ بِهِ عَلَينَا مَصَآئِبَ الدُّنْيَا ،

Allāhumma-qsim lanā min khashyatika mā taḥūlu bihi baynanā wa bayna maʿāṣīk, wa min ṭāʿatika mā tuballighunā bihi Jannatak, wa min-l-yaqīni mā tuhawwinu bihi ʿalaynā maṣā•iba-d-dunyā§

O Allah, grant for us the reverent fear of You which will intervene between us and acts of disobedience to You, and the obedience by which we may reach Your heaven, and the certainty that will ease for us the tribulations of this world

§ This supplication is attributed to the Prophet ﷺ in the collections of al-Suyūṭī, al-Tirmidhī, al-Nasā'ī, and others, usually related by ʿUmar ؓ with the words, "The Messenger of Allah would rarely rise from a gathering (*majlis*) without making this prayer for his companions."

اللّٰهُمَّ مَتِّعْنَا بِأَسْمَاعِنَا وَأَبْصَارِنَا وَقُوَّتِنَا مَا أَحْيَيْتَنَا ، وَاجْعَلْهُ الْوَارِثَ مِنَّا ، وَاجْعَلْ ثَأْرَنَا عَلَى مَنْ ظَلَمَنَا ، وَانْصُرْنَا عَلَى مَنْ عَادَانَا وَلَا تَجْعَلْ مُصِيبَتَنَا فِي دِينِنَا ، وَلَا تَجْعَلِ الدُّنْيَا أَكْبَرَ هَمِّنَا ، وَلَا مَبْلَغَ عِلْمِنَا، وَلَا غَايَةَ رَغْبَتِنَا وَلَا إِلَى النَّارِ مَصِيرَنَا ، وَلَا تُسَلِّطْ عَلَيْنَا بِذُنُوبِنَا مَنْ لَا يَخَافُكَ وَلَا يَرْحَمُنَا ،

[يَا أَرْحَمَ الرَّاحِمِينَ] (3)

Allāhumma matti^cnā bi asmā^cinā wa abṣārinā wa quwwatinā mā aḥyaytanā, wa-j^calhu-l-wāritha minnā, wa-j^cal tha•ranā ^calā man ẓalamanā, wa-nṣurnā ^calā man ^cādānā, wa lā taj^cal muṣībatanā fī dīninā, wa lā taj^cali-d-dunyā akbara hamminā, wa lā mablagha ^cilminā, wa lā ghāyata raghbatinā, wa lā ila-n-nāri maṣīranā, wa lā tusalliṭ ^calaynā bi dhunūbinā man lā yakhāfuka wa lā yarḥamunā.
[Yā Arḥama-r-Rāḥimīn] (3)

O Allah, benefit us in our hearing, sight, and strength as long as You give us life, and make them our heirs. Place our vengeance only upon one who would oppress us, and be our ally against any who would harm us, and do not place tribulations for us in our religion, and do not make this world our greatest concern or the extent of our knowledge, or the limit of our aspirations, nor make the Fire our final destination. And do not give authority over us – due to our sins – to one who does not fear You and is not merciful towards us. O Most Merciful of those who are merciful.

اللّٰهُمَّ يَا رَبِّ بِجَاهِ نَبِيِّكَ الْمُصْطَفَى ، وَرَسُولِكَ الْمُرْتَضَى ، طَهِّرْ قُلُوبَنَا مِنْ كُلِّ وَصْفٍ يُبَاعِدُنَا عَنْ مُشَاهَدَتِكَ وَمَحَبَّتِكَ ، وَأَمِتْنَا عَلَى السُّنَّةِ وَالْجَمَاعَةِ وَالشَّوْقِ إِلَى لِقَآئِكَ ،

[يَاذَا الْجَلَالِ وَالإِكْرَامِ] (3)

Allāhumma yā Rabbi, bi jāhi Nabiyyika-l-Muṣṭafā, wa Rasūlika-l-Murtaḍā, ṭahhir qulūbanā min kulli waṣfin yubāʿidunā ʿan mushāhadatika wa maḥabbatik, wa amitnā ʿalā-s-sunnati wa-l-jamāʿati, wa-sh-shawqi ilā liqā·ik
[Yā Dha-l-Jalāli wa-l-Ikrām] (3)

O Allah, by the honor of Your chosen Prophet, and the Messenger with whom You are pleased: cleanse our hearts from every attribute which removes us from being aware of You and loving You, and cause us to die in orthodoxy, with a longing for the meeting with You. O You who possesses Majesty and Generosity.

﴿فَسُبْحَانَ اللهِ حِينَ تُمْسُونَ وَحِينَ تُصْبِحُونَ * وَلَهُ الْحَمْدُ فِي السَّمَاوَاتِ وَالأَرْضِ وَعَشِيًّا وَحِينَ تُظْهِرُونَ * يُخْرِجُ الْحَيَّ مِنَ الْمَيِّتِ وَيُخْرِجُ الْمَيِّتَ مِنَ الْحَيِّ وَيُحْيِي الأَرْضَ بَعْدَ مَوْتِهَا * وَكَذَٰلِكَ تُخْرَجُونَ﴾

Fa subḥāna-Llāhi ḥīna tumsūna wa ḥīna tuṣbiḥūn, wa lahu-l-ḥamdu fī-s-samāwāti wa-l-arḍi, wa ʿashīyyan wa ḥīna tuẓhirūn. Yukhriju-l-ḥayya mina-l-mayyiti, wa yukhriju-l-mayyita mina-l-ḥayy wa yuḥyī-l-arḍa baʿda mawtihā,
wa kadhālika tukhrajūn.§

So glory be to Allah when you reach the evening and in the morning when you arise. His is the praise in the heavens and upon earth, and in the late afternoons, and at midday. He brings the living forth from the dead, and the dead forth from the living, And He brings the earth back to life after its death; even thus will you be brought forth. (30:16-18)

اللّٰهُمَّ إِنَّا نَسْأَلُكَ رِضَاكَ وَالْجَنَّةَ ، وَمَا يَقَرِّبُ إِلَيْهِمَا مِنْ قَوْلٍ وَعَمَلٍ وَنَعُوذُ بِكَ مِنْ سَخَطِكَ وَالنَّارِ ، وَمَا يُقَرِّبُ إِلَيْهِمَا مِنْ قَوْلٍ وَعَمَلٍ

Allāhumma, innā nas•aluka riḍāka wa-l-Janna, wa mā yuqarribu ilayhimā min qawlin wa ʿamal, wa naʿūdhu bika min sakhaṭika wa-n-nār, wa mā yuqarribu ilayhimā min qawlin wa ʿamal.

§ In a ḥadīth narrated by Ibn ʿAbbās, the Prophet ﷺ is reported to have said, "He who recites (this verse) upon waking in the morning shall catch up with whatever he misses in that day, and he who recites it in the evening shall catch up with whatever he misses in that night." In the *Sunan* of Abū Dāwūd, *al-Duʿā'* of al-Ṭabarānī, ʿ*Amal al-yawm w'al-layla* of Ibn al-Sunnī, and several other sources.

O Allah, we ask You for Your contentment and heaven, and for words and deeds that bring (us) near them, And we seek refuge in You from Your anger and from the Fire, and from words and deeds that bring us near them.

اللّٰهُمَّ يَا سَابِغَ النِّعَم ، وَيَا دَافِعَ النِّقَم ، وَيَا فَارِجَ الْغُمَم ، وَيَا كَاشِفَ الظُّلَم وَيَآ أَعْدَلَ مَنْ حَكَمَ ، وَيَا حَسْبَ مَنْ ظَلَمَ ، وَيَا وَلِيَّ مَنْ ظُلِمَ ، يَآ أَوَّلاً بِلاَ بِدَايَةٍ يَآ آخِراً بِلاَ نِهَايَةٍ ، يَا مَنْ لَهُ إِسْمٌ بِلاَ كُنْيَةٍ ، فَرِّجْ عَنَّا وَعَنْ جَمِيعِ الْمُسْلِمِينَ مَا هُمْ فِيهِ ، بِسِرِّ اسْمِكَ الْمَخْزُونِ الْمَكْنُونِ الْمُبَارَكِ الطَّاهِرِ الْمُطَهَّرِ الْمُقَدَّسِ ، إِنَّكَ عَلَى كُلِّ شَيْءٍ قَدِيرٌ وَبِالإِجَابَةِ جَدِيرٌ

Allāhumma, yā Sābigha-n-niʿam, wa yā Dāfiʿa-n-niqam, wa yā Fārija-l-ghumam, wa yā Kāshifa-ẓ-ẓulam, wa ya̱ aʿdala man ḥakam, wa yā ḥāsba man ẓalam, wa yā Walīyya man ẓulim. Ya̱ Awwalan bilā bidāya, ya̱ A̱khiran bilā nihāya, ya man lahu Ismun bilā kunya, farrij ʿannā wa ʿan jamīʿi- l-muslimīna mā hum fih, bi Sirri-ismika-l-Makhzūni-l-Maknūni-l-Mubāraki-ṭ-Ṭāhiri-l-Muṭahhari-l-Muqaddas. Innaka ʿalā kulli shay'in Qadīr wa bi-l-ijābati Jadīr.§

§ In Ibn al-Najjār's history, where he speaks of the life of Muḥammad ibn ʿUmar al-Ḥanbalī, Anas b. Mālik said, "I was seated with ʿĀ'isha ﷺ to convey to her the good news that revelation had come exonerating her, when she said to me, 'By Allah, both those near to me and far had left me alone, even the cat had left me alone, and I was not offered food or drink. I lay down to sleep hungry and I saw in my sleep a youth who said, "Why are you sad?" I said, "I am sad about what people are saying." He answered, "Pray to Allah with these (words) and He will relieve you." I said, "What are they?" He said, "They are the supplication of relief (*duʿā' al-faraj*): O Allah! You are the One Who abounds in blessings, defends against malice, relieves tribulation, dispels the darkness; You are the One Who is the Most Just to judge, the One Who brings to reckoning the oppressor and is the

O Allah! You are the One Who abounds in blessings, defends against malice, relieves tribulation, dispels the darkness; You are the One Who is the Most Just to judge, the One Who brings to reckoning the oppressor and is the Guardian of the oppressed, the First without beginning, the Last without end, the One Who has a Name with no last name, Relieve us and all Muslims in whatever (hardship) they may be in, by the mystery of Your treasured, concealed, blessed, pure, purifying, and holy Name. You, over all things, have Power and are the most reliable to answer prayers.

﴿سُبْحَانَ رَبِّكَ رَبِّ الْعِزَّةِ عَمَّا يَصِفُونَ ٭ وَسَلَامٌ عَلَى الْمُرْسَلِينَ ٭
وَالْحَمْدُ لِلَّهِ رَبِّ الْعَالَمِينَ﴾

Subḥāna Rabbika Rabbi-l-ʿizzati ʿammā yaṣifūn, wa salāmun ʿala-l-mursalīn, wa-l-ḥamdu li-Llāhi Rabbi-l-ʿālamīn

Glorified be your Lord, Lord of Honor, above all they attribute to Him and peace be upon all the Messengers, and Praise be to Allah, Lord of the Worlds.

Guardian of the oppressed, the First without beginning, the Last without end, the One Who has a Name with no last name, give me in my plight relief and a way out." Then I woke up, my thirst had been quenched and my hunger satisfied, and Allah had revealed my innocence and relief had come to me.'"

-1-

التائية في الورد الشريف

On the Meanings and Merits of the Noble Litany

يَقُولُ عُبَيْدُ اللهِ أَعْنِي مُحَمَّداً هُوَ ابْنُ حَبِيبٍ قَاصِداً لِلنَّصِيحَةِ

Yaqūlu ʿubaydu-Llāhi aʿnī Muḥammadan
huwa-bnu Ḥabībin qāṣidan li-n-naṣīḥati

Thus says Allah's humble servant Muḥammad,
son of Ḥabīb for the purpose of true counsel:

أَيَا صَاحِبِي عِشْ فِي هَنَاءٍ وَنِعْمَةِ إِذَا كُنْتَ فِينَا ذَا اعْتِقَادٍ وَنِيَّةِ

A yā ṣāḥibī ʿish fī hanā•in wa niʿmatin
idha kunta fīnā dhāʿtiqādin wa niyyati

O my companion, live in happiness and grace
if you are among us with good intent and faith,

وَأَخْلَصْتَ فِي الْوُدِّ الَّذِي هُوَ رُكْنُنَا فِي سَيْرِ طَرِيقِ اللهِ مِنْ غَيرِ مِرْيَةِ

Wa akhlaṣta fi-l-wuddi-l-ladhī huwa ruknunā
fī sayri ṭarīqi-Llāhi min ghayri miryati

And if you are sincere in love, which is our mainstay
without doubt, in travelling Allah's way.

وَكُنْتَ قَوِيَّ العَزْمِ في الْوِرْدِ حَاضِراً   بِقَلْبٍ لِتَحْقِيقِ الْمَعَانِي الدَّقِيقَةِ

Wa kunta qawiyya-l-ʿazmi fi-l-wirdi ḥāḍiran
bi qalbin li taḥqīqi-l-maʿāni-d-daqīqati

And if you are strong in resolve towards the litany,
and present with your heart to realise its subtle meanings

وَأَحْضَرْتَ مَعْنَى الذِّكْرِ فِي كُلِّ مَرَّةٍ   تَكُونُ مُعَاناً فِي الْأُمُورِ بِسُرْعَةِ

Wa aḥḍarta maʿna-dh-dhikri fī kulli marratin
takūnu muʿānan fi-l-umūri bi surʿati

And present to the meaning of every invocation –
then you will be aided swiftly in all things.

فمِفْتَاحُ وِرْدٍ قُلْ صَلَاةٌ تَعَوُّذٌ   وَبَسْمِلْ وَحَوْقِلْ تُكْفَ كُلَّ بَلِيَّةِ

Fa miftāḥu wirdin qul ṣalātun taʿawwudhun
wa basmil wa ḥawqil tukfa kulla baliyyati

The opening of the litany is a prayer upon the Prophet, then seeking refuge,
the basmala, *followed by the* ḥawqala *which suffices in all trials.*

فَتَبْدَا بِالْإِسْتِغْفَارِ أَوَّلَ وِرْدِنَاَ   تَحُوزُ بِهِ نَيْلاً لِكُلِّ فَضِيْلَةِ

Fa tabdā bi-l-istighfāri awwala wirdinā
taḥūzu bihi naylan li kulli faḍīlati

Then you start the litany asking forgiveness
by which you may attain to every virtue.

وَمَعْنَاهُ سِتْرُ اللهِ لِلْعَبْدِ عَنْ ذَنْبٍ   فَيَحْفَظُهُ مِنْ كُلِّ هَوْلٍ وَفِتْنَةِ

Fa maʿnāhu sitru-l-Llāh li-l-ʿabdi ʿan dhanbin
fa yaḥfaẓuhu min kulli hawlin wa fitnati

It means that Allah veils the servant from sin,
protecting him from all terror and tribulation.

فَلاَ هَمَّ يَبْقَى مَعْ دَوَامِكَ ذِكْرَهُ   وَلاَ رَيْبَ فِي تَسْهِيلِ رِزْقٍ بِكَثْرَةِ

Fa lā hamma yabqā maʿ dawāmika dhikrahu
wa lā rayba fī tas·hīli rizqin bi kathrati

If you invoke Him with constancy, no worry will last,
nor doubt that your provision will come with ease and abundance.

وَبَعْدَ الْفَرَاغِ مِنْهُ صَلِّ عَلَى النَّبِيِّ   صَلاَةَ مُحِبٍّ رَاسِخٍ فِي الْمَحَبَّةِ

Wa baʿda-l-farāghi minhu ṣalli ʿala-n-Nabiyy
ṣalāta muḥibbin rāsikhin fi-l-maḥabbati

After completing this, pray that Allah bless the Prophet
with the prayer of a lover deeply rooted in love.

وَمَعْنَاهَا رَحْمَةٌ تُنَاسِبُ قَدْرَهُ   وَقَدْرُهُ يَعْلُو قَدْرَ كُلِّ الْخَلِيقَةِ

Wa maʿnāhā raḥmatun tunāsibu qadrahu
wa qadruhu yaʿlū qadra kulli-l-khalīqati

Its meaning is mercy as vast as his rank,
and his rank is more exalted than every other creature's.

وَشَخِّصْهُ فِي مِرْآةِ قَلْبِكَ دَائِماً   وَعَوِّلْ عَلَيْهِ فِي الْوُصُولِ لِحَضْرَةِ

Wa shakhkhiṣ•hu fī mir•āti qalbika dā•iman
wa ʿawwil ʿalayhi fi-l-wuṣūli li ḥaḍrati

Picture him always in the mirror of your heart,
and depend on him as the way to enter the Presence,

وَهَيْلَلَةٌ بَعْدَ الصَّلَاةِ عَلَى النَّبِيِّ   فَتَنْفِي بِهَا وَهْماً عَنْ عَيْنِ الْبَصِيرَةِ

Wa haylalatun baʿda-ṣ-ṣalāti ʿala-n-Nabiyy
fa tanfī bihā wahman ʿan ʿayni-l-baṣīrati

Following the prayer upon the Prophet comes the haylala.
By it you will cleanse your inner vision of illusion,

وَتُسْرِعُ فِي نَفْيِ السِّوَى وَهْوَ قَاطِعٌ   لِقَوْمِ طَرِيقَ الْحَقِّ مِنْ غَيرِ مِرْيَةِ

Wa tusriʿu fī nafyi-s-siwā wa h'wa qāṭiʿun
li qawmi ṭarīqa-l-Ḥaqqi min ghayri miryati

And you will swiftly negate the existence of what is "other",
which is a thief who robs the people on the path of truth without doubt.

وَتَشْهَدُ رَبّاً قَدْ تَجَلَّتْ صِفَاتُهُ   بِأَسْرَارِ أَكْوَانٍ وَأَنْوَارِ جَنَّةِ

Wa tash•hadu Rabban qad tajallat ṣifātuhu
bi asrāri akwānin wa anwāri jannati

And you will witness a Lord Whose attributes appear
in the mysteries of creation and the lights of Heaven,

وَتُدْرِكُ سِرًّا لَيْسَ يَعْرِفُ قَدْرَهُ   سِوَى عَارِفٍ بِاللهِ صَاحِبِ نَظْرَةِ

Wa tudriku sirran laysa yaʿrifu qadrahu
siwā ʿārifin bi-Llāhi ṣāḥibi naẓrati

And you will understand a mystery of the greatest worth
known to none except the gnostic with inner vision.

وَسَبِّحْ بِتَسْبِيحِ الإِلٰهِ فِي كُتْبِهِ   وَإِيَّاكَ تَنْزِيهاً بِعَقْلٍ وَفِكْرَةِ

Wa sabbiḥ bi tasbīḥi-l-ilāhi fī kutbihi
wa iyyāka tanzīhan bi ʿaqlin wa fikrati

Then glorify Allah with the glorification in His Books
and beware lest it be beyond the mind and thought.

وَنَزِّهْ بِمَا قَدْ نَزَّهَ الْحَقُّ نَفْسَهُ   وَفَوِّضْ وَنَزِّهْ عَنْ حُدُوثٍ وَشِرْكَةِ

Wa nazzih bi mā qad nazzaha-l-Ḥaqqu nafsahu
wa fawwiḍ wa nazzih ʿan ḥudūthin wa shirkati

Exalt Him above all else as He exalts Himself.
Accept (this) and exalt Him above temporality and partners.

وَكُنْ حَامِداً مُسْتَحْضِرَ الْعَجْزِ فِي الثَّنَا   كَمَا جَاءَ وَارِداً عَنْ خَيْرِ الْخَلِيقَةِ

Wa kun ḥāmidan mustaḥḍira-l-ʿajzi fi-th-thanā
kamā jāʾa wāridan ʿan khayri-l-khalīqati

Be one who praises (Him) knowing you cannot (truly) praise (Him),
as the best of creation is recorded to have said.

وَحَسْبَلَةٌ بَعْدَ الْفَرَاغِ مِنَ الْوِرْدِ فَتَذْكُرُ مِنْهَا عَدَّ سَجْيٍ بِنِيَّةِ

Wa ḥasbalatun baᶜda-l-farāghi mina-l-wirdi
fa tadhkuru minhā ᶜadda sajyin bi niyyati

Upon completing the wird invoke the ḥasbala,
seventy-three times with intention.

وَقَدْ وَعَدَ الْحَقُّ الْجَلِيلُ كِفَايَةً لِذَاكِرِهَا مِنْ غَيْرِ قَيْدٍ بِحَالَةِ

Wa qad waᶜada-l-Ḥaqqu-l-Jalīlu kifāyatan
li dhākirihā min ghayri qaydin bi ḥālati

Allah, the Truth, has promised sufficiency
to one who invokes it, regardless of his state.

فَقَدْ طُفِأَتْ نَارُ الْخَلِيلِ بِسِرِّهَا وَنَالَ الْحَبِيبُ مِنْهَا كُلَّ فَضِيلَةِ

Fa qad ṭufi•at nāru-l-Khalīli bi sirrihā
wa nāla-l-Ḥabību minhā kulla faḍīlati

The fire in which they put Allah's intimate friend
was extinguished by its mystery, and the beloved one attained every grace.

فَفِي وَقْتِنَا هَذَا يُرَجَّحُ ذِكْرُهَا عَلَى الذِّكْرِ بِالأَحْزَابِ أَوْ بِوَظِيفَةِ

Fa fī waqtinā hādhā yurajjaḥu dhikruhā
ᶜala-dh-dhikri bi-l-aḥzābi aw bi waẓīfati

In this, our age, its invocation is preferred
to the recitation of [other] litanies or [other] practices.

وَإِنْ شِئْتَ إِسْرَاعاً لِفَهْمِ الْحَقِيقَةِ   فَوَاظِبْ عَلَى الإِسْمِ الْعَظِيمِ بِهِمَّةِ

Wa in shi-ta israʿan li fahmi-l-ḥaqīqati
fa wāẓib ʿala-l-Ismi-l-ʿaẓīmi bi himmati

If you wish to understand the Inner Truth in the shortest time,
regularly invoke with fervor the Supreme Name.

وَشَخِّصْ حُرُوفَ الإِسْمِ فِي الْقَلْبِ دَائِماً   وَرَاجِعْهُ فِي النِّسْيَانِ فِي كُلِّ مَرَّةِ

Wa shakhkhiṣ ḥurūfa-l-Ismi fi-l-qalbi dā-iman
wa rājiʿhu fī-n-nisyāni fī kulli marrati

Picture the letters of Allah's Name constantly
in your heart and bring them back every time you forget.

وَلاَ تَلْتَفِتْ لِلْغَيْرِ إِنَّهُ قَاطِعٌ   وَلَوْ كَانَ مَحْمُوداً فَأَحْرَى لِظُلْمَةِ

Wa lā taltafit li-l-ghayri, innahu qāṭiʿun
wa law kāna maḥmūdan, fa aḥrā li ẓulmati

And do not be distracted by what is other. It is a thief,
even when it is laudable and more so if it is darkness.

فَذِكْرُهُ عِنْدَ الْقَوْمِ يُغْنِي عَنْ غَيْرِهِ   وَلاَ عَكْسَ إِنْ كُنْتَ صَاحِبَ هِمَّةِ

Fa dhikruhu ʿinda-l-qawmi yughni ʿan ghayrihi
wa lā ʿaksa in kunta ṣāḥiba himmati

For the Folk, this invocation replaces anything else
but not the opposite, so understand if you aspire!

وَرَاقِبْهُ عِنْدَ الذِّكْرِ وَافْنَ عَنْ غَيْرِهِ   وَلاَ غَيْرَ إِلاَّ مِنْ تَوَهُّمِ كَثْرَةِ

Wa rāqibhu ʿinda-dh-dhikri wa-fna ʿan ghayrihi
wa lā ghayra illā min tawahhumi kathrati

Be attentive to it in the invocation and absent from all else
– there is nothing else except the illusion of many,

وَمَا هِيَ إِلاَّ وَحْدَةٌ قَدْ تَكَثَّرَتْ   بِمُقْتَضَى أَسْمَاءٍ وَآثَارِ قُدْرَةِ

Wa mā hiya illā waḥdatun qad takaththarat
bi muqtaḍā asmāʾin wa āthāri qudrati

Which is only oneness multiplied in accordance with the Names
and traces (in creation) of Divine Power.

وَمَظْهَرُهَا الْأَعْلَى الرَّسُولُ مُحَمَّدٌ   عَلَيْهِ صَلاَةُ اللهِ فِي كُلِّ لَحْظَةِ

Wa maẓharuha- l-aʿlā-r-Rasūlu Muḥammadun
ʿalayhi ṣalātu-Llāhi fī kulli laḥẓati

Its highest manifestation is the Messenger Muḥammad,
upon whom be Allah's blessing at every instant!

وَآلِهِ وَالْأَصْحَابِ مَا حَنَّ ذَاكِرٌ   لِذِكْرِ إِلَهِ الْعَرْشِ فِي كُلِّ حَالَةِ

Wa ālihi wa-l-aṣḥābi mā ḥanna dhākirun
li dhikri Ilāhi-l-ʿarshi fī kulli ḥālati

And upon his family and Companions as long as an invoker is moved
by the invocation of the God of the Throne in every state.

طَرِيقَتُنَا تَعْلُو الطَّرَائِقَ كُلَّهَا   لِتَحْرِيرِنَا الْمَقْصُودَ أَوَّلَ مَرَّةِ

Ṭarīqatunā taʿlu-ṭ-ṭarā•iqa kullahā
li taḥrīrina-l-maqṣūda awwala marrati

Our path is above all the other paths
For we have made clear its purpose from the very start.

وَلِلْجَمْعِ بَيْنَ الْمَشْهَدَيْنِ بِلَا رَيْبِ   فَمَشْهَدُ حَقٍّ ثُمَّ مَشْهَدُ شِرْعَةِ

Wa li-l-jamʿi bayna-l-mash•hadayni bilā raybi
fa mash•hadu ḥaqqin thumma mash•hadu shirʿati

And since it joins both aspects without any doubt:
the aspect of the [inner] Truth and of the Law.

وَأَسْأَلُ رَبِّ اللهَ فَتْحًا إِلَهِيًا   لِكُلِّ مُرِيدٍ صَادِقٍ فِي الطَّرِيقَةِ

Wa as•alu Rabbi-Llaha fatḥan ilāhiyyan
li kulli murīdin ṣādiqin fi-ṭ-ṭarīqati

I ask Allah, my Lord, that a Divine Opening
may come to each sincere seeker in the Way.

وَأَنْ يُرْشِدَ الْإِخْوَانَ لِلْجَمْعِ دَائِماً   عَلَى كُلِّ مَا يُرْضِي إِلَهَ الْبَرِيَّةِ

Wa an yurshida-l-ikhwāna li-l-jamʿi dā-iman
ʿalā kulli mā yurḍī Ilāha-l-barīyyati

And that the brethren be always guided to stay united
in what is pleasing to the God of creation.

وَأُهْدِي سَلَامِي لِلَّذِينَ تَعَلَّقُوا بِأَذْكَارِ خَيْرِ الْخَلْقِ مِنْ كُلِّ فِرْقَةِ

Wa uhdī salāmī li-l-ladhīna taʿallaqū
bi adhkāri khayri-l-khalqi min kulli firqati

And I give greetings to those in every group
attached to the invocations from the Best of Creation.

فَتَابِعْهُ إِنْ كُنْتَ الْمُحِبَّ لِرَبِّنَا يُثِبْكَ عَلَى ذَاكَ الْإِلٰهُ بِنَظْرَةِ

Fa tābiʿhu in kunta-l-muḥibba li Rabbinā
yuthibka ʿalā dhāka-l-Ilāhu bi naẓrati

Follow him if you are one who loves our Lord
that perchance He may reward you for that with a glance.

فَقَدْ كَمُلَتْ مُسْتَغْفِراً مِنْ تَوَهُّمٍ لِغَيْرِ وُجُودِ الْحَقِّ فِي كُلِّ لَمْحَةِ

Fa qad kamulat mustaghfiran min tawahhumi
li ghayri wujūdi-l-Ḥaqqi fī kulli lamḥati

This is completed with my asking forgiveness for the illusion
of anything other than the Truth in every glance.

-2-

التائية الكبرى

If You Would Ascend the Path of Lovers

فَإِنْ شِئْتَ أَنْ تَرْقَى رُقِيَّ الْأَحِبَّةِ   فَعَرِّجْ عَلَى لَيْلَى بِصِدْقِ الْمَوَدَّةِ

Fa in shi•ta an tarqā ruqiyya-l-aḥibbati
fa ʿarrij ʿalā Laylā bi ṣidqi-l-mawaddati

If you would ascend the path of lovers,
then, with sincere love, visit Layla on the way,

وَكُلَّ عَذُولٍ فِي مَحَبَّتِهَا انْبُذَنْ   وَسَافِرْ إِلَى الأَحْبَابِ فِي كُلِّ بَلْدَةِ

Wa kulla ʿadhūlin fī maḥabbatihā-nbudhan
wa sāfir ilā-l-aḥbābi fī kulli baldati

And pay no heed to those who blame you for loving her,
and journey to lovers in every land.

وَلَو أَنَّ صِدْقَ الْحُبِّ فِيكَ حَقِيقَةً   رَأَيْتَ بِهَا الأَحْبَابَ مِنْ غَيْرِ رِحْلَةِ

Wa law anna ṣidqa-l-ḥubbi fīka ḥaqīqatan
ra•ayta biha-l-aḥbāba min ghayri riḥlati

Were sincere love a reality within you,
you would see those lovers without a journey.

وَلَوْ أَنَّ عَيْنَ الْقَلْبِ مِنْكَ تَطَهَّرَتْ   لَأَبْصَرَتِ الْأَنْوَارَ مِنْهَا تَجَلَّتِ

Wa law anna ᶜayna-l-qalbi minka taṭahharat
la abṣarati-l-anwāra minhā tajallati

And were the eye of your heart truly cleansed,
it would behold the Lights that from her shine forth.

فَكُنْ عَبْدَهَا شُكْراً بِلاَ رُؤْيَةِ السِّوَا   وَمَا بِكَ مِن نُعْمَى فَمِنْهَا تَبَدَّتِ

Fa kun ᶜabdahā shukran bilā ru•yati-s-siwā
wa mā bika min nuᶜmā fa minhā tabaddati

So be her servant in gratitude, seeing none other.
All the graces you have arise from her.

وَإِيَّاكَ تَلْبِيسَ الْخَوَاطِرِ إِنَّهَا   تُمَوِّهُ نُصْحاً وَهْوَ أَعْظَمُ فِرْيَةِ

Wa iyyāka talbīsa-l-khawāṭiri innahā
tumawwihu nuṣḥan wa h'wa aᶜẓamu firyati

And beware of the confusion of passing thoughts
which disguise themselves as counsel but are the biggest of lies.

فَخَالِلْ أَخَا صِدْقٍ يُمَيِّزُ بَيْنَهَا   وَيُذْهِبُ عَنْكَ مَا أَتَاكَ بِشُبْهَةِ

Fa khālil akhā ṣidqin yumayyizu baynahā
wa yudh•hibu ᶜanka mā atāka bi shubhati

Make your dearest friend an honest brother who can
discern between them and help you to be free of doubtful things.

وَهَيْلَلَةٌ تَنْفِي جَمِيعَ الْوَسَاوِسِ   بِتَلْقِينِ شَيخٍ عَارِفٍ بِالْحَقِيقَةِ

Wa haylalatun tanfī jamīʿa-l-wasāwisi
bi talqīni shaykhin ʿārifin bi-l-ḥaqīqati

The invocation of the shahāda dispells all whisperings
when imparted by a master who knows the inner truth.

وَآيَاتُهُ نُورٌ يَلُوحُ بِظَاهِرٍ   وَسِرٌّ بَدَا مِنْ بَاطِنٍ مَعَ هِمَّةِ

Wa āyātuhu nūrun yalūḥu bi-ẓāhirin
wa sirrun badā min bāṭinin maʿa himmati

And the signs of [such a one] are: a light that shines outwardly,
a secret that shows from within, and high aspiration.

وَتَرْقِيَةٌ بِاللَّحْظِ قَبْلَ تَلَفُّظٍ   فَإِنْ كَانَ مِنْهُ اللَّفْظُ جَاءَ بِحُلَّةِ

Wa tarqiyatun bi-l-laḥẓi qabla talaffuẓin
fa in kāna minhu-l-lafẓu jāʾa bi ḥullati

Just to see him uplifts you before a single word is uttered,
and should speech come forth from him, it comes forth in a robe,

وَأَعْنِي بِهَا الْأَنْوَارَ تَسْرِي بِسُرْعَةٍ   لِقَلْبِ مُرِيدِ الْحَقِّ مِنْ غَيْرِ شِرْكَةِ

Wa aʿnī biha-l-anwāra tasrī bi surʿatin
li qalbi murīdi-l-ḥaqqi min ghayri shirkati

By which I mean lights which run straight to the heart
of the one who aspires to Allah, the Truth, without partner.

وَزُهْدُهُ فِي الْأَكْوَانِ عُمْدَةُ سَيْرِهِ وَشُغْلٌ بِإِفْرَادِ الْحَبِيبِ بِرُؤْيَةِ

Wa zuhduhu fi-l-akwāni ʿumdatu sayrihi
wa shughlun bi ifrādi-l-Ḥabībi bi ru•yati

Detachment from what creatures might possess is the mainstay of his journey;
he has been chosen to be occupied with a vision of the Beloved Friend.

وَتَصْرِيحُهُ بِالْإِذْنِ مِنْ خَيرِ أُمَّةٍ عَلَيْهِ اعْتِمَادُ الصَّادِقِينَ الْأَجِلَّةِ

Wa taṣrīḥuhu bi-l-idhni min khayri ummati
ʿalayhi-ʿtimādu-ṣ-ṣādiqīna-l-ajillati

And his speech is by permission of the Best of this community,
upon whom the greatest of the saintly depend.

فَإِنْ حَصَلَ الْمَقْصُودُ مِمَّا ذَكَرْتُهُ فَبَادِرْ وَأَعْطِ النَّفْسَ مِنْ غَيْرِ مُهْلَةِ

Fa•in ḥaṣala-l-maqṣūdu mim-mā dhakartuhu
fa bādir wa aʿṭi-n-nafsa min ghayri muhlati

If you've found such a one as we have mentioned,
then go ahead and give yourself without hesitation.

وَلاَ تَعْتَبِرْ شَيئاً سِوَى مَا رَسَمْتُهُ فَفِيهِ الَّذِي يُغْنِي وَكُلُّ الْمَسَرَّةِ

Wa lā taʿtabir shay•an siwā mā rasamtuhu
fa fīhi-l-ladhī yughnī wa kullu-l-masarrati

And do not consider other than what I have written,
for therein is sufficiency and therein every joy.

فَإِنْ لَمْ تَجِدْ مِمَّا ذَكَرْتُ فَإِنَّنِي سَأَشْرَحُ نَهْجَ الْحَقِّ مِنْ غَيْرِ مِرْيَةِ

Fa in lam tajid mimmā dhakartu fa innanī
sa•ashraḥu nahja-l-Ḥaqqi min ghayri miryati

But if you've not found the one I have mentioned,
then I'll explain the way to God, the Truth, without any doubt:

فَأَوَّلُ فِعْلِ الْمَرْءِ فِي بَدءِ سَيْرِهِ مُجَانَبَةُ الأَشْرَارِ مِنْ كُلِّ فِرْقَةِ

Fa awwalu fiʿli-l-mar•i fī bad•i sayrihi
mujānabatu-l-ashrāri min kulli firqati

The first thing to do at the beginning of the journey
is stay clear of the bad people in every group.

وَشُغْلٌ بِذِكْرِ اللهِ جَلَّ جَلَالُهُ فَفِيهِ الدَّوَا مِنْ كُلِّ عَيْبٍ وَعِلَّةِ

Wa shughlun bi dhikri-Llāhi Jalla Jalāluhu
fa fīhi-d-dawā min kulli ʿaybin wa ʿillati

And make your work the invocation of Allah, the Majestic.
for therein is the remedy for every ailment and flaw.

وَخِدْمَةُ خَيْرِ الْخَلْقِ أَعْظَمُ قُرْبَةٍ فَفِيهَا مِنَ الْخَيْرَاتِ أَعْلاَ مَزِيَّةِ

Wa khidmatu khayri-l-khalqi aʿẓamu qurbatin
fa fīhā mina-l-khayrāti aʿlā mazīyyati

To serve the Best of Creation is the greatest path of approach;
the goodness it contains is the highest gain.

فَشَاهِدْهُ فِي الْأَكْوَانِ قَدْ عَمَّ نُوْرُهُ   وَمِنْهُ أَتَى الْإِمْدَادُ فِي كُلِّ لَحْظَةِ

Fa shāhidhu fī-l-akwāni qad ʿamma nūruhu
wa minhu atā-l-imdādu fī kulli laḥẓati

Witness him in creation – his light spread far and wide.
From him comes support at every moment.

وَحَكِّمْهُ فِي التَّشْرِيعِ دُوْنَ تَكَاسُلٍ   وَجَانِبْ مُرَادَ النَّفْسِ أَصْلُ الْبَلِيَّةِ

Wa ḥakkimhu fī-t-tashrīʿi dūna takāsulin
wa jānib murāda-n-nafsi aṣlu-l-balīyati

Judge by his law without being lazy,
and turn aside from selfish goals which are the source of tribulation.

وَغَلِّبْ جَنَابَ الْحَقِّ عِنْدَ نِزَاعِهَا   وَلاَ تَغْتَرِرْ بِالْعِلْمِ إِلاَّ بِخَشْيَةِ

Wa ghallib janāba-l-Ḥaqqi ʿinda nizāʿihā
wa lā taghtarir bi-l-ʿilmi illā bi khashyati

Side with the Truth in the struggle with the ego,
and be not taken in by knowledge that lacks fear.

وَأَعْظَمُ ذَنْبِ الْعَبْدِ رُؤْيَةُ نَفْسِهِ   فَفِيهَا مِنَ الأَخْبَاثِ كُلُّ شَنِيعَةِ

Wa aʿẓamu dhanbi-l-ʿabdi ru•yatu nafsihi
fa fīhā mina-l-akhbāthi kullu shanīʿati

The servant's biggest sin is to see only himself:
in that sin lies all that is ugly.

وَوَحْدَةُ فِعْلِ اللهِ تَنْفِي رُسُومَهَا   وَتَطْوِي جَمِيعَ الْكَوْنِ عَنْهَا فِي لَحْظَةِ

Wa waḥdatu fiᶜli-Llāhi tanfī rusūmahā
wa taṭwī jamīᶜa-l-kawni ᶜanhā fī laḥẓati

In the oneness of Allah's deeds the ego's traces dissolve
and the entire cosmos is enfolded in an instant.

فَعَوِّلْ عَلَى التَّوْحِيدِ وَاتْرُكْ شُكُوكَهَا   تَفُزْ بِالَّذِي قَدْ فَازَ كُلُّ الْأَجِلَّةِ

Fa ᶜawwil ᶜala-t-tawḥīdi wa-truk shukūkahā
tafuz bi-l-ladhī qad fāza kullu-l-ajillati

Depend on that Oneness and leave your ego's doubts behind,
and you will succeed in the journey the way the greatest saints have done.

فَإِنْ تَصْدُرِ الْأَعْمَالُ مِنْهُمْ كَآلَةٍ   تُحَرِّكُهَا الْأَقْدَارُ مِنْ غَيْرِ رِيْبَةِ

Fa in taṣduri-l-aᶜmālu minhum ka-ālatin
tuḥarrikuha-l-aqdāru min ghayri rībati

If deeds arise from them, they see themselves as tools
whose movements, without doubt, are by Allah's Decrees.

فَتَوْبَتُهُمْ لِلهِ بِاللهِ مُطْلَقاً   وَخَوفُهُمُ تَعْظِيمُ عِزٍّ وَهَيْبَةِ

Fa tawbatuhum li-Llāhī bi-Llāhi muṭlaqan
wa khawfuhumu taᶜẓīmu ᶜizzin wa haybati

So their repentance is on-going, for Allah and by Allah;
their fear is veneration of His mightiness and awe.

رَجَاءُهُمُ حُسْنُ الْيَقِينِ بِوَعْدِهِ   وَشِدَّةُ إِتْعَابِ الْجُسُومِ فِي خِدْمَةِ

Rajāʾuhumu ḥusnu-l-yaqīni bi waʿdihi
wa shiddatu itʿābi-l-jusūmi fī khidmati

Their hope is the beauty of being sure of His promise
and the weariness of their bodies given to service.

وَشُكْرُهُمُ شُغْلٌ بِرُؤْيَةِ مُنْعِمٍ   وَغَيْبَتُهُمْ عَنْ كُلِّ ضَيْقٍ وَنِعْمَةِ

Wa shukruhumu shughlun bi ruʾyati munʿimi
wa ghaybatuhum ʿan kulli ḍayqin wa niʿmati

Their gratitude is to be occupied with a vision of the Giver
and to be detached from both hardship and comfort;

وَصَبْرُهُمُ حُسْنُ الرِّضَى بِمَقَادِيرٍ   وَلَيْسَ لَهُمْ تَدْبِيرُ سُقْمٍ وَصِحَّةِ

Wa ṣabruhumu ḥusnu-r-riḍā bi maqādīrin
wa laysa lahum tadbīru suqmin wa ṣiḥḥati

Their patience is the beauty of their contentment with decrees,
knowing they control neither sickness nor health.

تَوَكُّلُهُمْ تَفْوِيضُ كُلِّ أُمُورِهِمْ   لِمَنْ هُوَ أَدْرَى بِالْأُمُورِ الْخَفِيَّةِ

Tawakkuluhum tafwīḍu kulli umūrihim
liman Huwa adrā bi-l-umūri-l-khafīyyati

Their trust is to place their concerns in the Hands
of the One Who best knows the most hidden of our cares.

وَزُهْدُهُمُ يَأْسٌ مِمَّا لَمْ يَكُنْ لَهُمْ بِسَابِقِ عِلْمِ اللهِ مِنْ بَرْمِ قِسْمَةِ

Wa zuhduhumu ya•sun mimmā lam yakun lahum
bi sābiqi ʿilmi-Llāhi min barmi qismati

Their renouncement is to give up what in Allah's fore-knowledge,
was not to be part of their immutable lot in life.

مَحَبَّتُهُمْ سُكْرٌ بِحُسْنِ جَمَالِهِ وَفِيهَا مَقَامُ الْأُنْسِ أَشْرَفُ حِلْيَةِ

Maḥabbatuhum sukrun bi ḥusni jamālihi
wa fīhā maqāmu-l-unsi ashrafu ḥilyati

Their love is to be drunk with the goodliness of His beauty
and there is the station of intimacy – the noblest adornment –

وَبَسْطٌ وَإِدْلَالٌ وَتَكْلِيمُ حِبِّهِمْ وَأَسْرَارُهَا تَسْرِي إِلَى غَيْرِ غَايَةِ

Wa basṭun wa idlālun wa taklīmu Ḥibbihim
wa asrāruhā tasrī ilā ghayri ghāyati

And expansion and unrestraint and discourse with the Beloved:
the mysteries of love flow forth without end.

فَنَافِسْهُمُ فِيهَا بِحُسْنِ تَأَدُّبٍ وَأَحْسِنْ لِأَحْبَابِ الْحَبِيبِ بِفَضْلَةِ

Fa nāfis•humu fīhā bi ḥusni ta•addubin
wa aḥsin li aḥbābi-l-Ḥabībi bi faḍlati

So vie with them in it through beautiful manners
and be ever generous to the lovers of the Friend

فَلَوْ عَرَفَ الْإِنْسَانُ قِيمَةَ قَلْبِهِ لَأَنْفَقَ كُلَّ الْكُلِّ مِنْ غَيْرِ فَتْرَةِ

Fa law ʿarafa-l-insānu qīmata qalbihi
la anfaqa kulla-l-kulli min ghayri fatrati

For if a person truly knew the worth of his heart,
he would give all he had without hesitation.

وَلَوْ أَدْرَكَ الْإِنْسَانُ لَذَّةَ سِرِّهِ لَقَارَنَ أَنْفَاسَ الْخُرُوْجِ بِعَبْرَةِ

Wa law adraka-l-insānu ladhdhata sirrihi
la qārana anfāsa-l-khurūji bi ʿabrati

And if a person came to know the bliss within his soul,
he would shed a tear of joy with every breath he took.

وَطَارَ مِنَ الْجِسْمِ الَّذِي صَارَ قَفْصَهُ بِأَجْنِحَةِ الْأَفْكَارِ مُنْتَهَى سِدْرَةِ

Wa ṭāra mina-l-jismi-l-ladhī ṣāra qafṣahu
bi ajniḥati-l-afkāri muntahā sidrati

He would fly forth from the body that had become his cage
on wings of meditation to the Lote-Tree of the Boundary.

وَجَالَ نَوَاحِي الْعَرْشِ وَالْكُرْسِيِّ الَّذِي تَضَاءَلَتِ الْأَجْرَامُ عَنْهُ كَحَلْقَةِ

Wa jāla nawāḥi-l-ʿarshi wa-l-kursīyyi-l-ladhī
taḍā•alati-l-ajrāmu ʿanhu ka-ḥalqati

And would range the expanses of the Footstool and Throne
where the galaxies appear but a tiny ring.

وَشَاهَدَ أَفْلَاكاً وَسِرَّ بُرُوجِهَا   وَشِدَّةَ إِفْرَاطِ الْمُرُوْرِ بِسُرْعَةِ

Wa shāhada aflākan wa sirra burūjihā
wa shiddata ifrāṭi-l-murūri bi surᶜati

He would see the planets' orbits and the mystery of their houses,
and the immensity of the speed at which they pass

وَزَالَ حِجَابُ اللَّوحِ عَنْ طَيِّ سِرِّهِ   فَفَاحَتْ عُلُومُ الْكَشْفِ مِن غَيرِ سُتْرَةِ

Wa zāla ḥijābu-l-Lawḥi ᶜan ṭayyi sirrihi
fa fāḥat ᶜulūmu-l-kashfi min ghayri sutrati

And the veil of the Tablet would be lifted from the mystery it enfolds,
and the knowledge it contains would waft forth uncovered

فَلَوْ كَانَتِ الْأَشْجَارُ أَقْلَامَ كَتْبِهَا   وَمِدَادُهَا الْبَحْرُ الْمُحِيْطُ لَجَفَّتِ

Fa law kānati-l-ashjāru aqlāma katbihā
wa midāduhā-l-baḥru-l-muḥīṭu la jaffati

Such that were all the trees on earth pens to record it
and the ocean their ink, they would run dry.

وَزَارَ مِنَ الْمَعْمُورِ أَمْلَاكَهُ الَّتِي   تَنُوفُ عَلَى الْأَعْدَادِ مِنْ غَيْرِ غَايَةِ

Wa zāra mina-l-maᶜmūri amlākahu-l-latī
tanūfu ᶜalā-l-aᶜdādi min ghayri ghāyati

And he would visit angels from this world's abode
whose ranks are numberless, without limit.

وَوَافَى دُخُولَ حَضْرَةِ الْقُدْسِ طَالِباً   لِتَطْهِيرِ سِرِّ السِّرِّ مِنْ كُلِّ وَقْفَةِ

Wa wāfā dukhūla Ḥaḍrati-l-Qudsi ṭāliban
li taṭhīri sirri-s-sirri min kulli waqfati

And be granted entry into the Presence as a seeker,
to cleanse the inmost soul of any obstacles that remained.

فَهٰذَا مَحَطُّ الْقَوْمِ عِنْدَ سُرَائِهِمْ   بِأَرْوَاحِهِمْ مَحَلُّ كَتْمٍ وَحَيْرَةِ

Fa hādhā maḥaṭṭu-l-qawmi ʿinda surā•ihim
bi arwāḥihim maḥallu katmin wa ḥayrati

This station of the folk on the journey of their souls
is a place of silence and speechless wonder.

وَمِنْ بَعْدِهَا الْعِلْمُ الَّذِي لاَ يَبُثُّهُ   سِوَى مَنْ لَهُ الإِذْنُ الصَّرِيْحُ بِرُؤْيَةِ

Wa min baʿdihā-l-ʿilmu-l-ladhī lā yabuththuhu
siwā man lahu-l-idhnu-ṣ-ṣarīḥu bi ru•yati

And beyond it is a teaching which may only be mentioned
by one who – in a vision – is permitted to speak.

وَفِي الْأَرْضِ آيَاتٌ لِكُلِّ مُفَكِّرٍ   عَجَائِبُهَا تَمْضِي إِلَى أَعْلاَ عِبْرَةِ

Wa fi-l-arḍi āyātun li kulli mufakkirin
ʿajā•ibuhā tamḍī ilā aʿlā ʿibrati

On earth there are signs for all who reflect
and their marvels range to the loftiest teachings

فَأَسْمَاءُ رَبِّ الْعَرْشِ قَدْ عَمَّ نُورُهَا   بِأَجْزَائِهَا مَا بَيْنَ خَافٍ وَشُهْرَةِ

Fa asmā•u Rabbi-l-ʿArshi qad ʿamma nūruhā
bi ajzā•ihā mā bayna khāfin wa shuhrati

The light of the Names of the Lord has encompassed
every part of creation whether hidden or known

فَلَوْجُلْتَ فِي الْمِيَاهِ مَعْ أَصْلِ نَشْئِهَا   وَتَرْبِيَةِ الْأَشْيَاءِ مِنْهَا بِحِكْمَةِ

Fa law julta fi-l-miyāhi maʿ aṣli nash•ihā
wa tarbīyati-l-ashyā•i minhā bi ḥikmati

If you consider the waters and the source from which they come
and how creatures have been formed from them by Wisdom

حَكَمْتَ بِعَجْزِ الْكُلِّ عَنْ دَرْكِ سِرِّهَا   وَبُحْتَ بِتَخْصِيصِ الْإِلٰهِ بِقُدْرَةِ

Ḥakamta bi ʿajzi-l-kulli ʿan darki sirrihā
wa buḥta bi takhṣīṣi-l-ilāhi bi qudrati

You'd reckon that all are helpless to grasp their secret,
and would affirm that Power is Allah's alone.

وَأَطْلِقْ عِنَانَ الْفِكْرِ عِنْدَ جِبَالِهَا   تَجِدْهَا هِيَ الْأَوْتَادُ مِنْ غَيْرِ مِرْيَةِ

Wa aṭliq ʿināna-l-fikri ʿinda jibālihā
tajidhā hiya-l-awtādu min ghayri miryati

Then let your thoughts range free before the mountains
and you will find them, without doubt, to be the mainstays of the earth.

وَمَا حَوَتِ الْأَزْهَارُ مِنْ حُسْنِ مَنْظَرٍ   وَكَثْرَةِ تَنْوِيعِ الثِّمَارِ الْبَدِيْعَةِ

Wa mā ḥawati-l-azhāru min ḥusni manẓarin
wa kathrati tanwīʿi-th-thimāri-l-badīʿati

And consider the beauty of the trees in blossom
and the wondrous multitude of fruits they bear!

وَمَا أَظْهَرَتْ مِنْ كُلِّ شَيءٍ يُرَى بِهَا   وَكُلٌّ أَتَى مِنْ عَيْنِ عِزٍّ وَسَطْوَةِ

Wa mā aẓharat min kulli shay•in yurā bihā
wa kullun atā min ʿayni ʿizzin wa saṭwati

And what each thing manifests in the way it is seen:
all from a Source of power and strength.

فَشَاهِدْ جَمَالَ الْحَقِّ عِنْدَ لِحَاظِهَا   وَإِيَّاكَ تَنْكِيفاً عَلَى أَدْنَى ذَرَّةِ

Fa shāhid jamāla-l-Ḥaqqi ʿinda liḥāẓihā
wa iyyāka tankīfan ʿalā adnā dharrati

So witness Allah's beauty with every glance [you take]
and do not disdain even the tiniest of creatures.

فَمَا قَامَتِ الأَشْيَاءُ إِلاَّ بِرَبِّهَا   فَيَا حَيُّ يَا قَيُّومُ أَبْلَغُ حُجَّةِ

Fa mā qāmati-l-ashyā•u illā bi Rabbihā
fa Yā Ḥayyu Yā Qayyūmu ablaghu ḥujjati

For nothing exists except by its Lord's [decree].
O Living! O Eternal! is the clearest proof.

فَفِي النَّفْسِ آيَاتٌ لِكُلِّ مُفَكِّرٍ   فَفِيهَا انْطَوَى الْكَوْنُ الْكَبِيرُ بِرُمَّةِ

Fa fī-n-nafsi āyātun li kulli mufakkirin
fa fīhā-nṭawā-l-kawnu-l-kabīru bi rummati

In the soul are signs for all who reflect:
the entire cosmos is contained within it.

وَزَادَتْ بِوُسْعِ الْحَقِّ عِنْدَ تَطَهُّرٍ   وَذَا قُلْ بِلاَ كَيْفٍ وَأَيْنٍ وَشُبْهَةِ

Wa zādat bi wusʿi-l-Ḥaqqi ʿinda taṭahhurin
wa dhā qul bilā kayfin wa aynin wa shubhati

When purified it grows vast enough to contain Allah, the Truth:
say this, but not how, or where, or any likeness.

وَزَادَتْ بِتَحْمِيلِ الْإِلٰهِ أَمَانَةً   عَلَيْهَا فَمَا حَدَّ الْإِلٰهِ تَعَدَّتِ

Wa zādat bi taḥmīli-l-ilāhi amānatan
ʿalayhā fa mā ḥadda-l-ilāhi taʿaddati

It is increased to bear the trust that Allah placed upon it,
but may not exceed the limits that Allah has set.

وَقَدْ عَجَزَتْ عَنْهَا الْعِظَامُ مِنَ الْوَرَى   وَقَامَ بِهَا الْإِنْسَانُ أَرْفَعَ قَوْمَةِ

Wa qad ʿajazat ʿanha-l-ʿiẓāmu mina-l-warā
wa qāma bihā-l-insānu arfaʿa qawmati

The mightiest of creatures were too weak to bear it,
but man took it on as his loftiest duty.

فَيَا سَعْدَ مَنْ أَضْحَى يُتَابِعُ سَيِّداً رَسُوْلاً لَهُ أَعْلاَ الْمَزَايَا وَرُتْبَةِ

Fa yā saʿda man aḍḥā yutābiʿu Sayyidan
Rasūlan lahu aʿla-l-mazāyā wa rutbati

So blessed be the one who sets forth to follow a master,
a Messenger of highest merit and rank.

فَحَازَ مِنَ الْخَيْرَاتِ فَوْقَ نِهَايَةٍ وَأُمَّتُهُ أَرْبَتْ عَلَى كُلِّ أُمَّةِ

Fa ḥāza mina-l-khayrāti fawqa nihāyatin
wa ummatuhu arbat ʿalā kulli ummati

He was given goodness without limit or end
and his community was raised up above every people

فَلاَ أَحَدٌ يَرْقَى لِرُتْبَةِ قُرْبِهِ وَذَاكَ بِتَخْصِيصِ الْإِلٰهِ بِعَطْفَةِ

Fa lā aḥadun yarqā li rutbati qurbihi,
wa dhāka bi takhṣīṣi-l-ilāhi bi ʿaṭfati

There is no one else who may reach the degree of his nearness,
That is his alone as compassion from Allah.

فَلاَ كَسْبَ لِلإِنْسَانِ فِي دَرْكِ غَايَةٍ لِمَا خَصَّهُ الرَّحْمَانُ فِي أَصْلِ نَشْأَةِ

Fa lā kasba li-l-insāni fī darki ghāyatin
limā khaṣṣahu-r-Raḥmānu fī aṣli nash•ati

A human may not gain – however much he strives –
what the Most Merciful gave only to the Prophet at creation

عَلَيْهِ صَلاةُ اللهِ مَاجَآءَ وَارِدٌ   يُبَيِّنُ طُرْقَ الْحَقِّ مَعْ سَوْقِ مِنْحَةِ

ʿAlayhi ṣalātu-Llāhi mā jā•a wāridun
yubayyinu ṭurqa-l-Ḥaqqi maʿ sawqi minḥati

May Allah's blessings be upon him for as long as there are sent
those who make clear the sacred path and transmit the gift.

وَآلِهِ وَالأَصْحَابِ مَعْ كُلِّ مُرْشِدٍ   دَعَا لِطَرِيقِ اللهِ فِي كُلِّ حَالَةِ

Wa ālihi wa-l-aṣ•ḥābi maʿ kulli murshidin
daʿā li ṭarīqi-Llāhi fī kulli ḥālati

And upon his Family and Companions and all of the guides
who call to Allah's way in every condition.

وَأَسْأَلُ رَبِّ اللهَ إِلْقَاءَ سِرِّهِ   عَلَيَّ مَعَ الإِخْوَانِ فِي كُلِّ وِجْهَةِ

Wa as•alu Rabbi-Llāha ilqā•ā sirrihi
ʿalayya maʿa-l-ikhwāni fī kulli wijhatin

I ask the Lord, Allah, to grant me the secret
and to the brethren as well in every direction.

قَدْ وَافَقَتِ الإِسْمَ الْعَظِيمَ جَلاَلَةً   بِعَدٍّ فَنَافِسْ فِي افْتِتَاحٍ وَخَتْمَةِ

Qad wāfaqati-l-Isma-l-ʿAẓīma Jalālatan
bi ʿaddin fa nāfis fī-ftitāḥin wa khatmati

The number of its lines equals the Supreme Name of Majesty,
so treasure its beginning and its end.

-3-

التائية الوسطى

We Drank From the Lights

شَرِبْنَا مِنَ الْأَنْوَارِ فِي حَانِ حَضْرَةٍ   شَرَاباً أَزَالَ اللَّبْسَ مِنْ غَيْرِ مِرْيَةِ

Sharibnā mina-l-anwāri fī ḥāni ḥaḍratin
sharāban azāla-l-labsa min ghayri miryati

We drank from the lights in the tavern of the Presence
a wine that removed confusion without doubt

فَأَدْرَكْنَا أَنَّ الْفِعْلَ فِي كُلِّ ذَرَّةٍ   بِخَالِقِهَا الْمَعْبُودِ فِي كُلِّ وِجْهَةِ

Fa adraknā anna-l-fiʿla fī kulli dharratin
bi Khāliqiha-l-maʿbūdi fī kulli wijhati

And perceived that the action inside every atom
is by its Creator Who is Worshipped in every direction

وَحَقَّقْنَا أَنَّ اللهَ فِي الْكُلِّ ظَاهِرٌ   بِأَسْمَائِهِ الْحُسْنَى وَأَسْرَارِ قُدْرَةِ

Wa ḥaqqaqnā anna-Llāha fi-l-kulli ẓāhirun
bi asmā•ihi-l-ḥusnā wa asrāri Qudrati

And realized that Allah is manifest in all
by His beautiful Names and the mysteries of Power

وَلٰكِنَّ أَحْوَالَ الْوُجُودِ كَثِيرَةٌ بِهَا وَقَعَ الْحُجْبُ الْعَظِيمُ لِحِكْمَةِ

Wa lākinna aḥwāla-l-wujūdi kathīratun
bihā waqaʿa-l-ḥujbu-l-ʿaẓīmu li ḥikmati

But the states of existence are many indeed
and through them great veils – by Wisdom – befell

لِذَا أَرْسَلَ الرَّحْمَٰنُ خِيرَةَ خَلْقِهِ بَشِيرًا نَذِيْرًا دَاعِيًا بِالْبَصِيرَةِ

Li dhā arsala-r-Raḥmānu khīrata khalqihi
bashīran nadhīran dāʿiyan bi-l-baṣīrati

Thus did the Merciful send the Best of Creation
as a bearer of glad tidings, a warner, and one who calls with inner vision.

فَإِنْ شِئْتَ أَنْ تَحْظَى بِنَيْلِ سَعَادَةٍ فَحَكِّمْهُ تَحْكِيماً عَلَى كُلِّ خَطْرَةِ

Fa in shiʾta an taḥẓā bi nayli saʿādati
fa ḥakkimhu taḥkīman ʿalā kulli khaṭrati

So if you wish to be granted well-being and salvation
make him the standard by which you judge each passing thought.

وَقُلْ لِحُظُوظِ النَّفْسِ لَا تَذْهَبِي مَعِي وَلَا تَقْطَعِي سَيْرِي لِرَبِّ الْبَرِيَّةِ

Wa qul li ḥuẓūẓi-n-nafsī lā tadhhabī maʿī
wa lā taqṭaʿī sayrī li Rabbi-l-barīyyati

And say to the ego's claims: "Do not go with me,
and do not cut short my journey to the Lord of Creation!"

فَمَنْ كَانَ ذَا ذِكْرٍ وَفِكْرٍ وَهِمَّةٍ   تَرَقَّى عَنِ الأَغْيَارِ فِي كُلِّ لَحْظَةِ

Fa man kāna dhā dhikrin wa fikrin wa himmatin
taraqqā ʿani-l-aghyāri fī kulli laḥẓati.

For the one with invocation, reflection, and aspiration
rises, at each moment, above the illusion of otherness,

وَحَازَ مِنَ الْعِرْفَانِ فَوْقَ مُرَادِهِ   وَحَقَّقَ أَسْرَارَ الْوُجُودِ بِسُرْعَةِ

Wa ḥāza mina-l-ʿirfāni fawqa murādihi
wa ḥaqqaqa asrāra-l-wujūdi bi surʿati

And be granted gnosis beyond what he'd hoped for,
and realize quickly the mysteries of being,

وَشَاهَدَ أَنَّ الْفَرْقَ مَحْضُ شَرِيعَةٍ   وَهِيَ عَلَى التَّحْقِيقِ عَيْنُ الْحَقِيقَةِ

Wa shāhada anna-l-farqa maḥḍu sharīʿatin
wa hiya ʿala-t-taḥqīqi ʿaynu-l-ḥaqīqati

And see that separation is purely the revealed Law,
and is one and the same with the Spiritual Truth.

لِذَا أَمَرَ الْقُرءَانُ بِالْفِكْرِ فِي الْوَرَى   وَجَاءَ بِتَوْحِيدٍ مُزِيلٍ لِرَيْبَةِ

Li dhā amara-l-Qur•ānu bi-l-fikri fi-l-warā
wa jā•a bi tawḥīdin muzīlin li raybati

Even thus does the Qur'ān bid reflection on creation,
while bringing affirmation of oneness that removes any doubt.

وَلَيْسَ يُرَى الرَّحْمٰنُ إِلاَّ فِي مَظْهَرٍ   كَعَرْشٍ وَكُرْسِيٍّ وَلَوحٍ وَسِدْرَةِ

Wa laysa yura-r-Raḥmānu illā fī maẓharin
ka ʿArshin wa Kursīyyin wa Lawḥin wa Sidrati

The Most-Merciful is not seen save in a theophany
like the Throne, Footstool, Tablet, and Lote-Tree

وَكُنْهُ صِفَاتِ الرَّبِّ لَيْسَ النُّهَى تَفِي   بِتَحْقِيقِهَا كَشْفاً فَأَحْرَى الْمَهِيَّةِ

Wa kunhu ṣifāti-r-Rabbi laysa-n-nuhā tafī
bi taḥqīqihā kashfan fa aḥra-l-mahīyyati

The mind cannot grasp what the Attributes of the Lord truly are
in their unveilings let alone in their essential state

فَكِرَّ عَلَى أَوْصَافِ نَفْسِكَ فَامْحُهَا   تُمَدُّ بِأَنْوَارِ الصِّفَاتِ الْقَدِيْمَةِ

Fakirra ʿalā awṣāfi nafsika famḥuhā
tumaddu bi anwāri-ṣ-ṣifāti-l-qadīmati

Repel the traits of your ego and then efface them
and by the lights of the Eternal Attributes you will be aided

لِذَاكَ تَرَى الْعُشَّاقَ قَدْ ثَمِلُوا بِهَا   وَأَحْسَنُهُمْ سُكْراً مَلِيكُ الْإِبَاحَةِ

Lidhāka tarā-l-ʿushshāqa qad thamilū bihā
wa aḥsanuhum sukran malīku-l-ibāḥati

And so you see lovers made drunk by these lights
yet the best of them in drunkenness still guards what he proclaims.

وَلَيْسَ عَلَى الْمَغْلُوبِ مِنْ حَرَجٍ وَلَا عَلَى أَهْلِ الْإِذْنِ مِنْ وُضُوحِ الْإِشَارَةِ

Wa laysa ʿala-l-maghlūbi min ḥarajin wa lā
ʿalā ahli-l-idhni min wuḍūḥi-l-ishārati

But on someone overcome there is no blame
nor on those with permission if they make clear the allusion

فَدُونَكَ قَوْماً قَدْ أَذَابُوا نُفُوسَهُمْ فَخَاضُوا بِحَارَ الْحُبِّ فِي كُلِّ لُجَّةِ

Fa dūnaka qawman qad adhābū nufūsahum,
fa khāḍū biḥāra-l-ḥubbi fī kulli lujjati

Keep company with a folk whose egos have melted away
so that they swim in love's oceans at all of its depths

فَسَلِّمْ لَهُمْ فِيمَا تَرَى مِنْ صَبَابَةٍ وَرَقْصٍ عَلَى ذِكْرِ الْحَبِيبِ بِنَغْمَةِ

Fa sallim lahum fī mā tarā min ṣabābatin
wa raqṣin ʿalā dhikri-l-Ḥabībi bi naghmati.

And accept it of them if you see them seized by love
and dancing at the mention of the Beloved in song.

فَلَوْ ذُقْتَ شَيْئاً مِنْ مَعَانِي كَلَامِنَا لَكُنْتَ مِنَ السُّبَّاقِ فِي كُلِّ حَالَةِ

Fa law dhuqta shay·an min maʿānī kalāminā
lakunta mina-s-subbāqi fī kulli ḥālati.

For were you to taste the meaning of our words,
you would be the first among them in all of their states.

وَأَغْضَيْتَ يَا أَخِي الْجُفُونَ عَنِ القَذَى   وَمَزَّقْتَ أَثْوَابَ الْحَيَا وَالْمَهَابَةِ

Wa aghḍayta yā akhi-l-jufūna ʿani-l-qadhā
wa mazzaqta athwāba-l-ḥayā wa-l-mahābati

And you would lower your eyelids against the mote in your vision, my brother,
and rend the robes of shyness and reserve.

وَقُلْتَ لِحَادِي الْقَوْمِ حَبِّبْنَا فِي اسْمِهِ   فَلاَ عَارَ فِي ذَاكَ الْحِدَا وَالصَّبَابَةِ

Wa qulta li ḥādī-l-qawmi: "ḥabbibnā fi-smihi !"
fa lā ʿāra fī dhāka-l-ḥidā wa-ṣ-ṣabābati.

And you would say to the chanter, "Make us lovers of His Name!"
for in that chant and that love there is no fault or blame.

وَلٰكِنَّ مَنْ قَدْ صَارَ مِلْكاً لِنَفْسِهِ   تَقَاعَدَ عَنْ أَسْرَارِ تِلْكَ الطَّرِيقَةِ

Wa lākinna man qad ṣāra milkan li nafsihi
taqāʿada ʿan asrāri tilka-ṭ-ṭarīqati

But the one who has fallen under the power of his ego
is kept back from [knowing] the mysteries of that Path.

فَأَعْدَى عَدُوٍّ فِي الْوَرَى نَفْسُكَ الَّتِي   تُعَطِّلُ عَنْ تَحْقِيقِ فَهْمِ الْحَقِيقَةِ

Fa aʿdā ʿaduwwin fi-l-warā nafsuka-l-latī
tuʿaṭṭilu ʿan taḥqīqi fahmi-l-ḥaqīqati

The worst enemy you have in this world is your ego
which holds you back from real understanding of the Truth

فَكَبِّرْ عَلَى الْأَكْوَانِ إِنْ شِئْتَ وَصْلَهُ   وَإِيَّاكَ أَنْ تَرْضَى بِنَيْلِ الْكَرَامَةِ

Fa kabbir ʿala-l-akwāni in shi•ta waṣlahu
wa iyyāka an tarḍā bi nayli-l-karāmati

So if you desire Union, pray the funeral prayer for this world
and beware of settling only for miracles you [might] gain.

فَيَا فَوْزَ قَوْمٍ قَدْ أَجَابُوا حَبِيبَهُمْ   لِدَعْوَتِهِ الْعُظْمَى فَفَازُوْا بِجَنَّةِ

Fa yā fawza qawmin qad ajābū ḥabībahum
li daʿwatihi-l-ʿuẓmā fa fāzū bi Jannati

The people who answered the Beloved's highest call –
what a victory they were given: they won the Garden!

وَأَعْنِي بِهِ الْعِرْفَانَ فِي حَضْرَةِ الدُّنَا   وَجَنَّةَ أَنْهَارٍ وَحُورٍ وَلَذَّةِ

Wa aʿnī bihi-l-ʿirfāna fī ḥaḍrati-d-dunā
wa Jannata anhārin wa ḥūrin wa ladhdhati

And by "Garden" I mean [both] gnosis in the Presence
and the Heaven of rivers, and houris, and delight.

عَلَى نَفْسِهِ فَلْيَبْكِ مَنْ صَارَ قَلْبُهُ   خَرَاباً مِنَ الْعِرْفَانِ فِي كُلِّ فِكْرَةِ

ʿAlā nafishi fa-l-yabki man ṣāra qalbuhu
kharāban mina-l-ʿirfāni fī kulli fikrati.

The one whose heart has been emptied of gnosis
should weep for his soul every time he reflects.

وَمَا لَذَّةُ الْعَيْشِ السَّلِيمِ مِنَ النَّغْصِ   وَرَبِّيَ إِلاَّ فِي تَحَقُّقِ وُصْلَةِ

Wa mā ladhdhatu-l-ʿayshi-s-salīmi mina-n-naghṣi
wa Rabbiya illā fī taḥaqquqi wuṣlati

For the sweetness of a life unburdened by trouble
comes only – by my Lord – in realizing union.

عَسَى نَظْرَةٌ تَشْفِي السَّقِيمَ مِنَ الضَّنَى   فَقَدْ عَزَّ إِدْرَاكٌ لِكُنْهِ الْحَقِيقَةِ

ʿAsā naẓratun tashfī-saqīma mina-ḍ-ḍanā
fa qad ʿazza idrākun li kunhi-l-ḥaqīqati

It might be that only a glance would cure the patient of his weakness
for the essence of the Truth is hard to the mind.

فَأَطْيَبُ أَوْقَاتِي اتِّصَافِي بِذِلَّةٍ   وَعَجْزٍ وَفَقْرٍ وَانْسِلاَبِ إِرَادَةِ

Fa aṭyabu awqātī-ttiṣāfī bi dhillati
wa ʿajzin wa faqrin wa-nsilābi irādati

The best of my moments are in my lowliness and weakness,
my neediness, and when the will is eclipsed.

فَتِلْكَ أُصُولٌ فِي طَرِيقَتِنَا الْمُثْلَى   فَكُنْهُ وَجَنِّبْ عَنْ عُلُوٍّ وَرِفْعَةِ

Fa tilka uṣūlun fī ṭarīqatina-l-muthlā
fa kunhu wa jannib ʿan ʿulūwwin wa rifʿati

These are the principles of our most perfect path.
Be thus, and turn away from high rank and fame

وَكُلُّ صِفَاتِ الرَّبِّ فَاهْرُبْ لِضِدِّهَا تَكُونُ بِفَضْلِ اللهِ أَغْنَى الْبَرِيَّةِ

Wa kullu ṣifāti-r-Rabbi fa-hrub li ḍiddihā
takūnu bi faḍli-Llāhi aghna-l-bariyyati

From each Attribute of the Lord, flee to its opposite
and you will be, by Allah's grace, the richest of creatures

فَأَوْصَافُهُ الْعِلْمُ الْمُحِيطُ وَقُدْرَةٌ وَ أَوْصَافُنَا جَهْلٌ وَعَجْزٌ عَنْ ذَرَّةِ

Fa•awṣāfuhu-l-ᶜilmu-l-muḥīṭu wa qudratun
wa awṣāfunā jahlun wa ᶜajzun ᶜan dharrati

His Attributes are all-encompassing knowledge and power;
while ours are ignorance and weakness over the smallest matters

وَإِنْ شِئْتَ قَصْدَ الْعَارِفِينَ بِأَسْرِهِمْ فَخُذْهُ وَكُنْ يَا صَاحِ صَاحِبَ هِمَّةِ

Wa in shi•ta qaṣda-l-ᶜārifīna bi asrihim
fa khudh hu wa kun yā ṣāḥi ṣāḥiba himmati

If you wish, O friend, to reach the goal of the gnostics
then take [this advice] and be a person of aspiration.

عُبُودِيَّةٌ لِلهِ صَادِقَةٌ وَمَعْ قِيَامٍ بِحَقِّ الرَّبِّ فِي كُلِّ لَحْظَةِ

ᶜUbūdiyyatun li-Lāhi ṣādiqatun wa maᶜ
qiyāmin bi ḥaqqi-r-Rabbi fī kulli laḥẓati

Servanthood that is sincere is for Allah [alone]
along with maintaining what is due to the Lord at each moment.

وَأَعْنِي بِهَا التَّجْرِيدَ مِنْ كُلِّ قُوَّةٍ وَحَوْلٍ وَأَسْبَابٍ وَنَيلِ الْمَزِيَّةِ

Wa aʿnī biha-t-tajrīda min kulli quwwati
wa ḥawlin wa asbābin wa nayli-l-mazīyyati

And by servanthood I mean giving up all [pretensions]
of power, strength, and means, and of gaining distinction.

لِأَنَّ بِهَا يَصْفُو الْفُؤَادُ مِنَ الْعَمَى وَيُمْلَأُ بِالْأَنْوَارِ فِي كُلِّ فِكْرَةِ

Li anna bihā yaṣfu-l-fuʾādu mina-l-ʿamā,
wa yumlaʾu bi-l-anwāri fī kulli fikrati

Through servanthood the heart is cleansed of blindness
and its every reflection is filled with lights.

فَقَدْ كَمُلَتْ وَالْحَمْدُ فِي الْبَدْءِ وَالْخَتْمِ عَلَى نِعْمَةِ الْإِمْدَادِ مِنْ خَيْرِ أُمَّةِ

Fa qad kamulat wa-l-ḥamdu fi-l-badʾi wa-l-khatmi
ʿalā niʿmati-l-imdādi min khayri ummati.

[This ode] is completed. I give thanks at its start and end
for the gift of help from the best of this people.

عَلَيْهِ صَلَاةُ اللهِ فِي كُلِّ لَحْظَةٍ وَآلِهِ وَالْأَصْحَابِ أَهْلِ الْعِنَايَةِ

ʿAlayhi ṣalātu-Llāhi fī kulli laḥẓatin
wa ālihi wa-l-aṣʾḥābi ahli-l-ʿināyati.

Upon him may there always be the blessings of Allah
and upon his Family and Companions, the people of providence.

وَنَاظِمُهَا الْمَعْرُوفُ أَعْنِي مُحَمَّداً   هُوَ ابْنُ حَبِيبٍ طَالِبًا لِلْعُبُودَةِ

Wa nāẓimuhā-l-maʿrūfu aʿnī Muḥammadan
huwa-bnu Ḥabībin ṭāliban li-l-ʿubūdati

Its writer is known: I mean Muḥammad,
son of Ḥabīb, who seeks total worship

فَبَلِّغْهُ يَاذَا الْفَضْلِ مِنْكَ بِنَفْحَةٍ   تَسُحُّ عَلَى الْأَكْوَانِ فَيْضَ الْحَقِيقَةِ

Fa balligh•hu yā dha-l-faḍli minka bi nafḥatin
tasuḥḥu ʿalā-l-akwāni fayḍa-l-ḥaqīqati

O You of Endless Grace, convey it with a breeze
that floods creation with overflowing Truth

-4-

سقاني حبي من صفاء محبة

My Beloved Gave Me to Drink

سَقَانِي حِبِّي مِنْ صَفَاءِ مَحَبَّةٍ   فَأَصْبَحْتُ مَحْبُوباً لَدَى كُلِّ نِسْبَةِ

Saqāniya ḥibbī min ṣafā•i maḥabbatin
fa aṣbaḥtu maḥbūban ladā kulli nisbati

My Beloved gave me to drink from the purity of love,
so that I became beloved to those of every order.

وَغَيَّبَنِي عَنِّي فَلَمْ أَرَ غَيْرَهُ   وَنَعَّمَ سِرِّي فِي مَظَاهِرِ حَضْرَةِ

Wa ghayyabanī ʿannī fa lam ara ghayrahu
wa naʿʿama sirrī fī maẓāhiri ḥaḍrati.

And He caused me to vanish from myself so that I saw naught but Him
and in theophanies of Presence, my soul found bliss.

فَفَرَّقْتُ فِي جَمْعِي وَجَمَعْتُ مَفْرُوْقِي   وَحَقَقْتُ تَوْحِيدِي بِإِفْرَادِ وَحْدَةِ

Fa farraqtu fī jamʿī wa jamaʿtu mafrūqī
wa ḥaqaqtu tawḥīdī bi ifrādi waḥdati.

Then in my union I separated and united what was separate within me,
and affirmed my unity by a unique oneness.

وَنِلْتُ مُرَادِي مِنْ شُهُودِ كَمَالِهِ   وَحَقَّقْتُهُ فِي كُلِّ مَعْنَى وَصُورَةِ

Wa niltu murādī min shuhūdi kamālihi
wa ḥaqqaqtuhu fī kulli maʿnā wa ṣūrati.

And I attained my desire: to witness His perfection
and affirmed it in every substance and form

وَمَزَّقْتُ وَهْمِي وَهْوَ أَعْظَمُ قَاطِعٍ   فَأَلْفَيْتُهُ قَيُّوماً فِي كُلِّ ذَرَّةِ

Wa mazzaqtu wahmī wa hwa aʿẓamu qāṭiʿin
fa alfaytuhu qayyūman fī kulli dharrati

I rent the veil of my illusion, which is the greatest of obstacles,
and found Him eternally present in every particle of existence.

وَحَكَّمْتُ شَرْعِي فِي تَجَلِّي صِفَاتِهِ   فَأَطْلَعَنِي رَبِّي عَلَى سِرِّ حِكْمَتِي

Wa ḥakkamtu sharʿī fī tajallī ṣifātihi,
fa aṭlaʿanī Rabbī ʿalā sirrī ḥikmatī.

I made the Law to be ruler over the unveiling of His Attributes,
so my Lord gave me knowledge of the mystery of Wisdom.

فَطَوْراً أَرَى الْأَكْوَانَ مَظْهَرَ أَحْمَدٍ   وَطَوْراً أَرَاهَا مِنْ مَظَاهِرِ عِزَّةِ

Fa ṭawran arā-l-akwāna maẓhara Aḥmadin
wa ṭawran arāhā min maẓāhiri ʿizzati.

At times I see creatures as the manifestation of Aḥmad,
and at times I see them as theophanies of might

وَ طَوْرًا يَفْنَى فِعْلِي بِرُؤْيَةِ فِعْلِهِ   وَطَوْراً أَرَى الأَوْصَافَ مِنْهُ تَبَدَّتِ

Wa ṭawran yafnā fiʿlī bi ru•yati fiʿlihi,
wa ṭawran arā-l-awṣāfa minhu tabaddati.

And at times my acts vanish in a vision of His acts
and at times I see the Attributes appearing from Him.

وَطَوْرًا أَغِيبُ عَنْ وُجُودِ مَجَازِيٍّ   فِي وَحْدَةِ حَقٍّ لاَ تُشَابُ بِشِرْكَةِ

Wa ṭawran aghību ʿan wujūdi majāziyyi
fī waḥdati ḥaqqin lā tushābu bi shirkati

And at times I pass away from my figurative existence
in the Oneness of a Truth untainted by partners.

وَمَا الْخَلْقُ إِلاَّ كَالْهَبَا فِي الْهَوَى لِمَنْ   تَغَيَّبَ فِي أَنْوَارِ ذِكْرِ الْحَقِيْقَةِ

Wa ma-l-khalqu illā ka-l-habā• fi-l-hawā liman
taghayyaba fī anwāri dhikri-l-ḥaqīqati

And creation is nothing but motes of floating dust
to one effaced in the lights of invoking the Inner Truth.

فَفِي ذِكْرِهَا الْفَتْحُ الْمُبِينُ لِتَائِبٍ   تَحَلَّى بِصَبْرٍ مَعْ تَحَقُّقِ نِعْمَةِ

Fa fī dhikriha-l-fatḥu-l-mubīnu li tā•ibin
taḥallā bi ṣabrin maʿ taḥaqquqi niʿmati

In its invocation is a clear opening for any who repents
And is adorned by patience, and has realized His benevolence

فَقَامَ بِشُكْرِ اللهِ لِكُلِّ نِعْمَةٍ تَجَلَّى بِهَا الْوَهَّابُ فِي كُلِّ حَالَةِ

Fa qāma bi shukri-Llāhi li kulli niʿmatin,
tajallā biha-l-Wahhābu fī kulli ḥālati.

And maintains gratitude to Allah for all of the gifts
which manifest the Giver in every condition.

فَأَوْرَثَهُ حُبُّ التَّفَرُّدِ دَائِماً تَحَقُّقَ إِمْدَادٍ أَتَتْ بِسَكِينَةِ

Fa awrathahu ḥubbu-t-tafarrudi dā•iman
taḥaqquqa imdādin atat bi sakīnati

And comes to love on-going solitude with Allah
realizing the aid which brings inner peace.

فَصَارَ يُحِبُّ اللهَ حَقًّا بِلاَ رَيْبٍ لِرُؤْيَتِهِ الإِحْسَانَ فِي كُلِّ لَحْظَةِ

Fa ṣāra yuḥibbu-Llaha ḥaqqan bilā raybin,
li ru•yatihi-l-iḥsāna fī kulli laḥẓati.

So he becomes one who loves Allah without any doubt
because he sees (Divine) excellence at every single instant.

فَكُلُّ مَقَامَاتِ الْيَقِينِ قَدِ انْطَوَتْ فِي صَبْرٍ وَحُبٍّ خَالِصٍ مِنْ مَشُوبَةِ

Fa kullu maqāmāti-l-yaqīni qadi-nṭawat
fī ṣabrin wa ḥubbin khāliṣin min mashūbati

All the stations of certitude are contained
in a patience and love free of taint.

وَ لاَ بُدَّ فِي ذَا مِنْ إِمَامٍ لِسَالِكٍ   يَدُلُّ عَلَى بِرٍّ وَتَقْوَى وَسُنَّةِ

Fa lā budda fī dhā min imāmin li sālikin
yadullu ʿalā birrin wa taqwā wa sunnati.

And in this the traveller must have an imām
to guide him in goodness, piety, and the Sunna.

وَدَعْ عَنْكَ مَحْجُوباً غَفُولاً عَنْ رَبِّهِ   جَهُولاً بِطُرْقِ اللهِ مِنْ فَرْطِ ظُلْمَةِ

Wa daʿ ʿanka maḥjūban ghafūlan ʿan Rabbihi
jahūlan bi ṭurqi-Llāhi min farṭi ẓulmati.

Stay clear of the veiled one who is negligent of his Lord,
ignorant of Allah's paths in his excess of darkness.

وَ إِيَّاكَ أَنْ تَرْضَى بِصُحْبَةِ فِرْقَةٍ   تَمَكَّنَ مِنْهَا الشَّرُّ فِي كُلِّ قَوْلَةِ

wa iyyāka an tarḍā bi ṣuḥbati firqatin
tamakkana minha-sh-sharru fī kulli qawlatin.

And beware of accepting to be part of any group
who enable evil through all that they say.

يَقُولُونَ بِالْأَفْوَاهِ مَا لَيْسَ فِي الْحَشَا   وَيَاتُونَ مِنْ أَفعَالِ كُلَّ قَبِيحَةِ

Yaqūlūna bi-l-afwāhi mā laysa fi-l-ḥashā,
wa yātūna min afʿāli kulla qabīḥati

They say with their mouths what is not in their hearts;
their actions bring about all that is ugly.

نَصَحْتُكَ بَعْدَ الْبَحْثِ إِنْ كُنْتَ سَامِعاً   فَمَا الدِّينُ إِلاَّ نُصْحُ كُلِّ الْخَلِيقَةِ

Naṣaḥtuka baᶜda-l-baḥthi in kunta sāmiᶜan,
fa mā-d-dīnu illā nuṣḥu kulli-l-khalīqati

I counsel you in this based on study, if you are listening,
and what is religion if not good counsel to every creature?

فَكَمْ قَدْ أَزَاغُوا مِنْ عُقُولٍ بَسِيطَةٍ   خَلَتْ عَنْ تَوْفِيقِ نُورِ رَبِّ الْبَرِيَّةِ

Fa kam qad azāghū min ᶜuqūlin basīṭatin,
khalat ᶜan tawfīqi nūri Rabbi-l-bariyyati.

How many of the simple-minded have deviated from the way,
devoid of Divine accord from the light of the Lord.

وَ قَدْ صَارَتِ الْأَعْرَاضُ فِي هَتْكِهَا لَهُمْ   قَبَائِحَ أَغْرَاضٍ هِيَ شَرُّ فِتْنَةِ

Wa qad ṣārati-l-aᶜrāḍu fī hatkihā lahum
qabā•iḥa aghrāḍin hiya sharru fitnati

Shattering reputations has become for them
their vile intent – the worst of tribulations.

وَقَدْ أَمَرَ الشَّرْعُ الْمُبِينُ بِتَعْظِيمِ   لِمَنْ كَانَ ذَا نَفْعٍ بِإِرْشَادِ أُمَّةِ

Wa qad amara-sh-sharᶜu-l-mubīnu bi taᶜẓīmi,
li man kāna dhā nafᶜin bi irshādi ummati.

While the clear Law has enjoined veneration towards all
who serve the community by giving them guidance.

وَطُوبَى لِمَشْغُولٍ بِتَهْذِيبِ نَفْسِهِ   يُجَاهِدُهَا بِالذِّكْرِ فِي كُلِّ حَالَةِ

Wa ṭūbā li mashghūlin bi tahdhībi nafsihi
yujāhiduhā bi-dh-dhikri fī kulli ḥālati.

So blessed be the one who works to train his ego
and makes efforts against it with invocation in every state

وَيَتْلُو كِتَابَ اللهِ بِالْجِدِّ دَائِماً   وَيَقْتَبِسُ الْأَنْوَارَ مِنْ كُلِّ آيَةِ

Wa yatlū kitāba-Llāhi bi-l-jiddi dā•iman,
wa yaqtabisu-l-anwāra min kulli āyati

And regularly recites with sincerity the Book of Allah
and kindles lights from each and every verse.

يُحَكِّمُهُ فِي كُلِّ مَا هُوَ فَاعِلٌ   وَيَتْبَعُ أَخْلَاقاً لِخَيْرِ الْخَلِيقَةِ

Yuḥakkimuhu fī kulli mā huwa fāʿilun,
wa yatbaʿu akhlāqan li khayri-l-khalīqati.

And makes it a standard in all he is doing
and follows the character of the best of creation.

فَهُوَ الصِّرَاطُ الْمُسْتَقِيمُ لِمَنْ دَرَى   وَهُوَ الَّذِي أَتَى بِأَفْضَلِ مِلَّةِ

Fa huwa-ṣ-ṣirāṭu-l-mustaqīmu li man darā,
wa huwa-l-ladhī atā bi afḍali millati.

For he is the Straight Path for anyone who knows
And he is the one who brought the most excellent of creeds.

عَلَيهِ صَلاةُ اللهِ مَعْ آلِهِ وَمَنْ   تَلَاهُمْ بِإِحْسَانٍ إِلَى يَوْمِ بِعْثَةِ

ʿAlayhi ṣalātu-Llāhi maʿ ālihi wa man
talāhum bi iḥsānin ilā yawmi biʿthati.

Upon him be the blessings of Allah and upon his Family
and those who follow them in goodness until Ressurection Day.

-5-

عقائد التوحيد

The Tenets of Unity

يَقُولُ عَبْدُ رَبِّهِ مُحَمَّدُ ابنُ الْحَبِيبِ رَبَّهُ يُوَحِّدُ

Yaqūlu ʿabdu Rabbihi Muḥammadu
Ibnu-l-Ḥabībi Rabbahu yuwaḥḥidu:

Thus says the Lord's servant, Muḥammad,
son of al-Ḥabīb, affirming his Lord's oneness:

بِاسْمِ الإِلٰهِ فِي الأُمُورِ أَشْرَعُ إِلَيْهِ بَدْؤُهَا كَذَاكَ الْمَرْجَعُ

Bismi-l-Ilāhi fi-l-umūri ashraʿu
ilayhi bad•uhā kadhāka-l-marjaʿu

In the Name of God do I commence all things.
His are their beginning and return.

مَعْنَى الإِلٰهِ الْغَنِيُّ عَنْ سِوَاهُ وَلَهُ يَفْتَقِرُ مَا عَدَاهُ

Maʿna-l-ilāhi–l–Ghanīyyu ʿan siwāhu,
wa lahu yaftaqiru mā ʿadāhu.

"God" means the One Who is independent
of all else while all else depends upon Him.

لِلاِسْتِغْنَا عَنْ كُلِّ مَا سِوَاهُ   يَجٍّ مِنَ الأَوْصَافِ لاَ تَنْسَاهُ

Li-l-istighnā ʿan kulli mā siwāhu
yajjin mina-l-awṣāfi lā tansāhu:

This independence from all else besides Him
has thirteen Attributes – do not forget them:

وُجُودٌ ثُمَّ قِدَمٌ ثُمَّ الْبَقَا   مُخَالَفَةْ ثُمَّ غِنَاهُ مُطْلَقَا

Wujūdun thumma qidamun thumma-l-baqā,
mukhālafah thumma ghināhu muṭlaqā

Existence, beginninglessness, and endlessness,
incomparability, and absolute independence,

وَالسَّمْعُ وَالْبَصَرُ وَالْكَلاَمُ   وَالْكَوْنُ لاَزِمٌ لَهَا أَحْكَامُ

Wa-s-samʿu wa-l-baṣaru wa-l-kalāmu,
wa-l-kawnu lāzimun lahā aḥkāmu.

Hearing, sight, and speech [which must be understood]
according to the rules inherent to them.

وَعَدَمُ الأَغْرَاضِ فِي الأَفْعَالِ   كَذَاكَ فِي الأَحْكَامِ رُدَّ البَالِ

Wa ʿadamu-l-aghrāḍi fi-l-afʿāli,
kadhāka fi-l-aḥkāmi rudda-l-bāli.

In His acts and decrees there is nothing
which compels or constrains [Him]. Take heed.

جَوَازُ فِعْلٍ ثُمَّ تَرْكٍ أَلْحِقَا بِمَا ذَكَرْنَاهُ وَكُنْ مُحَقِّقَا

Jawāzu fiʿlin thumma tarkin alḥiqā,
bi mā dhakarnāhu wa kun muḥaqqiqā.

He is free to act or leave an act undone.
Hold fast to what we've mentioned and be certain.

وَلاِفْتِقَارِ كُلِّ مَا عَدَاهُ يَبٌّ مِنَ الأَوْصَافِ مُنْتَهَاهُ

Wa-l-iftiqāri kulli mā ʿadāhu
yabbun mina-l-awṣāfi muntahāhu:

The dependency of all else [upon Him]
is itself completed by twelve[other] attributes:

الْعِلْمُ وَالْقُدْرَةُ وَالْإِرَادَةْ ثُمَّ الْحَيَاةُ حَقِّقِ الْإِفَادَهْ

Al-ʿilmu wa-l-qudratu wa-l-irādah
thumma-l-ḥayātu ḥaqqiqi-l-ifādah

Knowledge, power, will, and also
life. Realize the benefit.

زِدْ قَادِراً وَمُرِيداً وَعَالِمْ حَيًّا فَلاَ تَكْتَفِي بِاللَّوَازِمْ

Zid qādiran, wa murīdan wa ʿālim
ḥayyan, falā taktafī bi-l-lawāzim

Add that He is the Able, Willing, Knowing One, and the Living –
do not stop with only the inherent.

وَحْدَةُ فِعْلٍ وَكَذَا وَصْفٍ وَذَاتْ   بِنَفْيِ كَمٍّ فَاسْئَلَنْ عَنْهَا الثِّقَاتْ

Waḥdatu fiʿlin wa kadhā waṣfin wa dhāt,
bi nafyi kammin fa-s•alan ʿanhā-th-thiqāt.

[Then] Oneness of Action, Attribute, and Essence
which negates all multiplicity – ask those you trust!

حُدُوثُ عَالَمٍ وَنَفْيُ تَأْثِيرِ   بِطَبْعٍ أَوْ بِقُوَّةٍ فَاعْتَبِرِ

Ḥudūthu ʿālamin wa nafyu ta•thīri
bi ṭabʿin aw bi quwwatin faʿtabiri.

The temporality of the world, and the negation
of its effects through nature or power – so reflect.

فَتِلْكَ خَمْسَةٌ وَعِشْرُونَ صِفَةْ   وَالضِّدُّ مِثْلُهَا فَفَصِّلْ عَدَدَهْ

Fa tilka khamsatun wa ʿishrūna ṣifah,
wa-ḍ-ḍiddu mithluhā fa faṣṣil ʿadadah.

Those are five and twenty Attributes
and their opposites number the same, so count each one.

وَلِلْإِيمَانِ بِالرَّسُولِ عَشَرَةْ   وَسِتَّةٌ مِنَ الصِّفَاتِ تَابِعَهْ

Wa li-l-īmāni bi-r-rasūli ʿasharah
wa sittatun mina-ṣ-ṣifāti tābiʿah

Belief in the Messenger comprises sixteen
attributes which are as follows:

الصِّدْقُ وَالتَّبْلِيغُ وَالأَمَانَةْ   وَجَوَازُ الأَعْرَاضِ لِلْإِفَادَةْ

Aṣ-ṣidqu wa-t-tablīghu wa-l-amānah,
wa jawāzu-l-aʿrāḍi li-l-ifādah.

That he is truthful, conveys the message, and is trusted
and that he may be prone to any human frailty.

وَ إِيمَانٌ بِكُتُبٍ وَأَنْبِيَا   وَرُسُلٍ وَأَمْلَاكٍ يَا ذَكِيَا

Wa īmānun bi kutubin wa anbiyā
wa rusulin wa amlākin yā dhakiyā.

And belief in Allah's books and in His Prophets
and Messengers, and angels, O you who are wise.

وَإِيمَانٌ بِيَومِ الآخِرِ فَعِ   أَضْدَادَهَا وَكُنْ لِنَفْيِهَا سَاعِي

Wa īmānun bi yawmi-l-ākhiri faʿi
aḍdādahā wa kun li nafyihā sāʿī

And belief in the Last Day, so be aware
of their opposites and be vigilant in negating them.

فَتِلْكَ سِتَّةٌ وَسِتُّونَ صِفَةْ   تَدْخُلُ فِي الْكَلِمَةِ الْمُشَرَّفَةْ

Fa tilka sittatun wa sittūna ṣifah
tadkhulu fi-l-kalimati-l-musharrafah

These are the six and sixty Attributes
contained in [the meaning] of the Noble Word.

فَاشْغَلْ بِهَا الأَوْقَاتَ بِالْحُضُورِ   تَرْقَى إِلَى الْمَعْنَى مَعَ السُّرُورِ

Fa-shghal biha-l-awqāta bi-l-ḥūḍūri,
tarqā ila-l-maᶜnā maᶜa-s-surūri.

Fill your moments invoking it with presence
and you'll ascend to its meaning full of joy.

دَلِيلُهَا النَّظَرُ فِي الْقُرْآنِ   وَجَوَلاَنُ الْعَقْلِ فِي الأَكْوَانِ

Dalīluha-n-naẓaru fi-l-Qur•āni,
wa jawalānu-l-ᶜaqli fi-l-akwāni.

Its proof is in looking in the Qur'an
and reflecting on creation with the mind.

يَا رَبَّنَا صَلِّ عَلَى مُحَمَّدٍ   وَآلِهِ وَكُلِّ عَبْدٍ مُقْتَدِي

Yā Rabbanā ṣalli ᶜalā Muḥammadin
wa ālihi wa kulli ᶜabdin muqtadī

Our Lord, shower blessings upon Muḥammad,
and his family and every servant who seeks to follow him.

وَانْفَعْ بِهَا يَا رَبِّ كُلِّ مَنْ قَرَا   وَسَامِعٍ وَأُمِّيٍّ وَمَنْ دَرَى

Wa-nfaᶜ bihā yā Rabbi kulli man qarā
wa sāmiᶜin wa ummiyyi wa man darā.

And, O Lord, benefit everyone who reads this
or hears it, both the learned and unlettered.

وَانْصُرْ أَمِيْرَنَا بِخَرْقِ الْعَادَةْ   وَاحْفَظْ أَنْجَالَهُ وَكُلَّ الْعَائِلَةْ

Wa-nṣur amīranā bi kharqi-lʿādah,
wa-ḥfaẓ anjālahu wa kulla-l-ʿā·ilah.

Grant our leader Your miraculous assistance
and keep his children and whole family in Your protection.

وَاجْعَلْهُ عَيْناً مِن عُيُونِ اللهِ   يَنْفَعُ فِي كُلِّ بِلَادِ اللهِ

Wa-jʿalhu ʿaynan min ʿuyūni-Llāhi,
yanfaʿu fī kulli bilādi-Llāhi.

Make of him a flowing spring from among the springs of Allah,
and a benefit to every land of Allah.

وَوَالِ مَنْ وَالَاهُ بِالإِحْسَانِ   وَمَنْ أَعَانَهُ بِلَا خِذْلَانِ

Wa wāli man wālāhu bi-l-iḥsāni,
wa man aʿānahu bilā khidhlāni.

Take care of those who care for him with excellence
and anyone who faithfully assists him.

وَاجْعَلْ لَهُ مِنْ عُلَمَاءِ الأُمَّةْ   مَنْ يُخْلِصُ النُّصْحَ وَلَهُ النِّيَّةْ

Wa-jʿal lahu min ʿulamā·i-l-ummah,
man yukhliṣu-n-nuṣḥa lahu wa-n-niyyah.

And make for him from among the learned of this people
those who give sincere advice with good intent.

وَوَفِّقِ الْوُلَاةَ لِلْمُسَاعَدَهْ لِكُلِّ مَا فِيهِ صَلاَحُ الْعَمَلَةْ

Wa waffiqi-l-wulāta li-l-musāʿadah
li kulli mā fīhi ṣalāḥu-l-ʿamalah

Accord to those who govern the means to help
with all that can benefit those who labor.

وَاخْتِمْ لَنَا يَا رَبِّ بِالسَّعَادَةْ وَارْفُقْ بِنَا عِنْدَ قِيَامِ السَّاعَةْ

Wa-khtim lanā yā Rabbi bi-s-saʿāda,
wa-rfuq binā ʿinda qiyāmi-s-sāʿa.

And let the end of our lives, O Lord, be one of happiness
and be clement towards us when the final Hour arises.

-6-

براق الطريق

Burāq of the Way

يَقُولُ أَفْقَرُ الْوَرَى مُحَمَّدُ   إِبْنُ الْحَبِيبِ قَوْلُهُ مُسَدَّدُ

Yaqūlu afqaru'l-warā Muḥammadu
ibnu-l-Ḥabībi qawluhu musaddadu

Thus says Muḥammad, the neediest of creatures,
son of al-Ḥabīb – words brief and to the point.

اَلْحَمْدُ لِلّٰهِ الَّذِي بِخَيْرِهِ   عَمَّ الْوَرَى فِي بَرِّهِ وَبَحْرِهِ

Al-ḥamdu li-Llāhi-l-ladhī bi khayrihi
ʿamma-l-warā fī barrihi wa baḥrihi

Praise be to Allah Who in His goodness
spread creatures in His land and His sea

وَأَرْسَلَ الرُّسُلَ بِالشَّرَائِعْ   وَمُعْجِزَاتٍ مَا لَهَا مِنْ دَافِعْ

Wa arsala-r-rusula bi-sh-sharā•iʿ
wa muʿjizātin mā lahā min dāfiʿ

And sent the Messengers with Laws
and with miracles that could not be denied.

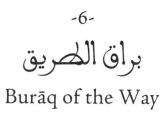

فَلُبُّهَا تَصَوُّفٌ مُحَرَّرُ   عَلَى كِتَابٍ سُنَّةٍ مُقَرَّرُ

Fa lubbuhā taṣawwufun muḥarraru
ʿalā kitābin sunnatin muqarraru

The heart [of all this] is pure sufism
based on the Book and Sunna

فَهَاكَ مِنْهَا نُبْذَةً تُقَرِّبُ   طَرِيقَهُ وَسَيْرَهُ تُحَبِّبُ

Fa hāka minhā nubdhatan tuqarribu
ṭariqahu wa sayrahu tuḥabbibu

So take this summary of it that you might approach
its path and love to travel on it.

سَمَّيْتُهَا بِبُرَاقِ الطَّرِيقِ   تُسْرِعُ بِالْمُرِيدِ لِلتَّحْقِيقِ

Sammaytuhā bi burāqi-ṭ-ṭarīqi
tusriʿu bi-l-murīdi li-t-taḥqīqi

I have called it the Burāq of the Way,
for it takes a disciple swiftly to realization

فَإِنْ تُرِدْ سُلُوكَكَ الطَّرِيقَا   فَاعْتَمِدِ اللهَ وَسَلْ تَوفِيقَا

Fa in turid sulūkaka-ṭ-ṭarīqā
faʿtamidi-l-Lāha wa sal tawfīqā

If you truly desire to follow the Way
depend [first] upon Allah and ask (His) accord

وَأَرِحِ النَّفْسَ مِنَ التَّدْبِيرِ فَإِنَّ ذَا يَجْلُبُ لِلتَّنْوِيرِ

Wa ariḥi-n-nafsa mina-t-tadbīri
fa inna dhā yajlubu li-t-tanwīri

Then rest your soul from self-direction
and that will bring ever more light

إِيَّاكَ أَنْ تَهْتَمَّ بِالْأَرْزَاقِ لِأَنَّهَا فِي ضَمَانِ الْخَلَّاقِ

Iyyāka an tahtamma bi-l-arzāqi
li annahā fī ḍamāni-l-khallāqi

Avoid becoming careworn over your provision
for it has been promised [you] by the Creator

وَخَصْلَتَانِ لَيْس شَيْءٌ يُوْجَدُ فَوْقَهُمَا مِنَ الْخَيْرَاتِ يُحْمَدُ

Wa khaṣlatāni laysa shay›un yūjadu
fawqahumā mina-l-khayrāti yuḥmadu

And two qualities above which there is nothing higher
in praiseworthy good are these:

حُسْنُ ظَنٍّ بِاللهِ ثُمَّ بِالْعِبَادْ فَكُنْ هُمَا وَجَنِّبَنَّ لِلْعِنَادْ

Ḥusnu ẓannin bi-Llāhi thumma bi-l-ʿibād
fa kun humā wa jannibanna l-l-ʿinād

The best opinion of Allah and then of His servants.
make these part of you and stay clear of intransigence.

وَأَقْرَبُ الطُّرُقِ عِنْدَ اللهِ   أَنْ تُكْثِرَ الذِّكْرَ بِإِسْمِ اللهِ

Wa aqrabu-ṭ-ṭuruqi ʿinda-Llāhi
an tukthira-dh-dhikra bi-ismi-Llāhi

The shortest of paths in the presence of Allah
is that you invoke with abundance the Name Allāh.

لِأَنَّهُ الْإِسْمُ الْعَظِيْمُ الْأَعْظَمُ   عَلَى الْأَصَحِّ مِنْ خِلاَفٍ يُعْلَمُ

Li annahu-l-ismu-l-ʿaẓīmu-l-aʿẓamu
ʿala-l-aṣaḥḥī min khilāfin yuʿlamu

For it is the Greatest and the Supreme Name,
according to the soundest view, beyond dispute.

وَفَرِّغِ الْقَلْبَ مِنَ الْأَغْيَارِ   عِنْدَ التَّوَجُّهِ لِذِكْرِ الْبَارِي

Wa farrighi-l-qalba mina-l-aghyāri
ʿinda-t-tawajjuhi li dhikri-l-Bārī

Empty your heart of everything else
when you turn towards invocation of the Creator.

وَانْظُرْ لِأَسْرَارِ الْحَكِيمِ وَاعْتَبِرْ   وَجَنِّبِ الْخَوضَ وَلاَ تَكُنْ تُصِرْ

Wa-nẓur li asrāri-l-Ḥakīmi waʿtabir
wa jannibi-l-khawḍa wa lā takun tuṣir

Behold the mysteries of the Infinitely Wise and reflect,
stay clear of vain chatter; do not persist in sin.

بَلْ عَقِّبِ الذَّنْبَ بِالْإِسْتِغْفَارِ   وَبِالتَّضَرُّعِ وَالْإِنْكِسَارِ

Bal, ʿaqqibi-dh-dhanba bi-l-istighfāri
wa bi-t-taḍarruʿi wa-l-inkisāri

Rather, follow sin by seeking forgiveness,
And by humility and by lowliness.

وَانْظُرْ لِمَا مَنَّ بِهِ عَلَيْكَا   مِنْ كُلِّ طَاعَةٍ سَعَتْ إِلَيْكَا

Wa-nẓur limā manna bihi ʿalaykā
min kulli ṭāʿatin saʿat ilaykā

And behold the grace that Allah gives you
in every act of obedience that's come to you.

وَاحْمَدْهُ فِي السَّرَّاءِ وَالضَّرَّاءِ   لأَنَّهُ الْفَاعِلُ فِي الْأَشْيَاءِ

Wa-ḥmadhu fi-s-sarrā•i wa-ḍ-ḍarrā•i
li annahu-l-fāʿilu fi-l-ashyā•i

Praise Him both in comfort and in hardship
for in truth He is the Doer in [all] things

وَحَرِّكِ الْهِمَّةَ بِالْأَشْوَاقِ   وَلاَ تَكُنْ تَرْضَى بِدُونِ الْبَاقِي

Wa ḥarraki-l-himmata bi-l-ashwāqi
wa la takun tarḍā bi dūni-l-Bāqī

And let the yearning of love be what moves your aspiration
do not settle for less than the Eternal One.

وَلاَ تَقِفْ مَعَ الْبَوَارِقِ وَلاَ مَعْ غَيْرِهَا مِنْ كُلِّ شَيْءٍ حَصَلاَ

Wa lā taqif maʿa-l-bawāriqi wa lā
maʿ ghayrihā min kulli shay•in ḥaṣalā

Nor cease [your journey] at glimmers of light,
nor at anything else you might reach [along the way]

وَاسْأَلْهُ أَنْ يَطْوِي لَكَ الطَّرِيقَا حَتَّى تَذُوقَ ذَلِكَ التَّحْقِيقَا

Wa-s•alhu an yaṭwī laka-ṭ-ṭarīqā
ḥattā tadhūqa dhālika-t-taḥqīqā

And ask Him to shorten for you the Path
that you might taste that realization.

فَاللهُ يَجْتَبِي مِنَ الْعَبِيدِ مَنْ شَاءَهُ لِحَضْرَةِ التَّفْرِيدِ

Fa-Llāhu yajtabī mina-l-ʿabīdi
man shā•ahu li ḥaḍrati-t-tafrīdi

For Allah chooses from His servants
Whom He wishes to bring into His Solitary Presence

إِيَّاكَ أَنْ تَسْتَبْعِدَ الطَّرِيقَا فَإِنَّ ذَا يُكْسِبُكَ التَّعْوِيقَا

Iyyāka an tastabʿida-ṭ-ṭarīqā,
fa inna dhā yuksibuka-t-taʿwīqā

And be careful not to make the Way too long,
that will only bring you hindrance.

وَاسْلُكْ بِنَفْسِكَ سَبِيلَ الرِّفْقِ لِكَيْ يَكُونَ سَيْرُهَا بِالشَّوْقِ

Wa-sluk bi nafsika sabīla-r-rifqi
li kay yakūna sayruhā bi-sh-shawqi

Conduct your soul along the path of kindness,
that its journey might be one of love and longing.

فَإِنَّ رَكْعَتَيْنِ مِنْ مُحِبٍّ أَفْضَلُ مِنْ أَلْفٍ مِنْ غَيْرِ حُبِّ

Fa inna rakʿatayni min muḥibbi
afḍalu min alfin min ghayri ḥubbi

Two bowings of prayer offered by a lover
are better than a thousand that are lacking in love.

وَالْأَدَبَ اجْعَلَنَّهُ رَفِيقَا فِي أَخْذِكَ التَّشْرِيعَ وَالتَّحْقِيقَا

Wa-l-adaba-j-ʿalannahu rafīqā
fī akh•dhika-t-tashrīʿa wa-t-taḥqīqā

Make beautiful conduct your [constant] companion
in whatever you take of the Law and Inner Truth

فَمَثَلُ الْأَدَبِ فِي الْأُمُورِ كَخَلْطِكَ الْحَدِيدَ بِالْإِكْسِيرِ

Fa mathalu-l-adabi fi-l-umūri
ka khalṭika-l-ḥadīda bi-l-iksīri.

Approaching all matters with beautiful conduct
is like mixing the Elixir into [molten] iron.

أَمَا تَرَاهُ يُقْلِبُ الْحَدِيدَا فِي لَحْظَةٍ بِذَهَبٍ جَدِيدَا

A mā tarāhu yuqlibu-l-ḥadīdā
fī laḥẓatin bi dhahabin jadīdā

Do you not see how that transmutes the iron
in an instant into new and precious gold?

كَذٰلِكَ الأَدَبُ لِلقُلُوبِ يَنْقُلُهَا لِحَضْرَةِ الْغُيُوبِ

Kadhālika-l-adabu lil-qulūbi
yanquluha li-ḥaḍrati-l-ghuyūbi

Even thus does beautiful conduct act upon hearts
and transports them into the Realm of the Unseen.

فَكَمْ مُجِدٍّ عَمَلاً قَدْ وَكَلَهْ لِنَفْسِهِ وَكَمْ أَدِيبٍ قَرَّبَهْ

Fakam mujiddin ʿamalan qad wakalah
li nafsihi wa kam adībin qarrabah.

For how many a zealot is left only to his practice
and how many a humble servant through his conduct is brought near?

فَأَدَبُ النَّظَرِ فِي الأَكْوَانِ شُهُودُ بَارِيهَا بِغَيْرِ ثَانِ

Fa•adabu-n-naẓari fi-l-akwāni
shuhūdu Bārīhā bi ghayri thāni

Beautiful conduct when looking at creation
means to witness its Creator without any other.

فَتُبْصِرُ الْخَالِقَ فِي الْمَخْلُوقِ وَتُبْصِرُ الرَّازِقَ فِي الْمَرْزُوقِ

Fatubṣiru-l-Khāliqa fi-l-makhlūqi
wa tubṣiru-l-Rāziqa fi-l-marzūqi

So you see the Creator in the created
and you see the Provider in the one He provides for.

وَالْحَقُّ لاَ يُرَى فِي غَيْرِ مَظْهَرِ لِأَحَدٍ مِنْ مَلَكٍ أَوْ بَشَرِ

Wa-l-Ḥaqqu lā yurā fī ghayri maẓharin
li aḥadin min malakin aw bashari

No one – whether angel or human kind
sees Allah the Truth apart from a theophany

فَالْمَظْهَرُ الْأَوَّلُ نُورُ أَحْمَدَا عَلَيْهِ أَفْضَلُ الصَّلَاةِ سَرْمَدَا

Fa-l-maẓharu-l-awwalu nūru Aḥmadā,
ʿalayhi afḍalu-ṣ-ṣalāti sarmadā

And the first theophany is the Light of Aḥmad,
may the most excellent of blessings be upon him, always.

قَدْ مَلأَ الْحَقُّ بِهِ الْأَكْوَانَ وَكُلَّ مَا يَكُونُ أَوْ قَدْ كَانَا

Qad mala•a-l-Ḥaqqu bihi-l-akwāna,
wa kulla mā yakūnu aw qad kānā.

With this light, the Truth has filled creation,
and all there is and all there ever has been.

فَاشْهَدْهُ فِي النَّفْسِ وَفِي الْأَفَاقِ   وَامْزُجْ بِذَاكَ رُؤْيَةَ الْخَلَّاقِ

Fash-had-hu fi-n-nafsi wa fi-l-afāqi
wā-mzuj bi dhāka ru•yata-l-Khallāqi

Witness it in the soul and upon the horizons
and then immerse it in a vision of the Creator

تُكْفَى بِذَا الشُّهُودِ كُلَّ عَيْبِ   فِي النَّفْسِ وَالْقَلْبِ وَغَيْبِ الْغَيْبِ

Tukfā bi dha-sh-shuhūdi kulla ʿaybi
fi-n-nafsi wa-l-qalbi wa ghaybi-l-ghaybi

And that vision will suffice you from seeing every fault in the self,
and the heart and in the hidden of the hidden.

وَذَكِّرِ النَّفْسَ بِحُسْنِ نِيَّةِ   وَاقْرِنْهَا بِالسُّكُونِ وَالْحَرَكَةِ

Wa dhakkiri-n-nafsa bi ḥusni niyyati,
wa-qranhā bi-sukūni wa-l-ḥarakati.

Remind the soul with the best of intentions
and join that to your stillness and movement.

وَنَمِّهَا تَنْمِيَةً وَكَثِّرَا   لَهَا تَحُوزُ فَضْلَهَا بِلَا مِرَا

Wa nammihā tanmiytan wa kaththirā
lahā taḥūzu faḍlahā bilā mirā

Give to it in abundance what will nourish its growth,
you will bring forth its virtues without doubt.

وَاخْتَصِرِ الطَّرِيقَ بِالتَّعْظِيمِ   لِكُلِّ مَا شُرِعَ مِنْ مَرْسُومِ

Wa-khtaṣiri-ṭ-ṭarīqa bi-t-taʿẓīmi
li kulli mā shuriʿa min marsūmi

Shorten the Path by having respect
for everything that has been ordained by the Law.

وَلَا تَكُنْ تَحْقِرْ مِنَ الْأَعْمَالِ   شَيْئًا أَتَى وَلَا مِنَ الْأَقْوَالِ

Wa lā takun taḥqir mina-l-aʿmāli
shay•an atā wa lā mina-l-aqwāli

And do not underestimate anything that has come
be it actions [to accomplish] or words.

طَرِيقَةُ الْأَبْدَالِ جُوعٌ سَهَرُ   صَمْتٌ وَعُزْلَةٌ وَذِكْرٌ حَرَّرُوا

Ṭarīqatu-l-abdāli jūʿun saharu
ṣamtun wa ʿuzlatun wa dhikrun ḥarrarū

The Way of the great saints, clearly explained,
is hunger, vigils, silence, solitude, and invocation.

قَدِ انْتَهَتْ نُبْذَةُ ذَا التَّصَوُّفِ   وَالْحَمْدُ لِلَّهِ عَلَى التَّعَرُّفِ

Qadi-n-tahat nubdhatu dha-t-taṣawwufi
wa-l-ḥamdu li-Llāhi ʿalā-t-taʿarrufi

Thus is completed this summary of Sufism,
and may praise be to Allah for making it known.

وَأُصَلِّي عَلَى النَّبِيِّ الْمُمِدِّ صَلاَةَ رَبِّنَا بِغَيْرِ حَدِّ

Wa uṣallī ʿala-n-Nabiyyi-l-mumiddi
ṣalāta Rabbinā bi ghayri ḥaddi.

I ask blessings upon the Prophet, the one who gives support–
blessings of our Lord without limit.

وَآلِهِ وَصَحْبِهِ الثِّقَاتِ السَّالِكِينَ سُبُلَ النَّجَاةِ

Wa ālihi wa ṣaḥbihi-th-thiqāti,
as-sālikīna subula-n-najāti.

And upon his Family and his trusted Companions
travellers on the paths of salvation

وَأَسْأَلُ اللهَ صَلاَحَ الْحَالِ لَنَا وَلِلْأَحْبَابِ فِي الْمَآلِ

Wa as•alu-Llāha ṣalāḥa-l-ḥāli
lanā wa li-l-aḥbābi fi-l-ma'āli

And I ask Allah to make good our states
and those of our friends at the Final Return.

وَأَنْ يُزِيلَ عَنَّا كُلَّ رَيْبِ بِجَاهِ كُلِّ عَارِفٍ مُرَبِّي

Wa an yuzīla ʿannā kulla raybin
bi jāhi kulli ʿārifin murabbī

And to remove from our souls every doubt
by the honor of every gnostic who teaches.

وَالْحَمْدُ لِلهِ عَلَى التَّمَامِ وَالشُّكْرُ لِلهِ عَلَى الْخِتَامِ

Wa-l-ḥamdu li-Llāhi ʿala-t-tamāmi
wa-sh-shukru li-Llāhi ʿala-l-khitāmi

Praise be to Allah for its completion;
thanks be to Allah at its closing.

-7-

خوارق الطريق

The Extraordinary Gifts of the Path

اَلْحَمْدُ لِلّٰهِ وَصَلَّى اللهُ عَلَى النَّبِيِّ مُحَمَّدِ الأَوَّاهُ

Al-ḥamdu li-Llāhi wa ṣalla-Llāhu
ʿala-n-Nabīyi Muḥammadi-l-awwāhu

All praise be to Allah and may He bless
the Prophet Muhammad who cries out to his Lord.

قَالَ أَبُو حَامِدٍ الصُّوفِيُّ حُجَّةُ الإِسْلاَمِ هُوَ الطُّوسِيُّ

Qāla Abū Ḥāmidin aṣ-Ṣūfīyyu
ḥujjatu-l-Islāmi huwa-ṭ-Ṭūsīyyu

Thus said Abū Ḥāmid the Sufi,
the Proof of Islam, whose birthplace was Ṭūs:

كَرَامَةُ الدَّاخِلِ فِي الطَّرِيقِ عِشْرُونَ فِي الدُّنْيَا عَلَى التَّحْقِيقِ

Karāmatu-d-dākhili fi-ṭ-ṭarīqi
ʿishrūna fi-d-dunyā ʿala-t-taḥqīqi.

The gifts of honor given one who enters the Path
have been confirmed as twenty in this world.

أَوَّلُهَا يَذْكُرُهُ الْإِلٰهُ   كَمَا يَلِيقُ بِهِ يَا بُشْرَاهُ

Awwaluhā yadhkuruhu-l-ilāhu
kamā yalīqu bihi yā bushrāhu

The first of these is that God remembers him
in the manner that befits Him. What glad tidings!

ثَانِيهَا تَعْظِيمُهُ بَيْنَ الْأَنَامْ   وَالثَّالِثُ الْحُبُّ لَهُ بِلَا مَلَامْ

Thāniyuhā taᶜẓīmuhu bayna-l-anām
wa-th-thālithu-l-ḥubbu lahu bilā malām.

The second is that Allah esteems him among people,
and the third is [His] love for him, without reproach.

وَكُلُّ مَنْ أَحَبَّهُ الْإِلٰهُ   أَحَبَّهُ الْخَلْقُ فَيَا سَعْدَاهُ

Wa kullu man aḥabbahu-l-Ilāhu
aḥabbahu-l-khalqu fa yā saᶜdāhu

And anyone who is Allah's beloved
His creatures love as well – what a blessing!

رَابِعُهَا يُدَبِّرُ الْأُمُورَا   لَهُ فَيَبْقَى دَائِمًا مَسْرُورَا

Rābiᶜuhā yudabbiru-l-umūrā
lahu fa yabqā dā·iman masrūrā

The fourth is that Allah takes charge of his life,
such that he remains constantly joyful.

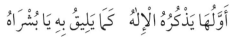

خَامِسُهَا تَسْهِيلُهُ الرِّزْقَ لَهُ   بِلاَ مَشَقَّةٍ فِيهِ تَلْحَقُهُ

Khāmisuhā tas·hīluhu-r-rizqa lahu
bilā mashaqqatin fīhi talḥaquhu

The fifth is that his provision is made easy
and comes to him without toil and worry.

سَادِسُهَا يَنْصُرُهُ عَلَى الْعِدَا   بِخَرْقِ عَادَةٍ مَعْ حِفْظٍ أَبَدَا

Sādisuhā yanṣuruhu ʿala-l-ʿidā
bi kharqi ʿādatin maʿ ḥifẓin abadā

The sixth is that Allah aids him against all foes
by extraordinary means and ceaseless protection.

سَابِعُهَا يَكُونُ أُنْسَهُ فَلاَ   وَحْشَةَ تَاتِيهِ مِنْ شَيْءٍ نَزَلاَ

Sābiʿuhā yakūnu unsahu fa lā
waḥshata tātīhi min shay·in nazalā

The seventh is he is granted such intimacy with Allah,
that nothing which befalls him can estrange him.

ثَامِنُهَا الْعِزُّ لَهُ فِي النَّفْسِ   فَالْكَوْنُ يَخْدُمُهُ دُونَ لَبْسِ

Thāminuha-l-ʿizzu lahu fi-nafsi
fa-l-kawnu yakhdumuhu dūna labsi

The eighth is the dignity within his soul
such that the world serves him without doubt.

تَاسِعُهَا الرَّفْعُ لِهِمَّةٍ لَهُ   عَنْ كُلِّ شَيْءٍ فَاتِنٍ يَشْغَلُهُ

Tāsiʿuha-r-rafʿu li himmatin lahu
ʿan kulli shay•in fātinin yashghaluhu

The ninth is that his soul's aspiration is raised above
the lures of this world that might entice him.

عَاشِرُهَا الْغِنَى لِقَلْبِهِ مَعَ   تَسْهِيلِ أَمْرِهِ الَّذِي فِيهِ سَعَى

ʿĀshiruha-l-ghinā li qalbihi maʿa
tas•hīli amrihi-l-ladhī fīhi saʿā

Tenth is that his heart is given independence
and anything he strives for is made easy.

وَهَاكَ بَاقِيهَا مَعَ اخْتِصَارِ   بِعَطْفِ بَعْضِهَا فَخُذْ يَا قَارِي

Wa hāka bāqīhā maʿa-khtiṣāri
bi ʿaṭfi baʿḍihā fa khudh yā qārī

The rest of them are mentioned here briefly,
a few at more length, so receive them.

تَنْوِيرُ قَلْبٍ يَهْتَدِي بِنُورِهِ   لِفَهْمِ أَسْرَارٍ بِفَضْلِ رَبِّهِ

Tanwīru qalbin yahtadī bi nūrihi
li fahmi asrārin bi faḍli Rabbihi

His heart is enlightened and by it he is guided
to the understanding of divine mysteries by the grace of his Lord;

وَشَرْحُ صَدْرِهِ فَلاَ يَهْتَمُّ   بِكُلِّ مِحْنَةٍ بِهِ تَلِمُّ

Wa sharḥu ṣadrihi falā yahtammu
bi kulli miḥnatin bihi talimmu

*Expansion of his breast so that he is not distressed
by any sort of trial that might befall him.*

مَهَابَةٌ لَهُ وَحُسْنُ مَوْقِعِ   فِي نُفُوسِ النَّاسِ بِغَيْرِ دَافِعِ

Mahābatun lahu wa ḥusnu mawqiʿi
fī nufūsi-n-nāsi bi ghayri dāfiʿi

*And undeniable veneration and good standing
in the souls of people around him.*

تَحْبِيبُهُ لِكُلِّ خَلْقٍ فِي الْوَرَى   بِوَعْدِ رَبِّنَا لَهُ بِلا مِرَا

Taḥbībuhu li kulli khalqin fi-l-warā
bi waʿdi Rabbinā lahu bilā mirā

*A love for him from every human being
by the promise of our Lord to him without doubt.*

تَبَرُّكٌ بِهِ مَعَ الْأَدَابِ   مَعْهُ وَلَوْ نُقِلَ لِلتُّرَابِ

Tabarrukun bihi maʿa-l-adābi
maʿhu wa law nuqila li-t-turābi

*People seek blessing through him with proper manners,
even should he be transferred to the earth.*

تَسْخِيرُهُ الْأَرْضَ لَهُ فَيَذْهَبُ   حَيْثُ يَشَا بِسُرْعَةٍ لَا يَرْهَبُ

Taskhīruhu-l-arḍa lahu fa yadh•habu
ḥaythu yashā bi surʿatin lā yarhabu

Allah subjects the earth to him so he journeys
wherever he wishes quickly and without fear

وَالْبَرُّ وَالْبَحْرُ مَعَ الْهَوَاءِ   خَادِمَةٌ لَهُ بِلَا امْتِرَاءِ

Wa-l-barru wa-l-baḥru maʿa-l-hawā•i
khādimatun lahu bila-mtirā•i

And the land and sea and air as well
become his servants without doubt.

وُحُوشٌ ثُمَّ سِبَاعٌ مَعَ الْهَوَامْ   سَخَّرَهَا الرَّبُّ لَهُ عَلَى الدَّوَامْ

Wuḥūshun thumma sibāʿun maʿa-l-hawām
sakhkharaha-r-Rabbu lahu ʿala-d-dawām

Wild animals, beasts of prey, and reptiles
the Lord always puts under his control.

مَفَاتِيحُ الْكُنُوزِ وَالْمَعَادِنْ   تَطْلُبُهُ وَهُوَ عَنْهَا بَائِنْ

Mafātīḥu-l-kunūzi wa-l-maʿādin
taṭlubuhu wa huwa ʿanhā bā•in

The keys to treasures and mines would seek him out
were he not indifferent to them all.

تَوَسُّلُ النَّاسِ بِجَاهِهِ إِلَى   إِلٰهِهِ فِي كُلِّ شَيْءٍ نَزَلَا

Tawassulu-n-nāsi bi jāhihi ilā
ilāhihi fī kulli shay•in nazalā

People supplicate God by his honor
in everything that might befall them.

فَيَقْضِيهِ الرَّبُّ بِلَا تَعْسِيرِ   بِفَضْلِهِ الْمَصْحُوبِ بِالتَّيْسِيرِ

Fa yaqḍīhi-r-Rabbu bilā taʿsīri
bi-faḍlihi-l-maṣḥūbi bi-t-taysīri

Then the Lord fulfills it without difficulty
by His grace along with ease.

وَذَاكَ مَوْكُولٌ إِلَى اخْتِيَارِ   إِلٰهِهِ فِي سَابِقِ الْأَقْدَارِ

Wa dhāka mawkūlun ilā-khtiyāri
Ilāhihi fī sābiqi-l-aqḍāri

And that is a thing entrusted to God's choice
in all that was eternally pre-ordained.

فَلَا تَقُلْ دَعَوْتُهُ فَلَمْ يُجِبْ   فَذَاكَ شَأْنُ كُلِّ غَافِلٍ مُرِيبْ

Falā taqul daʿawtuhu falam yujib
fa dhāka sha•nu kulli ghāfilin murīb

So say not, "I prayed to Him but He did not answer,"
as do the heedless and the doubter.

أَمَّا الْكَرَامَةُ لَهُ فِي الآخِرَةْ   عِشْرُونَ أَيْضاً هَا كَهَا مُتَّبَعَةْ

Amma-l-karāmatu lahu fi-l-ākhira
ʿishrūna ayḍan hākahā muttabaʿa

As for the gifts of honor in the Next World,
these also number twenty and are as follows:

تَسْهِيلُ مَوْتِهِ مَعَ الْخِتَامِ   عَلَى الإِيمَانِ فَازَ بِالْمَرَامِ

Tas•hīlu mawtihi maʿa-l-khitāmi
ʿala-l-īmāni fāza bi-l-marāmī

His death will be easy and he will end with faith,
and thus attain the hoped-for goal.

تَبْشِيرُهُ بِالرَّوْحِ وَالرَّيْحَانِ   وَالأَمْنِ مِنْ خَوْفٍ مَعَ الرِّضْوَانِ

Tabshīruhu bi-rawḥi wa-r-rayḥāni
wa-l-amni min khawfin maʿa-r-riḍwāni

He will be given tidings of rest and sustenance,
Allah's good pleasure and safety from fear,

كَذَا الْخُلُودُ فِي الْجِنَانِ أَبَدَا   فِي جِوَارِ الرَّحْمَانِ دَأْباً سَرْمَدَا

Kadha-l-khulūdu fi-l-jināni abadā
fī jiwāri-r-Raḥmāni da•ban sarmadā

And will dwell in Heaven perpetually and forever
in nearness to Allah, the Most Merciful.

لِرُوحِهِ الْعُرُوجُ وَالْإِكْرَامُ   مِنَ الْمَلَائِكَةِ وَالْإِنْعَامُ

Li rūḥihi-l-ʿurūju wa-l-ikrāmu
mina-l-malāʾikati wa-l-inʿāmu

His soul will be allowed to ascend
and be given honor and graces among the angels

وَالنَّاسُ تَزْدَحِمُ لِلصَّلَاةِ   عَلَيْهِ إِذْ كَانَ مِنَ الثِّقَاتِ

Wa-n-nāsu tazdaḥimu li-ṣ-ṣalāti
ʿalayhi idh kāna mina-th-thiqāti

As people throng to pray the funeral prayer upon him
for among them he had been one of the trusted.

يُلَقَّنُ الصَّوَابَ فِي السُّؤَالِ   فَلَا يَخَافُ شِدَّةَ الْأَهْوَالِ

Yulaqqanu-ṣ-ṣawāba fi-s-suʾāli
falā yakhāfu shiddata-l-ahwāli

He will have the right answers when the questioning occurs
so that he need not fear the terrors [of the grave].

تَوْسِعَةُ الْقَبْرِ لَهُ فِي رَوْضَةِ   يَكُونُ فِيهَا ءَامِنًا مِنْ فِتْنَةِ

Tawsiʿatu-l-qabri lahu fī rawḍati
yakūnu fīhā āminan min fitnati

And his grave will be widened into one of Heaven's meadows
and therein he will be safe from tribulation.

وَإِينَاسٌ لِرُوحِهِ وَجِسْمِهِ   إِذْ تَأْتِيهِ الْبُشْرَى لَهُ مِنْ رَبِّهِ

Wa īnāsun li rūḥihi wa jismihi
idh ta•tīhi-l-bushrā lahu min Rabbihi

Both his soul and body will be comforted
as good tidings come to him from his Lord.

تَحْمِلُهُ الطُّيُورُ فِي أَجْوَافِهَا   فِي جَنَّةٍ حَيْثُ يَشَا فِي عَرْضِهَا

Taḥmiluhu-ṭ-ṭuyūru fī ajwāfihā
fī jannatin ḥaythu yashā fī ʿarḍiha

And he is carried within the birds of Heaven
to whatever part of its vast expanse he wishes.

وَالْحَشْرُ فِي الْعِزِّ مَعَ الْكَرَامَةْ   وَالتَّاجِ وَالْحُلَلِ وَالشَّفَاعَةْ

Wa-l-ḥashru fi-l-ʿizzi maʿa-l-karāma
wa-t-tāji wa-l-ḥulali wa-sh-shafāʿa

Glory and honor will be his at the Gathering,
and a crown, and robes, and intercession.

بَيَاضُ وَجْهِهِ وَنُورُهُ ظَهَرْ   لِكُلِّ مَنْ بِمَوْقِفٍ قَدِ انْتَشَرْ

Bayāḍu wajhihi wa nūruhu ẓahar
li kulli man bi mawqifin qadi-ntashar

His face will be made bright and its light will appear
to all who are gathered at the Place of Standing.

وَهَوْلُ مَوقِفٍ فَلاَ يَرَاهُ   وَالآخِذُ الْكُتْبَ لَهُ يُمْنَاهُ

Wa hawlu mawqifin falā yarāhu
wa-l-ākhidhu-l-kutba lahu yumnāhu

And the terrors of that place he will not see,
and by his right hand he will take his book.

فَلاَ يُحَاسَبُ حِسَابَ عُنْفِ   بَلْ يُبْتَدَى بِجَمِيلٍ وَلُطْفِ

Fa lā yuḥāsabu ḥisāba ʿunfi
bal yubtadā bi jamīlin wa luṭfi

And he will not be reckoned harshly.
Rather, it will proceed with beauty and kindness.

أَعْمَالُهُ تَثْقُلُ عِنْدَ الْوَزْنِ   وَالشُّرْبُ مِنْ حَوْضِ نَبِيٍّ يُغْنِي

Aʿmāluhu tathqulu ʿinda-l-wazni
wa-sh-shurbu min ḥawḍi Nabiyyin yughnī

His deeds will weigh heavy in the balance
and a drink from the pond of the Prophet will suffice him.

جَوَازُهُ الصِّرَاطَ بِالإِسْرَاعِ   لِجَنَّةِ الْخُلْدِ بِلاَ نِزَاعِ

Jawāzuhu-ṣ-ṣirāṭa bi-l-isrāʿi
li jannati-l-khuldi bilā nizāʿi

His passage over the Span will be swift
and it will bring him to the eternal Garden without doubt.

فَلاَ يُحَاسَبُ وَلاَ يُلاَمُ   فِي مَوْقِفِ الْمِيزَانِ لاَ يُضَامُ

Fa lā yuḥāsabu wa lā yulāmu
fī mawqifi-l-mīzāni lā yuḍāmu

So he will be neither reckoned [harshly] nor rebuked
in the place of the Balance, and he will not be wronged.

يَشْفَعُ فِي الْأَهْلِ وَفِي الْإِخْوَانِ   وَيُكْتَسَى مِنْ حُلَلِ الرِّضْوَانِ

Yashfaʿu fi-l-ahli wa fi-l-ikhwāni
wa yuktasā min ḥulali-r-riḍwāni

He will intercede for his Family and his Brethren
and don the robes of Allah's perfect pleasure.

ثُمَّ لِقَاءُ اللهِ بِالْمُعَايَنَةْ   مِنْ غَيْرِ تَكْيِيفٍ وَ لاَ مُشَابَهَةْ

Thumma liqā•u-Llāhi bi-l-muʿāyana
min ghayri takyīfin wa lā mushābaha

Then the meeting with Allah face to face –
beyond all manner and all likeness –

وَهْيَ أَجَلُّ مِنْ دُخُولِ الْجَنَّة   كَمَا أَتَى فِي كِتَابٍ وَ سُنَّةْ

Wa-hya ajallu min dukhūli-l-janna
kamā atā fī kitābin wa sunna

Which is greater than entering Heaven,
as is stated in the Book and the Sunna.

وَشَرْطُ مَنْ يَمْنَحُهُ الإِلٰهُ   بِهَذِهِ الْخِلَعِ لاَ تَنْسَاهُ

Wa sharṭu man yamnaḥuhu-l-Ilāhu
bi hādhihi-l-khilaʿi lā tansāhu

But do not forget the condition
upon which God grants these robes of honor:

الْعِلْمُ وَالْعَمَلُ مَعْ إِخْلاَصٍ   وَالذِّكْرُ يُوذِنُ بِالإِخْتِصَاصِ

Al-ʿilmu wa-l-ʿamalu maʿ ikhlāṣi
wa-dh-dhikru yūdhinu bi-l-iktiṣāṣi

Knowledge, practice, sincerity, and invocation
proclaim the station of the elect.

فَغَايَةُ الطَّرِيقِ فِي اسْتِغْرَاقِ   فِي شُهُودٍ لِمَالِكٍ خَلاَّقِ

Fa ghāyatu-ṭ-ṭarīqi fi-stighrāqī
fī shuhūdin li mālikin khallāqi

Thus, the ultimate goal of the Path is to be immersed
in an on-going vision of the Sovereign Creator.

إِيَّاكَ أَنْ تَصْغَى لِطَاعِنٍ فِيهَا   لِجَهْلِهِ بِعِلْمِهَا وَفَضْلِهَا

Iyyāka an taṣghā li ṭāʿinin fīhā
li jahlihi bi ʿilmihā wa faḍlihā

And pay no heed to those who deny our way
out of ignorance of its science and its excellence.

فَسَهِّلَنْ يَا رَبِّ لِلإِخْوَانِ سُلُوكَهَا فَضْلاً بِلاَ تَوَانِ

Fa sahhilan yā Rabbi li-l-ikhwāni
sulūkahā faḍlan bilā tawāni

O my Lord, by Your grace, make it easy for my brethren
to follow this Path without flagging.

قَدِ انْتَهَتْ خَوَارِقُ الطَّرِيقِ لِمَنْ مَشَى فِيهَا عَلَى التَّحْقِيقِ

Qadi-ntahat khawāriqu-ṭ-ṭarīqi
li man mashā fīhā ʿala-t-taḥqīqi

This completes [our mention] of the extraordinary gifts
which come to the one who really walks the Path.

فَارْحَمْ مُفِيدَهَا وَجَامِعاً لَهَا وَمَنْ تَصَدَّى مَعَنَا لِنَشْرِهَا

Farḥam mufīdahā wa jāmiʿan lahā
wa man taṣaddā maʿanā li nashrihā

Mercy be upon the one who recorded them, the one who collected them,
and any who help us make them known.[11]

نَاظِمُهَا مُحَمَّدُ ابْنُ الْحَبِيبْ يَطْلُبُ لِلأُمَّةِ فَتْحاً فِي الْقَرِيبْ

Nāẓimuhā Muḥammadu-bnu-l-Ḥabīb
yaṭlubu li-l-ummati fat•ḥan fi-l-qarīb

Muḥammad ibn al-Ḥabīb, who has put them into rhyme,
asks that Allah grant this community a victory at hand.

وَنُصْرَةً لِظِلِّنَا الْمَحْبُوبِ   تُظْفِرُهُ بِجَمِيعِ الْمَرْغُوبِ

Wa nuṣratan li ẓillina-l-maḥbūbi
tuẓfiruhu bi jamīʿi-l-marghūbi

And may Allah grant aid to our beloved ruler
by which he may achieve all that is desirable.

ثُمَّ صَلَاةُ اللهِ تَتْرَى أَبَدَا   عَلَى مُحَمَّدٍ وَمَن بِهِ اقْتَدَى

Thumma ṣalātu-Llāhi tatrā abadā
ʿalā Muḥammadin wa man bihi-qtadā

Then may the blessings of Allah be eternally
upon Muḥammad and those who follow him.

كَذَلِكَ الْآلِ مَعَ الصِّحَابِ   السَّالِكِينَ سُبُلَ الصَّوَابِ

Kadhālika-l-āli maʿa-ṣ-ṣiḥābi
as-sālikīna subula-ṣ-ṣawābi

And also upon his Family and Companions
who journeyed the paths towards what is right.

-8-

في فضائل الاسم الأعظم

On the Merits of the Supreme Name

تَجَرَّدْ عَنِ الْأَغْيَارِ تَحْظَى بِقُرْبِهِ   وَتَرْقَى مَرَاقِي الْقَوْمِ فِي كُلِّ مَشْهَدِ

Tajarrad ʿani-l-aghyāri taḥẓā bi qurbihi
wa tarqā marāqi-l-qawmi fī kulli mash•hadi

Be empty of all that is other than Allah.
You will be graced by His nearness
and ascend to the ranks of the folk in every station.

وَعَمِّرْ بِذِكْرِ اللهِ أَنْفَاسَكَ الَّتِي   تُحَاسَبُ عَنْهَا يَوْمَ حَشْرٍ وَمَوْعِدِ

Wa ʿammir bi dhikri-Llāhi anfāsaka-l-latī
tuḥāsabu ʿanhā yawma ḥashrin wa mawʿidi

And let the invocation of Allah fill your breaths
for which you'll be reckoned on the Appointed Day of Gathering.

وَعَظِّمْ جَمِيعَ الْكَوْنِ مِنْ حَيْثُ إِنَّهُ   تَكَوَّنَ مِنْ نُورِ النَّبِيِّ مُحَمَّدِ

Wa ʿaẓẓim jamīʿa-l-kawni min ḥaythu innahu
takawwana min nūri-n-Nabiyyi Muḥammadi

Esteem the whole of creation for the fact that it is
fashioned from the Light of the Prophet Muḥammad.

وَلاَحِظْهُ أَنْوَارًا لِأَسْمَاءِ رَبِّنَا   وَغِبْ عَنْ كَثَافَةٍ وَعَنْ قَوْلِ مُلْحِدِ

Wa lāḥiẓhu anwāran li asmā•i Rabbinā
wa ghib ʿan kathāfatin wa ʿan qawli mulḥidi

See it as the lights of the Names of our Lord,
and turn away from denseness and the speech of deniers.

وَأَحْبِبْ بِحُبِّ اللهِ وَابْغَضْ بِبُغْضِهِ   فَذَاكَ مِنَ التَّشْرِيعِ فَاحْفَظْهُ سَيِّدِي

Wa aḥbib bi ḥubbi-Llahi wa-bghaḍ bi bughḍihi
fa dhāka mina-t-tashrīʿi faḥfaẓhu sayyidī

Love what Allah loves, abhor what He abhors:
such is the Law, so keep it my dear sir.

وَكُنْ بَرْزَخَ الْبَحْرَينِ حَقٍّ وَشِرْعَةٍ   تَحُزْ رُتْبَةَ التَّعْرِيفِ فِي كُلِّ مَقْعَدِ

Wa kun barzakha-l-baḥrayni ḥaqqin wa shirʿatin
taḥuz rutbata-t-taʿrīfi fī kulli maqʿadi

And be an isthmus between the two seas of Inner Truth and Law.
You'll be granted the rank of gnostic at every stage.

وَدُلَّ عِبَادَ اللهِ بِاللهِ مُعْلِنًا   بِتَحْسِينِ طُرْقِ اللهِ فِي كُلِّ مَسْجِدِ

Wa dulla ʿibāda-Llāhi bi-Llāhi muʿlinan
bi taḥsīni ṭurqi-Llāhi fī kulli masjidi

Direct Allah's servants to the beauty of His paths.
Do so by Allah, openly, in every mosque.

وَإِنْ شِئْتَ إِسْرَاعًا لِحَضْرَةِ رَبِّنَا فَحَسِّنْ بِخَلْقِ اللهِ ظَنًّا وَمَجِّدِ

Wa in shi•ta isrāʿan li ḥaḍrati Rabbinā
fa ḥassin bi khalqi-Llāhi ẓannan wa majjidi

And if you wish the quickest path to the Presence of our Lord,
then think best of Allah's creatures and honor them.

وَوَاظِبْ عَلَى الْإِسْمِ الْعَظِيمِ الْمُعَظَّمِ بِحُسْنِ سَرِيرَةٍ وَصِدْقٍ وَمَقْصِدِ

Wa wāẓib ʿala-l-Ismi-l-ʿaẓīmi-l-muʿaẓẓami
bi ḥusni sarīratin wa ṣidqin wa maqṣidi

Make invoking the Supreme Name your regular practice
with the best of your soul, sincerity, and purpose.

وَشَاهِدْ جَمَالَ الذَّاتِ فِي كُلِّ مَظْهَرٍ فَلَوْلَاهَا لَمْ يَثْبُتْ وُجُودٌ لِمُوجِدِ

Wa shāhid jamāla-dh-dhāti fī kulli maẓharin
fa law lā hā lam yathbut wujūdun li mūjidi

Be conscious of the beauty of the Essence in all Its manifestations –
were it not for that Essence, all existence would vanish.

وَكُلُّ صِفَاتِ النَّفْسِ تَفْنَى بِذِكْرِهِ وَيَبْقَى نَعِيمُ الْقَلْبِ أَحْلَى مِنَ الشَّهْدِ

Wa kullu ṣifāti-n-nafsi tafnā bi dhikrihi
wa yabqā naʿīmu-l-qalbi aḥlā mina-sh-shahdi

Every trait of the ego passes away in His Remembrance
leaving a joy in the heart that is sweeter than honey in the hive.

وَكُلُّ تَحَلٍّ بِالْمَقَامَاتِ نَاشِئٌ عَنِ الذِّكْرِ بِالْإِسْمِ الْعَظِيمِ مَعَ الْجِدِّ

Wa kullu taḥallin bi-l-maqāmāti nāshi•un
ʿani-dh-dhikri bi-l-Ismi-l-ʿaẓīm maʿa-l-jiddi

Every beauty that comes through the Stations of the Way
arises from the fervent invocation of His Name.

فَمِنْهُ يَكُونُ الْفَتْحُ لِكُلِّ سَالِكٍ وَمِنْهُ يَكُونُ الْفَيْضُ لِكُلِّ مُرْشِدِ

Fa minhu yakūnu-l-fatḥu li kulli sālikin
wa minhu yakūnu-l-fayḍu li kulli murshidi

From it is the Opening to each traveler on the path,
from it the outpouring of light to every guide;

وعَنْهُ تَكُونُ حَالَةُ السُّكْرِ وَالْفَنَا وَعَنْهُ تَكُونُ حَالَةُ الصَّحْوِ وَالْوَجْدِ

Wa ʿanhu takūnu ḥālatu-s-sukri wa-l-fanā
wa ʿanhu takūnu ḥālatu-ṣ-ṣaḥwi wa-l-wajdi

From it the states of intoxication and effacement,
from it the states of sobriety and rapture.

وَمَا نَالَ عِزًّا غَيْرُ مُنْفَرِدٍ بِهِ تَحَلَّى بِمَا يُرْضِيهِ مَعْ كَثْرَةِ الْحَمْدِ

Wa mā nāla ʿizzan ghayru munfaridin bihi
taḥallā bimā yurḍīhi maʿ kathrati-l-ḥamdi

And none attains true honor except in solitude with the Name,
adorned by what pleases Allah, abounding in praise.

فَمَا زَالَ يَرْقَى فِي مَهَامِهِ ذَاتِهِ وَيَفْنَى فَنَاءً لَيْسَ فِيهِ سِوَى الْفَقْدِ

Fa mā zāla yarqā fī mahāmihi dhātihi
wa yafnā fanā•an laysa fīhi siwa-l-faqdi

He ceaselessly ascends through the vastness of the Essence
and is effaced in an effacement where all else is gone.

فَإِنْ رُدَّ لِلْآثَارِ جَآءَ بِحُلَّةٍ تُنَادِي عَلَيهِ بِالْوِلَايَةِ وَالْمَجْدِ

Fa in rudda li-l-āthāri jā•a bi ḥullatin
tunādī ʿalayhi bi-l-wilāyati wa-l-majdi

And if he is returned to the traces of creation,
he comes in a robe that bespeaks sanctity and splendor.

فَكُنْ خَادِمًا عَبْداً لِمَنْ هَذَا وَصْفُهُ وَوَفِّ بِعَهْدِ اللهِ يَاتِكَ بِالْوَعْدِ

Fa kun khādiman ʿabdan liman hādhā waṣfuhu
wa waffi bi ʿahdi-Llāhi yātika bi-l-waʿdi

So to one who has these traits be a faithful servant,
keep your covenant with Allah and He will give you what is promised.

وَأَعْظَمُ خَلْقِ اللهِ فِي ذَاكَ رُسْلُهُ وَأَكْمَلُهُمْ فِيهِ النَّبِيُّ مُحَمَّدِ

Wa aʿẓamu khalqi-Llahi fī dhāka rusluhu
wa akmaluhum fīhi-n-Nabīyyu Muḥammadi

The greatest of Allah's creatures in this are His Messengers
the most perfect of whom is the Prophet Muḥammad.

فَظَاهِرُهُ نُورٌ وَبَاطِنُهُ سِرٌّ   كَمَالاَتُهُ لَيْسَتْ تُحَصَّلُ بِالْعَدِّ

Fa ẓāhiruhu nūrun wa bāṭinuhu sirrun
kamālātuhu laysat tuḥaṣṣalu bi-l-ʿaddi

Outwardly he is light, inwardly a mystery –
his virtues and perfections cannot be numbered

عَلَيْهِ صَلاَةُ اللهِ وَالْآلِ وَالصَّحْبِ   وَدَارِكْنَا بِالأَلْطَافِ مِنْ غَيْرِ مَاحَدِّ

ʿalayhi ṣalātu-Llāhi wa-l-āli wa-ṣ-ṣaḥbi
wa dāriknā bi-l-alṭāfi min ghayri mā ḥaddi

May Allah's blessings be upon him and his Family and companions,
and deliver us, O Allah, by Your infinite mercies.

-9-

الحمد

Praise

لَكَ الْحَمْدُ يَا ذَا الْحِلْمِ وَالْعَفْوِ وَالسِّتْرِ   وَحَمْدِيَ مِنْ نُعْمَاكَ يَا وَاسِعَ الْبِرِّ

Laka-l-ḥamdu yā Dha-l-Ḥilmi wa-l-ʿafwi wa-s-sitri
wa ḥamdiya min nuʿmāka yā Wāsiʿa-l-birri

Yours is (all) praise, in Your Gentleness and Pardon,
O You Who covers our faults,
You Whose goodness envelops all, my praise is part of Your grace.

لَكَ الْحَمْدُ عَدَّ الْقَطْرِ وَالرَّمْلِ وَالْحَصَى   وَعَدَّ نَبَاتِ الْأَرْضِ وَالْحُوتِ فِي الْبَحْرِ

Laka-l-ḥamdu ʿadda-l-qaṭri wa-r-ramli wa-l-ḥaṣā
wa ʿadda nabāti l-arḍi wa-l-ḥūti fi-l-baḥri

Yours is praise as abundant as raindrops, grains of sand, and pebbles,
as abundant as the plants of the earth, and the fish in the sea.

لَكَ الْحَمْدُ عَدَّ النَّمْلِ وَالْجِنِّ وَالْإِنْسِ   وَمِلْءَ السَّمَا وَالْعَرْشِ وَالْكَوْكَبِ الدُّرِّ

Laka-l-ḥamdu ʿadda-n-namli wa-l-jinni wa- l-insi
wa mil•a-s-samā wa-l-ʿarshi wa-l-kawkabi-d-durri

Yours is praise as abundant as the ants, the jinn, and humankind,
praise which fills the sky and the Throne and the stars that glisten above.

وَمِلْءَ الْفَضَا وَاللَّوْحِ وَالكُرْسِي وَالثَّرَى   وَعَدَّ جَمِيعِ الْكَائِنَاتِ إِلَى الْحَشْرِ

Wa mil•a-l-faḍā wal-l-Lawḥi wa-l-Kursī wa-th-tharā
wa ʿadda jamīʿi-l-kā•ināti ila-l-ḥashri

Praise which fills the vastness of space, the Tablet, the Chair, and the soil,
praise as abundant as all who exist till the Day of the Final Assembly.

لَكَ الْحَمْدُ يَا رَبِّي كَمَا أَنْتَ أَهْلُهُ   فَإِنِّيَ لاَ أُحْصِي الثَّنَاءَ مَدَى الدَّهْرِ

Laka-l-ḥamdu yā Rabbī kamā Anta ahluhu
fa inniya lā uḥṣī-th-thanā•a madā-d-dahri

Yours is praise, O my Lord, (praise) as is Your due.
I could not number Your praises, were I given all earthly time.

لَكَ الْحَمْدُ يَا مُعْطِي الْمَوَاهِبَ بِالفَضْلِ   وَمَانِحَ أَهْلِ اللهِ بِالفَتْحِ وَالنَّصْرِ

Laka-l-ḥamdu yā Muʿṭi-l-mawāhiba bi-l-faḍli
wa Māniḥa ahli-Llāhi bi-l-Fatḥi wa-n-Naṣri

Yours is praise, O Bestower of gifts, by way of Your infinite grace,
You are the One Who grants Allah's people the opening and the victory.

لَكَ الْحَمْدُ بِالْأَنْفَاسِ وَالْجِسْمِ وَالْقَلْبِ   تَفَضَّلْ عَلَى عَبدٍ تَحَيَّرَ فِي الأَمْرِ

Laka-l-ḥamdu bi-l-anfāsi, wa-l-jismi wa-l-qalbi
tafaḍḍal ʿalā ʿabdin taḥayyara fi-l-amri

Yours is praise, with (every) breath (we take), with the body and the heart:
so be benevolent towards a servant who is bewildered about the way.

فَإِنِّي وَإِنْ كَانَتْ ذُنُوبِي تَعُوقُنِي   فَلِي فِيكَ حُسْنُ الظَّنِّ يَجْبُرُ لِي كَسْرِي

Fa innī wa in kānat dhunūbī taʿūqunī
fa lī fīka ḥusnu-ẓ-ẓanni yajburu lī kasrī

Though my sins may surely weigh heavy upon me
still I trust in Your goodness to mend my brokenness.

فَمُنَّ عَلَيْنَا يَا غَفُورُ بِتَوْبَةٍ   تَجُبُّ الَّذِي قَدْ كَانَ فِي سَالِفِ الْعُمْرِ

Fa munna ʿalaynā yā Ghafūru bi tawbatin
tajubbu-l-ladhī qad kāna fī sālifi-l-ʿumri

Favor us, O Most-Forgiving Lord, with repentance
that effaces the mistakes which were made in times past.

وَزِدْنَا مِنَ النَّعْمَاءِ وَالنُّورِ وَالْكَشْفِ   وَمَكِّنَّا فِي الْإِرْشَادِ بِالْإِذْنِ وَالسِّرِّ

Wa zidnā mina-n-naʿmā•i, wa-n-nūri wa-l-kashfi
wa makkinnā fi-l-irshādi bi-l-idhni wa-s-sirri

And increase us in blessings, and light, and unveilings,
and enable us to guide with permission and the secret

وَأَيِّدْنَا فِي أَقْوَالِنَا وَفِعَالِنَا   وَيَسِّرْ لَنَا الْأَرْزَاقَ مِنْ حَيْثُ لَا نَدْرِي

Wa ayyidnā fī aqwālinā wa fiʿālinā
wa yassir lana-l-arzāqa min ḥaythu lā nadrī

Support us in what we say and do,
and ease for us our provision from a place we do not know.

فَهَا نَحْنُ فِي بَابِ التَّفَضُّلِ وَاقِفٌ   وَ مُنْتَظِرٌ عَطْفَ الْحَبِيبِ بِلاَ عُسْرِ

Fa hā naḥnu fī bābi-t-tafaḍḍuli wāqifun
wa muntaẓirun ʿaṭfa-l-Ḥabībi bilā ʿusri

Here we stand at the door of benevolence
awaiting without hardship the kindness of the Friend.

فَأَنْعِمْ عَلَينَا يَا مُجِيبُ بِسُرْعَةٍ   فَإِنَّكَ أَهْلُ الْجُودِ وَالْمَنِّ وَالْخَيرِ

Fa•anʿimʿalaynā yā Mujību bi surʿatin
fa innaka ahlu-l-jūdi wa-l-manni wa-l-khayri

You Who answers prayers, hasten Your grace upon us
You are truly the One full of generosity, goodness, and favor.

فَفَضْلُكَ مَوجُودٌ بِغَيرِ وُجودِنَا   وَجُودُكَ مَسْدُولٌ عَلَيْنَا بِلاَ نُكْرِ

Fa faḍluka mawjūdun bi ghayri wujūdinā
wa jūduka masdūlun ʿalaynā bi lā nukri

Your favor existed when we did not.
Your generosity undeniably rains down upon us.

وَ وَفِّقْنَا لِلشُّكْرِ الَّذِي هُوَ لاَزِمٌ   عَلَيْنَا وَيَسْتَدْعِي الْمَزِيدَ بِلاَ خُسْرِ

Wa waffiqnā li-sh-shukri-l-ladhī huwa lāzimun
ʿAlaynā wa yastadʿī-l-mazīda bilā khusri

Grant us the gratitude incumbent upon us
which beckons increase without any loss.

وَأَخْرِجْنَا مِنْ سِجْنِ الْجُسُومِ وَرَقِّنَا   لِحَضْرَةِ أَرْوَاحٍ ثَوَاباً عَلَى الشُّكْرِ

Wa akhrijnā min sijni-l-jusūmi wa raqqinā
Li ḥaḍrati arwāḥin thawāban ʿala-sh-shukri

Bring us forth from the prison of physical forms and raise us
to the realm of spirits as recompense for thanks.

وَأَشْهِدْنَا مَعْنَى الذَّاتِ فِي كُلِّ مَظْهَرٍ   لِيَقْوَى شُهُودِي فِي الشَّدَائِدِ وَالْيُسْرِ

Wa ash•hidnā maʿnā-dh-dhāti fī kulli maẓharin
Li yaqwā shuhūdī fi-sh-shadā•idi wa-l-yusri

And let us witness in every theophany the meaning of the Essence
that our vision might be strengthened both in hardship and in ease.

وَ أَفْنِنَا عَنَّا وَابْقِنَا بِكَ دَائِماً   لِنَلْحَقَ أَهْلَ الْإِرْثِ مِنْ حَضْرَةِ السِّرِّ

Wa afninā ʿannā wa-bqinā bika dā•iman
li nalḥaqa ahla-l-irthi min ḥaḍrati-s-sirri

Efface us from our egos and sustain us always in You,
that we might be among those who are heir to the realm of the secret.

فَأَمْرُكَ لِلأَشْيَاءِ فِي قَولِ كُنْ تَكُنْ   فَكَوِّنْ لَنَا الْأَشْيَاءَ عَزْماً بِلاَ مَكْرِ

Fa amruka li-l-ashyā•i fī qawli kun takun
fa kawwin lana-l-ashyā•a ʿazman bilā makri

For Your command to all things is "Be," and they are
So make things be resolutely for us without ruse.

وَ صَلِّ بِأَنْوَاعِ الْكَمَالاَتِ كُلِّهَا   عَلَى أَحْمَدَ الْهَادِي إِلَى حَضْرَةِ الطُّهْرِ

Wa ṣalli bi anwāʿi-l-kamālāti kullihā
ʿalā Aḥmada-l-Hādī ilā ḥaḍrati-ṭ-ṭuhri

And, O Lord, shower blessings in every mode of perfection
upon Aḥmad the Guide to the realm of Purity.

وَ آلِهِ وَالصَّحْبِ الْكِرَامِ وَمَنْ دَعَا   لِنَاظِمِ هَذَا النَّظْمِ بِالشَّرْحِ لِلصَّدْرِ

Wa ālihi wa-ṣ-ṣaḥbi-l-kirāmi wa man daʿā
li nāẓimi hadha-n-naẓmi bi-sh-sharḥi li-ṣ-ṣadri

And upon his people, and noble companions, and any who pray
that the rhymer of these verses be granted breadth of heart.

وَ يَا رَبِّ بِالْهَادِي الرَّؤُوفِ مُحَمَّدٍ   أَنِلْنَا عُلُومًا تَنْفَعُنَا يَومَ النَّشْرِ

Wa yā Rabbi bi-l-Hādi-r-Raʾūfi Muḥammadin
anilnā ʿulūman tanfaʿunā yawma-n-nashri

O Lord, by Muḥammad, the compassionate guide
grant us knowledge that will serve us on Resurrection Day.

وَقَوِّنَا بِالأَنْوَارِ فِي كُلِّ لَحْظَةٍ   وَثَبِّتْنَا عِنْدَ الْخَتْمِ وَالنَّزْعِ وَالْقَبْرِ

Wa qawwinā bi-l-anwāri fī kulli laḥẓatin
wa thabbitnā ʿinda-l-khatmi wa-n-nazʿi wa-l-qabri

Strengthen us with lights at every instant, and keep us steadfast
at the end, when the spirit is taken, and in the grave.

أيا من يرد قربا

O You Who Wish for Nearness

أَيَا مَنْ يُرِدْ قُرْباً مِنَ اللهِ عَنْ فَوْرٍ   عَلَيْكَ بِذِكْرِ اللهِ فِي السِّرِّ وَالْجَهْرِ

A yā man yurid qurban mina-Llāhi ʿan fawrin
ʿalayka bi-dhikri-Llāhi fi-s-sirri wa-l-jahri

O you who wish for nearness to Allah right away –
upon you I enjoin the Invocation, silently and aloud.

وَعَمِّرْ بِهِ الْأَوْقَاتَ تَسْمُو بِسُرْعَةٍ   إِلَى ذِرْوَةِ الْعِرْفَانِ مَعْ خَالِصِ الْفِكْرِ

Wa ʿammir bihi-l-awqāta tasmū bi surʿatin
ilā dhirwati-l-ʿirfāni maʿ khāliṣi-l-fikri

Fill your moments with it and you will swiftly climb
to the peaks of gnosis with purity of reflection.

لِتَصْقِيلِ مِرْءَا الْقَلْبِ يَنْكَشِفُ الْغِطَا   وَتَبْدُو لَهُ الْأَنْوَارُ مِنْ خَالِصِ الذِّكْرِ

Li taṣqīli mir•a-l-qalbi yankashifu-l-ghiṭā
wa tabdū lahu-l-anwāru min khāliṣi-l-dhikri

As the mirror of your heart is polished, the veil is lifted
and lights appear to it from the purity of invocation.

بِذِكْرِ إِلٰهِ الْعَرْشِ تَزْهَدُ فِي الْوَرَى   وَتَفْنَى عَنِ النَّفْسِ الْمُعَطِّلَةِ السَّيْرِ

Bi dhikri ilāhi-l-ʿarshi tazhadu fi-l-warā
wa tafnā ʿani-n-nafsi-l-muʿaṭṭilati-s-sayri

Invoking the God of the Throne you will withdraw from people
and be effaced from the ego which holds you back from the journey.

وَتَضْحى جَلِيسَ اللهِ مِنْ غَيرِ كُلْفَةِ   وَتَسْلَمُ مِنْ شَكٍّ وَشِرْكٍ وَمِنْ غَيْرِ

Wa taḍḥā jalīsa-Llāhi min ghayri kulfati
wa taslamu min shakkin wa shirkin wa min ghayri.

And you will be seated with Allah without formalities
and be delivered from doubt, association, and all others.

وَتَرْحَلُ عَنْ كَوْنٍ إِلَى حَضْرَةِ الْصَّفَا   وَتَشْهَدُ فِعْلَ اللهِ فِي الْخَلْقِ وَالأَمْرِ

Wa tarḥalu ʿan kawnin ilā ḥaḍrati-ṣ-ṣafā
wa tash·hadu fiʿla-Llāhi fi-l-khalqi wa-l-amri

You will travel from this world to a realm of clarity,
and witness the Act of Allah in the creation and command.

وَتَرْقَى إِلَى الأَسْمَاءِ تُسْقَى بِنُورِهَا   فَتَبْدُو لَكَ الأَوْصَافُ مِنْ غَيْرِ مَا سِتْرِ

Wa tarqā ila-l-asmā·i tusqā bi nūrihā
fa tabdū laka-l-awṣāfu min ghayri ma sitri

You will ascend to the Names, and be given to drink from their light,
and the Attributes will appear to you without a veil.

وَيَظْهَرُ مَعْنَى الذَّاتِ مِنْ كَامِلِ الْفَنَا   فَتَبْقَى غَنِيًّا بِالْإِلٰهِ مَدَى الْعُمْرِ

Wa yaẓharu maʿnā-dh-Dhāti min kāmili-l-fanā
wa tabqā ghanīyyan bi-l-Ilāhi madā-l-ʿumri

Your effacement complete, the meaning of the Essence will appear
and you will subsist by God, enriched for all your days.

فَإِنْ عَبِقَتْ فِي الْغَرْبِ أَنْفَاسُ ذِكْرِهِ   وَفِي الشَّرْقِ مَعْلُولٌ تَعَافَى مِنَ الضُّرِّ

Fa in ʿabiqat fi-l-gharbi anfāsu dhikrihi
wa fi-sh-sharqi maʿlūlun taʿāfā mina-ḍ-ḍurri

For if the west were perfumed by the breaths of His invocation,
the one suffering in the east would be relieved of pain.

عَلَيْهِ مَدَارُ الدِّينِ فِي كُلِّ قُرْبَةٍ   وَلاَ سِيَّمَا ذِكْرُ الْجَلَالَةِ مِنْ حُرِّ

ʿAlayhi madāru-d-dīni fī kulli qurbatin
wa lā siyyamā dhikru-l-jalālati min ḥurri

Upon it stands the axis of faith and all the means of approach,
and especially the invocation of Majesty by someone truly free.

فَمَا مِنْ وَلِيٍّ إِلاَّ هَامَ بِذِكْرِهِ   عَلَى عَدَدِ الْأَنْفَاسِ بِالرُّوحِ وَالسِّرِّ

Fa mā min waliyyin illā hāma bi dhikrihi
ʿalā ʿadadi-l-anfāsi bi-rūḥi wa-s-sirri

No saint has there been who was not taken up by its love
with every breath, with spirit and soul.

فَقَدْ كَانَ ذَاكِراً وَأَصْبَحَ مَذْكُوراً   يَتِيهُ عَلَى الأَكْوَانِ مِنْ غَيْرِ مَا فَخْرِ

Fa qad kāna dhākiran wa aṣbaḥa madhkūran
yatīhu ʿala-l-akwāni min ghayri ma fakhri

He had been one who mentioned Allah and became one who is mentioned,
exalted among creatures but without pride.

وَمَا الْفَخْرُ إِلاَّ بِالْعُبُودِيَّةِ الَّتِي   تَخَلَّصَتْ مِن حَوْلٍ وَقُوَى وَمِنْ مَكْرِ

Wa ma-l-fakhru illā bi-l-ʿubūdiyyati-l-latī
takhallaṣat min ḥawlin wa quwā wa min makri

For no pride there is save in servanthood that is free
from (the pretense of) strength, power, and guile.

نَتَائِجُ ذِكْرِ اللهِ لَيْسَ لَهَا حَصْرٌ   فَوَاظِبْ أَخِي وَلَوْ عَشِيًّا وَبِالْفَجْرِ

Natā•iju dhikri-Llāhi laysa lahā ḥaṣrun
fa wāẓib akhī wa law ʿashīyyan wa bi-l-fajri

The results, dear brother, of invoking Allah are boundless,
so make it your regular practice, even if only in the evening and at dawn.

لَقَدْ وَرَدَ الإِكْثَارُ مِنْهُ بِلَا حَدٍّ   تَصَفَّحْ كِتَابَ اللهِ مَعْ سُنَّةٍ تَدْرِي

La qad warada-l-ikthāru minhu bilā ḥaddin
taṣaffaḥ kitāba-Llāhi maʿ sunnatin tadrī

To be abdundant in it, without limit, has been passed down in the teachings.
Study the Book of Allah and the Sunna – you will know.

وَقَدْ وَعَدَ الْجَلِيلُ بِذِكْرِ مَنْ غَدَا   لَهُ ذَاكِرًا يَا فَوْزَ مَنْ خُصَّ بِالذِّكْرِ

Wa qad waʿada-l-Jalīlu bi dhikri man ghadā
lahu dhākiran yā fawza man khuṣṣa bi-dh-dhikri

The All-Mighty has promised to remember the one who becomes
one who remembers Him: blessed be the one chosen for remembrance!

وَمَنْ يَعْشُ عَنْ ذِكْرِ الْإِلٰهِ يَكُنْ لَهُ   قَرِينٌ مِنَ الشَّيْطَانِ يَفْتِنُ عَنْ سَيْرِ

Wa man yaʿshu ʿan dhikri-l-ilāhi yakun lahu
qarīnun mina-sh-shayṭāni yaftinu ʿan sayri

(But) whosoever turns blindly from God's remembrance
is given a devil as companion to lure him from the way.

فَلَا يَطْمَئِنُّ الْقَلْبُ إِلاَّ بِذِكْرِهِ   فَيَسْكُنَ عَنْ خَوْفِ الْخَلِيقَةِ وَالفَقْرِ

Fa lā yaṭma•innu-l-qalbu illā bi dhikrihi
Fa yaskuna ʿan khawfi-l-khalīqati wa-l-faqri.

The heart finds no rest except by Allah's remembrance –
it is calmed from fears of people and indigence.

وَلاَ تُبْسَطُ الْأَرْزَاقُ إِلاَّ لِمَنْ غَدَا   يُرَدِّدُهُ حَتَّى يُغَيَّبَ فِي الْوِتْرِ

Wa lā tubsaṭu-l-arzāqu illā li man ghadā
yuraddiduhu ḥattā yughayyaba fi-l-Witri

Nor is provision expanded save for one who becomes
among those who repeat the invocation until they vanish in the One.

وَهَذَا رَسُولُ اللهِ يَذْكُرُ دَائِماً عَلَى كُلِّ أَحْيَانٍ يُشَرِّعُ لِلْغَيْرِ

Wa hadhā Rasūlu-Llāhi yadhkuru dā•iman
ʿalā kulli aḥyānin yusharriʿu li-l-ghayri

And here is the Messenger of Allah remembering Him always,
and ordaining it for others in every state.

وَقَالَ اذْكُرُوا حَتَّى يَقُولُونَ إِنَّهُ يُرَائِي بِذِكْرِ اللهِ حِرْصاً عَلَى الْخَيْرِ

Wa qāla-dhkurū ḥattā yaqūlūna innahu
yurā'ī bi dhikri-Llāhi ḥirṣan ʿala-l-khayri

And he said, "Mention Allah until people say, It's ostentatious!"
(but really) it is for the sake of good.

عَلَيْكَ بِهِ فَالْقَوْمُ قَدْ سَكِرُوا بِهِ وَ أَفْنَوا فِيهِ الأَرْوَاحَ يَا لَهُ مِنْ ذُخْرِ

ʿAlayka bihi fa-l-qawmu qad sakirū bihi
wa afnaw fīhi-l-arwāḥa – yā lahu min dhukhri!

This I enjoin upon you – for the folk have been made drunk by it,
and their spirits effaced therein – what a treasure it holds!

فَكُلُّ مَقَامَاتِ الرِّجَالِ قَدِ انْطَوَتْ فِي حُبٍّ وَذِكْرِ اللهِ بِالْفَمِ وَالْصَّدْرِ

Fa kullu maqāmāti-r-rijāli qadi-nṭawat
fī ḥubbin wa dhikri-Llahī bi-l-fami wa-ṣ-ṣadri

All the (travellers') stations are contained in the Love of Allah
and His invocation with the voice and with the heart.

وَلاَ تَكْتَفِي بِالْوَارِدَاتِ عَنِ الْوِرْدِ   وَلاَ تَطْلُبَنْ إِلاَّ رِضَاهُ مَعَ السِّتْرِ

Wa lā taktafī bi-l-wāridāti ʿani-l-wirdi
wa lā taṭluban illā riḍāhu maʿa-s-sitri

And do not settle for inspirations in place of (accomplishing) the litany,
nor seek other than Allah's pleasure and the covering of your faults.

فَيَا رَبِّ وَفِّقْنَا لِصِدْقِ تَوَجُّهِ   بِجَاهِ الَّذِي قَدْ جَاءَ بِالْفَتْحِ وَالنَّصْرِ

Fa yā Rabbi waffiqnā li ṣidqi tawajjuhi
bi jāhi-l-ladhī qad jā•a bi-l-fatḥi wa-n-naṣri

O Lord, grant that we may turn with sincerity towards You
by the honor of the one who brought the opening and victory.

مُحَمَّدٌ أَصْلُ الْمَوْجُودَاتِ وَسِرُّهَا   وَخَاتِمُ رُسْلِ اللهِ وَالْأَنْبِيَا الْغُرِّ

Muḥammadun aṣlu-l-mawjūdāti wa sirruhā
wa khātimu Rusli-Llahī wa-l-anbiya-l-ghurri

Muhammad is the source and secret of all existence,
the seal of the Messengers and radiant Prophets of Allah.

عَلَيْهِ صَلاَةُ اللهِ مَا هَامَ ذَاكِرٌ   بِذِكْرِ مَوْلاَهُ فِي الشَّدَائِدِ وَالْيُسْرِ

ʿAlayhi ṣalātu-Llāhi mā hāma dhākirun
bi dhikri Mawlāhu fi-sh-shadā•idi wa-l-yusri.

May Allah's blessings be upon him as long as there is someone
taken up by the love of the invocation of the Lord both
in hardship and ease.

وَآلِهِ وَالْأَصْحَابِ مَعْ كُلِّ مُقْتَفٍ   مُتَابَعَةَ الْمُخْتَارِ فِي النَّهْيِ وَالْأَمْرِ

Wa ālihi wa-l-aṣ•ḥābi maᶜ kulli muqtafin
mutābaᶜata-l-Mukhtāri fi-n-nahyi wa-l-amri

And upon his people and Companions and each successor
following the Chosen Prophet in prohibition and command.

-11-

التفكّر

Reflection

تَفَكَّرْ جَمِيلَ الصُّنْعِ فِي الْبَرِّ وَالْبَحْرِ   وَجُلْ فِي صِفَاتِ اللهِ فِي السِّرِّ وَالْجَهْرِ

Tafakkar jamīla-ṣ-ṣunʿi fi-l-barri wa-l-baḥri
wa jul fī ṣifāti-Llāhi fi-s-sirri wa-l-jahri

Reflect upon the beauty of the artistry on land and sea
and journey through Allah's Attributes both hidden and open.

وَفِي النَّفْسِ وَالْآفَاقِ أَعْظَمُ شَاهِدٍ   عَلَى كَمَالَاتِ اللهِ مِن غَيْرِ مَا حَصْرِ

Wa fi-n-nafsi wa-l-āfāqi aʿẓamu shāhidin
ʿalā kamālāti-Llāhi min ghayri mā ḥaṣri

In the soul and on the horizons are the greatest of signs
of Allah's perfections without limit or end.

فَلَوْ جُلْتَ فِي الْأَجْسَامِ مَعْ حُسْنِ شَكْلِهَا   وَتَنْظِيمِهَا تَنْظِيمَ خَيْطٍ مِنَ الدُّرِّ

Fa law julta fi-l-ajsāmi maʿ ḥusni shaklihā
wa tanẓīmihā tanẓīma khayṭin mina-d-durri

If you consider forms and behold their beauties
and their order like pearls threaded on a string,

وَجُلْتَ فِي أَسْرَارِ اللِّسَانِ وَنُطْقِهِ   وَتَعْبِيرِهِ عَمَّا تُكِنُّهُ فِي الصَّدْرِ

Wa julta fī asrāri-l-lisāni wa nuṭqihi
wa taʿbīrihi ʿammā tukinnuhu fi-ṣ-ṣadri

And consider the mysteries of languages and speech
that give voice to what's hidden in a heart,

وَجُلْتَ فِي أَسْرَارِ الْجَوَارِحِ كُلِّهَا   وَتَسْخِيرِهَا لِلْقَلْبِ مِنْ غَيرِ مَا عُسْرِ

Wa julta fī asrāri-l-jawāriḥi kullihā
wa taskhīrihā li-l-qalbi min ghayri mā ʿusri

And consider the mysteries of the limbs of the body
and how the heart, without effort, may command them,

وَجُلْتَ فِي تَقْلِيبِ الْقُلُوبِ لِطَاعَةٍ   وَفِي بَعْضِ أَحْيَانٍ لِمَعْصِيَةٍ تَسْرِي

Wa julta fī taqlībi-l-qulūbi li ṭāʿatin
wa fī baʿḍi aḥyānin li maʿṣiyatin tasrī

And consider how that heart may turn in obedience
and then fall back into darkness and transgression,

وَجُلْتَ فِي أَرْضٍ مَعْ تَنَوُّعِ نَبْتِهَا   وَكَثْرَةِ مَا فِيهَا مِنَ السَّهْلِ والْوَعْرِ

Wa julta fī arḍin maʿ tanawwuʿi nabtihā
wa kathrati mā fīhā mina-s-sahli wa-l-waʿri

And consider the earth with its myriad plants
and its many flatlands and ascents,

وَجُلْتَ فِي أَسْرَارِ الْبِحَارِ وَحُوتِهَا   وَكَثْرَةِ أَمْوَاجٍ لَهَا حَاجِزٌ قَهْرِ

Wa julta fī asrāri-l-biḥāri wa ḥūtihā
wa kathrati amwājin lahā ḥājizun qahri

And the mysteries of the oceans and their fishes
and their numberless waves restrained by a barrier,

وَجُلْتَ فِي أَسْرَارِ الرِّيَاحِ وَجَلْبِهَا   لِغَيْمٍ وَسُحْبٍ قَدْ أَسَالَتْ مِنَ الْقَطْرِ

Wa julta fī asrāri-r-riyāḥi wa jalbihā
li ghaymin wa suḥbin qad asālat mina-l-qaṭri

And the mysteries of the winds and how they bring fog
and rainclouds streaming with drops,

وَجُلْتَ فِي أَسْرَارِ السَّمَاوَاتِ كُلِّهَا   وَعَرْشٍ وَكُرْسِيٍّ وَرُوحٍ مِنَ الْأَمْرِ

Wa julta fī asrāri-s-samāwāti kullihā
wa ʿarshin wa kursiyyin wa rūḥin mina-l-amri,

And the mysteries of the heavens and the Throne
and the Footstool and the Spirit by God's Command,

عَقَدْتَ عَلَى التَّوْحِيدِ عَقْدَ مُصَمِّمٍ   وَحُلْتَ عَنِ الْأَوْهَامِ وَالشَّكِّ وَالْغَيْرِ

ʿAqadta ʿala-t-tawḥīdi ʿaqda muṣammimin
wa ḥulta ʿani-l-awhāmi wa-sh-shakki wa-l-ghayri

You will affirm God's Unity with all of your being
and turn away from illusion, doubt, and otherness,

وَقُلْتَ إِلٰهِي أَنْتَ سُؤْلِي وَمَطْلَبِي   وَحِصْنِي مِنَ الْأَسْوَاءِ وَالضَّيْمِ وَالْمَكْرِ

Wa qulta ilāhī Anta su•lī wa maṭlabī
wa ḥiṣnī mina-l-aswā•i wa-ḍ-ḍaymi wa-l-makri

And will say, "Dear God, You are what I seek!
My refuge from wrong, and from injustice and deceit

وَأَنْتَ رَجَائِي فِي قَضَاءِ حَوَائِجِي   وَأَنْتَ الَّذِي تُنْجِي مِنَ السُّوءِ وَالشَّرِّ

Wa Anta rajā•ī fī qaḍā•i ḥawā•ijī
wa Anta-l-ladhī tunjī mina-s-sū•i wa-sh-sharri

You – my Hope in answering my needs
You – the One who will save me from evil and harm

وَأَنْتَ الرَّحِيمُ الْمُسْتَجِيبُ لِمَنْ دَعَاكَ   وَأَنْتَ الَّذِي تُغْنِي الْفَقِيرَ عَنِ الْفَقْرِ

Wa anta-r-Raḥīmu-l-Mustajību li man daʿāk
wa Anta-l-ladhī tughni-l-faqīra ʿani -l-faqri

You – the Compassionate Who answers those who call
You – the wealth of the needy in his need

إِلَيكَ رَفَعْتُ يَا رَفِيعُ مَطَالِبِي   فَعَجِّلْ بِفَتْحٍ يَا إِلٰهِي مَعَ السِّرِّ

Ilayka rafaʿtu yā Rafīʿu maṭālibī
faʿajjil bi fatḥīn yā Ilāhī maʿa-s-sirri

To You, the Sublime, I raise my voice in prayer:
Hasten to me with the Opening, dear God, and the Secret

بِجَاهِ الَّذِي يُرْجَى يَوْمَ الْكَرْبِ وَالْعَنَا   وَيَوْمَ وُرُودِ النَّاسِ لِلْمَوْقِفِ الْحَشْرِ

Bi jāhi-l-ladhī yurjā yawma-l-karbi wa-l-ʿanā
wa yawma wurūdi-n-nāsi li-l-mawqifi-l-Ḥashri

By the honor of the one [whose intercession] we hope for
on the day of distress, when we are brought to the Gathering,

عَلَيْهِ صَلاةُ اللهِ مَا جَالَ عَارِفٌ   فِي أَنْوَارِ ذَاتِهِ لَدَى كُلِّ مَظْهَرِ

ʿAlayhi ṣalātu-Llāhi mā jāla ʿārifun
fī anwāri dhātihi ladā kulli maẓhari

Upon him be the blessings of Allah as long as gnostics range
through the lights of His Essence in every theophany

وَآلِهِ وَالأَصْحَابِ مَعْ كُلِّ تَابِعٍ   لِسُنَّتِهِ الغَرَّاءِ فِي النَّهْيِ وَالأَمْرِ

Wa ālihi wa-l-aṣ•ḥābi maʿ kulli tābiʿin
li sunnatihi l-gharrā•i fi-n-nahyī wa-l-amri

And upon his people and companions and all those who follow
the Divine commandments by his shining way.

-12-

حلّة التقريب

The Robe of Nearness

قَدْ كَسَانَا ذِكْرُ الْحَبِيبِ جَمَالاً   وَبَهَاءً وَرِفْعَةً وَسُرُورَا

Qad kasānā dhikru-l-Ḥabībi jamālan
wa bahā•an wa rifᶜatan wa surūrā

*The Remembrance of the Beloved enrobed us in beauty
and in splendor, honor, and joy.*

وَخَلَعْنَا الْعِذَارَ عِنْدَ التَّدَانِي   وَجَهَرْنَا بِمَنْ نُحِبُّ افْتِخَارَا

Wa khalaᶜna-l-ᶜidhāra ᶜinda-t-tadānī
wa jaharnā bi man nuḥibbu-ftikhāra

*And as we drew near, we cast off all reserve
and proudly announced the One we love.*

وَسَقَانَا الْحَبِيبُ شُرْبَةَ حُبٍّ   قَدْ أَزَالَتْ سِوَى الْحَبِيبِ اضْطِرَارَا

Wa saqāna-l-Ḥabību shurbata ḥubbin
qad azālat siwā-l-Ḥabībi-ḍṭirārā

*And the Beloved gave us to drink from the wine of love
that made all else but Him disappear.*

وَشَهِدْنَا الْأَكْوَانَ مَحْضَ هَبَاءٍ   وَرَأَيْنَا الْأَنْوَارَ تَبْدُو جِهَارَا

Wa shahidna-l-akwāna maḥḍa habā•in
wa ra•ayna-l-anwāra tabdū jihārā

And we saw the world as motes of floating dust
and saw the lights openly appear.

وَرَجَعْنَا لِلْخَلْقِ بَعْدَ انْمِحَاقٍ   وَفَنَاءٍ فِي خَمْرَةٍ تُعْطِي نُورَا

Wa rajaʿnā li-l-khalqi baʿda-nmiḥāqin
wa fanā•in fī khamratin tuʿṭī nūrā

Then we came back to creatures after having passed away
and been effaced in that light-giving wine.

فَبِفَضْلٍ مِنَ الإِلٰهِ بَقِينَا   وَكَتَمْنَا الَّذِي نُحِبُّ اصْطِبَارَا

Fa bi faḍlin mina-l-ilāhi baqīnā
wa katamna-l-ladhī nuḥibbu-ṣṭibārā

And by the grace of God we were granted subsistence
and then concealed with patience the One we love.

كَمْ نَظَرْنَا فِي سَالِكٍ فَتَرَقَّى   لِمَقَامِ الَّذِينَ خَاضُوا الْبِحَارَا

Kam naẓarnā fī sālikin fa taraqqā
li maqāmi-l-ladhīna khāḍu-l-biḥārā

How many a wayfarer have we but looked upon
who then rose to the station of those who swim the seas!

وَشَفَيْنَا الْقُلُوبَ مِمَّا عَرَاهَا بِلَطِيفِ الْعُلُومِ ذَوْقاً فَطَارَا

Wa shafayna-l-qulūba mimmā ʿarāhā
bi laṭīfi-l-ʿulūmi dhawqan fa ṭārā

And hearts we have cured of what was ailing them
by a taste of subtle teachings, and they flew.

وَهَمَمْنَا بِالشَّيْءِ سِرًّا فَكَانَا وَأَتَانَا الَّذِي نُحِبُّ اخْتِيَارَا

Wa hamanā bi-sh-shayi sirran fa kānā
wa atāna-l-ladhī nuḥibbu-khtiyārā

And we have considered something secretly and it came to be,
and those we loved [as disciples] were brought to us as if by choice,

وَسَمِعْنَا مِنْ حَضْرَةِ الْغَيْبِ سِرًّا أَنْتَ مَحْبُوبٌ عِندَنَا كُنْ شَكُورَا

Wa samiʿnā min ḥaḍrati-l-ghaybi sirran
anta maḥbūbun ʿindanā kun shakūrā

And we heard in silence from the Unseen Presence:
"You are beloved to Me so be grateful!"

وأُذِنَّا بِسَقِي مَنْ جَاءَ شَوْقاً لِلِقَانَا وَلَمْ يَكُنْ ذَا اخْتِبَارَا

Wa udhinnā bi saqyi man jā•a shawqan
li-liqānā wa lam yakun dha-khtibārā

And we were allowed to quench the thirst of anyone who comes
yearning to meet us and not simply testing.

وَإِذَا كَانَتِ المَوَاهِبُ فَضْلاً   فَتَعَرَّضْ لَهَا وَكُنْ ذَا افْتِقَارَا

Wa idha kānati-l-mawāhibu faḍlan
fa taʿarraḍ lahā, wa kun dha-ftiqārā

If Divine gifts come to you by grace,
receive them gladly, yet as one who is needy.

وَتَذَلَّلْ لِأَهْلِهَا تُسْقَى مِنْهُمْ   وَتَقَرَّبْ لَهُمْ وَلاَ تَخْشَ عَارَا

Wa tadhallal li ahlihā tusqā minhum
wa taqarrab lahum wa lā takhsha ʿārā

Be humble towards those who bring them and from whom you drink,
and draw near to them and fear no blame.

وَتَجَرَّدْ مِنْ كُلِّ عِلْمٍ وَفَهْمٍ   لِتَنَالَ الَّذِي نَالُوهُ الْكِبَارَا

Wa tajarrad min kulli ʿilmin wa fahmin
li tanāla-l-ladhī nālūhu-l-kibārā

Renounce all the knowledge and understanding [you claim]
if you wish to attain what the saintly have attained.

وَابْذُلِ النَّفْسَ يَا مُحِبَّ الْوِصَالِ   وَاتْبَعِ الشَّيْخَ فِي الَّذِي قَدْ أَشَارَا

Wa-b-dhuli-n-nafsa yā muḥibba-l-wiṣāli
wa-tbaʿi-sh-shaykha fi-l-ladhī qad ashārā

And give freely of yourself, O you who love union,
and follow the teacher in what he has shown.

وَاشْهَدِ الْحَقَّ فِيهِ ذَاتاً وَقَلْبًا   وَافْنَ فِيهِ تَكُنْ بِهِ ذَا انْتِصَارَا

Wa-sh-hadi-l-ḥaqqa fīhi dhātan wa qalban
wa-fna fīhi takun bihi dha-ntiṣārā

Witness in him the truth that emanates from his heart
and be effaced in him – you will be given help.

فَهْوَ نُورُ الرَّسُولِ مِن كُلِّ وَجْهٍ   وَهْوَ طِبُّ الْقُلُوبِ سِرًّا وَجَهْـرَا

Fa hwa nūru-r-rasūli min kulli wajhin
wa hwa ṭibbu-l-qulūbi sirran wa jahrā

For in every way he is the light of the Messenger
and openly and secretly the medicine of hearts

فَالْحَظَنْهُ وَعَظِّمَنْهُ كَثِيرَا   وَاذْهَبَنْ عِنْدَهُ وَكُنْ ذَا انْكِسَارَا

Fa-lḥaẓanhu wa ʿaẓẓimanhu kathīrā
wa-dh-haban ʿindahu wa kun dha-nkisārā

Attend to him and esteem him in abundance.
Go to him and be humble in his presence

وَصَلَاةٌ عَلَى النَّبِيِّ وَآلٍ   وَصِحَابٍ وَمَنْ لَهُ قَدْ أَشَارَا

Wa ṣalātun ʿala-n-Nabīyyi wa ālin
wa ṣiḥābin wa man lahu qad ashārā

May blessings be upon the Prophet and his Family
and companions and those who've shown his way.

وَسَلَامٌ بِكُلِّ مِسْكٍ وَطِيبٍ   وَجَمَالٍ وَرِفْعَةٍ لَا تُجَارَا

Wa salāmun bi kulli miskin wa ṭībin
wa jamālin wa rifʿatin lā tujārā

And greetings of peace perfumed with musk and fragrance
and with beauty and honor that has no peer.

-13-

في روضة الرسول
In the Meadow of the Messenger

نَحْنُ فِي رَوْضَةِ الرَّسُولِ حُضُورٌ   طَالِبِينَ الرِّضَى وَحُسْنَ قَبُولِ

Naḥnu fī rawḍati-r-Rasūli ḥuḍūrun
ṭālibīna-r-riḍā wa ḥusna qabūli

We are present in the Meadow of the Messenger,
seeking Allah's contentment and most beautiful acceptance.

جِئْنَا يَا خَيْرَ مَنْ إِلَيْهِ الْمَلَاذُ   بِإِنْكِسَارٍ وَذِلَّةٍ وَذُهُولِ

Ji•nā yā khayra man ilayhi-l-malādhu
bi-nkisārin wa dhillatin wa dhuhūli

O you who are the best to turn to for shelter,
we come in humility, lowliness, and awe,

فَاسْأَلِ اللهَ فِينَا كُلَّ عِنَايَةْ   لِنَنَالَ الْمُنَى فِي وَقْتِ الحُلُولِ

Fas•ali-Llāha fīnā kulla ʿināya
li nanāla-l-munā fī waqti-l-ḥulūli

That you might ask Allah to grant us His help and protection
in reaching what we hope for at the time of reckoning.

لَكَ قَدْرٌ عَظِيمٌ لَيسَ يُضَاهَى   وَرِسَالَةْ تَفُوقُ كُلَّ رَسُولِ

Laka qadrun ʿaẓīmun laysa yuḍāhā
wa risālah tafūqu kulla rasūli

Yours is an immense station, beyond comparison,
and a message that is above every messenger.

أَنْتَ بَابُ الْإِلٰهِ فِي كُلِّ خَيْرٍ   مَنْ أَتَى فَازَ بِالرِّضَى وَالوُصُولِ

Anta bābu-l-Ilāhi fī kulli khayrin
man atā fāza bi-r-riḍā wa-l-wuṣūli

You are the door to God in all that is good.
Whoso comes to you gains acceptance and union.

كُلُّ سِرٍّ فِي الْأَنْبِيَا قَدْ أَتَاهُمْ   مِنْ عُلَاكُمْ مُؤَيَّدًا بِنُقُولِ

Kullu sirrin fi-l-anbiyā qad atāhum
min ʿulākum mu•ayyadan bi nuqūli

Every mystery of the prophets came from your sublimity
and then was confirmed by scriptures passed down.

قَدْ تَشَفَّعْتُ فِي أُمُورِي إِلَٰهِي   بِالنَّبِيِّ الْمُشَفَّعِ الْمَقْبُولِ

Qad tashaffaʿtu fī umūrī ilāhī
bi-n-Nabīyyi-l-mushaffaʿi-l-maqbūli

In every matter that confronts me I seek intercession with my God
from the Prophet, whose intercession is accepted.

كُلُّ مَنْ حَطَّ رَحْلَهُ بِكَرِيمٍ   نَالَ أَقْصَى الْمُنَى وَكُلَّ السُّولِ

Kullu man ḥaṭṭa raḥlahu bi-karīmin
nāla aqṣa-l-munā wa kulla-s-sūli

All who arrive at the abode of a noble
attain their greatest hopes and supplications.

قَدْ شَكَرْنَا الإِلَهَ فِي كُلِّ وَقْتٍ   حَيْثُ مَنَّ بِزَوْرَةٍ لِلرَّسُولِ

Qad shakarnā-l-Ilāhā fī kulli waqtin
ḥaythu manna bi zawratin li-r-Rasūli

We give thanks to God at every single moment
for having blessed us with this visit to the Messenger

وَكَذَاكَ لِكُلِّ مَنْ فِي بَقِيعٍ   مِنْ صِحَابٍ كَذَاكَ نَسْلُ الْبَتُولِ

Wa kadhāka li-kulli man fī baqīᶜin
min ṣiḥābin kadhāka naslu-l-batūli

And also a visit to all the Companions who rest
in the Baqīᶜ and the children of Fatima,

وَكَذَاكَ لِكُلِّ زَوْجٍ وَبِنْتٍ   وَابْنِ مُنْجِي الأَنَامِ يَوْمَ الْحُلُولِ

Wa kadhāka li-kulli zawjin wa bintin
wa-bni munjī-l-anāmi yawma-l-ḥulūli

And also a visit to all the wives and daughters
and the son of the deliverer on the Day of Reckoning.

وَكَذَاكَ لِكُلِّ مَنْ فِي أُحُدٍ   مِنْ شَهِيدٍ كَذَاكَ عَمُّ الرَّسُولِ

Wa kadhāka li kulli man fī Uḥudin
min shahīdin kadhāka ʿammu-r-Rasūli

And also a visit to the martyrs of Uḥud
and also to the uncle of the Messenger.

قَدْ طَلَبْنَا بِهِمْ تَمَامَ السَّلَامَةْ   فِي مَسِيرٍ لِأَرْضِنَا وَالدُّخُوْلِ

Qad ṭalabnā bihim tamāma-s-salāma
fī masīrin li arḍinā wa-d-dukhūli

We ask You by their sanctity for perfect peace and safety
on our journey back home and our arrival.

وَطَلَبْنَا النَّجَاةَ فِي يَوْمِ حَشْرٍ   وَسَلَاماً مِنْ كُلِّ فَظٍّ جَهُولِ

Wa ṭalabna-n-najāta fī yawmi ḥashrin
wa salāman min kulli faẓẓin jahūli

And we seek deliverance on the Day of Gathering
and safety from all who are ignorant and coarse.

رَبِّ صَلِّ عَلَى النَّبِيِّ وَآلٍ   وَصِحَابٍ وَتَابِعٍ بِشُمُولِ

Rabbi ṣalli ʿalā-n-Nabīyyi wa ālin
wa ṣiḥābin wa tābiʿin bi shumūli

My Lord send blessings that are all inclusive
upon the Prophet, his Family, his Companions, and their successors.

-14-

قد بدا
Qad badā

قَدْ بَدَا وَجْهُ الْحَبِيبِ   لاَحَ فِي وَقْتِ السَّحَرْ

Qad badā wajhu-l-Ḥabībi
laḥa fī waqti-s-saḥar

The Beloved's Face appeared
and shone in the hour before dawn.

نُورُهُ قَدْ عَمَّ قَلْبِي   فَسَجَدْتُ بِانْكِسَارْ

Nūruhu qad ʿamma qalbī
fa sajadtu bi-nkisār

Its light enveloped my heart
and humbly I prostrated

قَالَ لِي ارْفَعْ وَاسْأَلْنِّي   فَلَكُمْ كُلُّ وَطَرْ

Qāla li-r-faʿ wa-s•alannī
fa lakum kullu waṭar

He said: Arise and ask of Me!
Whatever you desire is yours.

قُلْتُ أَنْتَ أَنْتَ حَسْبِي   لَيْسَ لِي عَنْكَ اصْطِبَارْ

Qultu: Anta, Anta ḥasbī
laysa lī ʿanka-ṣṭibār

I said: You! You are all I need!
I cannot bear to be without You!

قَالَ عَبْدِي لَكَ بُشْرَى   فَتَنَعَّمْ بِالنَّظَرْ

Qāla ʿabdī laka bushrā
fa tanaʿʿam bi-n-naẓar

He said: My servant, glad tidings are yours.
rejoice in the vision you've been given!

أَنْتَ كَنْزٌ لِعِبَادِي   أَنْتَ ذِكْرَى لِلْبَشَرْ

Anta kanzun li ʿibādī
anta dhikrā li-l-bashar

You are a treasure for My servants.
You are a reminder for humanity.

كُلُّ حُسْنٍ وَجَمَالٍ   فِي الْوَرَى مِنِّي انْتَشَرْ

Kullu ḥusnin wa jamālin
fi-l-warā minnī-ntashar

Know that all goodness and beauty
in humanity spreads forth from Me.

بَطَنَتْ أَوْصَافُ ذَاتِي وَتَجَلَّتْ فِي الأَثَرْ

Baṭanat awṣāfu dhātī
wa tajallat fi-l-athar

The attributes of My Essence are hidden,
and unveiled in the traces (of creation).

إِنَّمَا الْكَوْنُ مَعَانٍ قَائِمَاتٌ بِالصُّوَرْ

Innama-l-kawnu maʿānin
qā•imātun bi-ṣ-ṣuwar

The cosmos is truly only spirit
existing in forms.

كُلُّ مَنْ يُدْرِكُ هَذَا كَانَ مِنْ أَهْلِ الْعِبَرْ

kullu man yudriku hādhā
kāna min ahli-l-ʿibar

All who grasp this (subtle allusion)
are among the people of wisdom,

لَمْ يَذُقْ لَذَّةَ عَيْشٍ اَلَّذِي عَنَّا انْحَصَرْ

Lam yadhuq ladhdhata ʿayshin
al-ladhī ʿannā-nḥaṣar

While no one who stays apart from us
can taste life's real sweetness.

رَبَّنَا صَلِّ عَلَى مَنْ نُورُهُ عَمَّ الْبَشَرْ

Rabbanā ṣalli ʿalā man
nūruhu ʿamma-l-bashar

Our Lord, bless the one
whose light envelops humanity.

-15-

محمد منشؤ الأنوار والظلل

Muḥammad is the Source of Light and Shade

مُحَمَّدٌ مَنْشَؤُ الأَنْوَارِ وَالظِّلَلِ   وَأَصْلُ تَكْوِينِهَا مِن حَضْرَةِ الأَزَلِ

Muḥammadun mansha•u-l-anwāri wa-ẓ-ẓilali
wa aṣlu takwīnihā min ḥaḍrati–l-azali

Muḥammad is the source of light and shade
and the origin of their creation from the Eternal Presence.

فَنُورُهُ أَوَّلُ الْأَنْوَارِ لَمَّا قَضَى   إِظْهَارَ أَسْمَائِهِ فِي الْعَالَمِ الْأَوَّلِ

Fa nūruhu awwalu-l-anwāri lammā qaḍā
iẓhāra asmā•ihi fi-l-ʿālami-l-awwali

His light was the first of the lights when Allah decreed
That His Names be manifest in the principial world.

مِنْهُ اكْتَسَتْ سَائِرُ الأَشْيَاءِ إِيجَادَهَا   وَمِنْهُ إِمْدَادُهَا مِنْ غَيْرِ مَا خَلَلِ

Minhu-ktasat sā•iru-l-ashyā•i ījādahā
wa minhu imdāduhā min ghayri mā khalali

From this light all things donned the raiment of existence,
and from it their being is ceaselessly sustained.

تَقَاطَرَ الْأَنْبِيَا وَالرُّسْلُ مِنْهُ كَمَا   تَقَاطَرَتْ سَائِرُ الْأَمْلَاكِ وَالْحُلَلِ

Taqāṭara-l-anbiyā wa-r-ruslu minhu kamā
taqāṭarat sā•iru-l-amlāki wa-l-ḥulali

From it flowed forth the stream of prophets and messengers;
from it all the angels and degrees of beauty.

فَنِسْبَةُ الْخَتْمِ وَالأَقْطَابِ مِنْ نُورِهِ   كَنُقْطَةٍ مِنْ بُحُورِ النُّوْرِ وَالْبَلَلِ

Fa nisbatu-l-khatmi wa-l-aqṭābi min nūrihi
ka nuqṭatin min buḥūri-n-nūri wa-l-balali

The Seal and the Poles in relation to his light
are like a droplet and the mist from luminous oceans.

وَالشَّمْسُ وَالْبَدْرُ وَالنُّجُومُ مِنْهُ بَدَتْ   كَالْعَرْشِ وَاللَّوْحِ وَالْكُرْسِيِّ وَالدُّوَلِ

Wa -sh-shamsu wa -l-badru wa-n-nujūmu minhu badat
ka-l-ʿarshi wa-l-lawḥi wa-l-kursīyyi wa-d-duwali

From it came forth the sun, moon, and stars,
the Throne, Tablet, Footstool, and all sublime domains.

فَشَاهِدِ النُّوْرَ قَدْ عَمَّ الْوُجُودَ وَلاَ   تَكُنْ تَرَى غَيْرَهُ تَصِلْ عَلَى عَجَلِ

Fa shāhidi-n-nūra qad ʿamma-l-wujūda wa lā
takun tarā ghayrahu taṣil ʿalā ʿajali

So see this light which envelops all existence –
see nothing else and you will quickly arrive.

لِأَنَّهُ المَظْهَرُ الأَعْلَى لِأَسْمَائِهِ وَسِرُّ أَوْصَافِهِ مِنْ غَيْرِ مَا عِلَلِ

Li annahu-l-maẓharu-l-aʿlā li asmā·ihi
wa sirru awṣāfihi min ghayri mā ʿilali

He is the highest manifestation of the Names;
he is the flawless mystery of the Qualities.

فَاللهُ إِخْتَارَهُ فِي عِلْمِهِ القَدِيمِ لِلْخَلْقِ أَرْسَلَهُ طُرًّا وَلِلرُّسُلِ

Fa-Llāhu ikhtārahu fī ʿilmihi-l-qadīmi
li-l-khalqi arsalahu ṭurran wa li-r-rusuli

Allah chose him in His eternal knowledge
and sent him for all creatures and all Messengers.

أَسْرَى بِهِ اللهُ لَيْلاً بَعْدَ مَبْعَثِهِ لِقَابِ قَوْسَيْنِ حَتَّى فَازَ بِالأَمَلِ

Asrā bihi-Llāhu laylan baʿda mabʿathihi
li qābi qawsayni ḥattā fāza bi-l-amali

After his advent, Allah conveyed him by night
to within two bow-lengths that his hope might be granted.

وَاسْتَبْشَرَ العَالَمُ العُلْوِيُّ لَمَّا رَقَى وَالْعَرْشُ قَدْ حَصَّلَ الْأَمَانَ مِنْ وَجَلِ

Wa-stabshara-l-ʿālamu-l-ʿulwiyyu lammā raqā
wa-l-ʿarshu qad ḥaṣṣala-l-amāna min wajali

And the sublime realm rejoiced when he ascended,
and the Throne gave him shelter from fear.

وَاخْتَرَقَ الْحُجْبَ وَالْأَنْوَارَ حَتَّى دَنَا وَنُودِيَ ادْنُ حَبِيبِي وَاسْكُنْ مِنْ خَجَلِ

Wa-khtaraqa- l-ḥūjba wa-l-anwāra ḥattā danā
wa nūdiya-dnu Ḥabībī wa-skun min khajali

And he pierced the veils and lights until he drew near
and was called to: "Approach, My Beloved, and be not shy."

وَمَتِّعِ اللَّحْظَ فِي أَنْوَارِنَا وَاطْلُبَنْ كُلَّ الَّذِي شِئْتَهُ تُعْطَ بِلاَ مَلَلِ

Wa mattiʿi-l-laḥẓa fī anwārinā wa-ṭluban
kulla-l-ladhī shi'tahu tuʿṭa bilā malali

"Let your gaze find pleasure in the vision of Our lights,
and ask all you desire. You will be given without stint."

فَأُرْجِعَ الْمُصْطَفَى بِكُلِّ مَكْرُمَةٍ وَأَخْبَرَ النَّاسَ بِالأَقْصَا وَبِالسُّبُلِ

Fa urjiʿa-l-Muṣṭafā bi kulli makrumatin
wa akhbara-n-nāsa bi-l-aqṣā wa bi-s-subuli

Then the Chosen One was returned bearing every honor,
and told people of the Furthest Mosque and the paths.

فَلُذْ بِهِ يَا أَخِي فِي كُلِّ مُعْضِلَةٍ يَضْحَى حَدِيثُكَ بَيْنَ النَّاسِ كَالعَسَلِ

Fa ludh bihi yā akhī fī kulli muʿḍilatin
yaḍḥā ḥadīthuka bayna-n-nāsi ka-l-ʿasali

So, my brother, keep to [his way] in the face of every problem
and your discourse among people will become like honey.

وَلَذِّذِ السَّمْعَ بِالأَخْلَاقِ وَالشِّيَمِ وَاذْكُرْ شَمَآئِلَهُ وَاحْذَرْ مِنَ الزَّلَلِ

Wa ladhdhidhi-s-samᶜa bi-l-akhlāqi wa-sh-shiyami
wa-dhkur shamā•ilahu wa-ḥdhar mina-z-zalali

Find delight in hearing of his character and person
speak about his qualities and be careful not to slip.

فَكَمْ خَوَارِقَ قَدْ جَاءَتْ عَلَى يَدِهِ فَأَعْجَزَتْ سَائِرَ الحُسَّادِ وَالمِلَلِ

Fa kam khawāriqa qad jā•at ᶜalā yadihi
fa aᶜjazat sā•ira-l-ḥussādi wa-l-milali

How many were the miracles that came to pass by his hand
that enviers and religions were powerless [to explain].

وَإِنَّ أَعْظَمَ خَارِقٍ لَهُ ظَهَرَا هَذَا الكِتَابُ الَّذِي قَدْ جَاءَ بِالعَمَلِ

Wa inna aᶜẓama khāriqin lahu ẓaharā
hādha-l-kitābu-l-ladhī qad jā•a bi-l-ᶜamali

And the greatest of miracles that through him appeared
is this Book which came with its practice.

فِي كُلِّ جَارِحَةٍ مِنْهُ فَوَائِدُ لاَ يُحْصِيهَا عَدٌّ وَلاَ تُدْرِكْهَا بِالمُقَلِ

Fī kulli jāriḥatin minhu fawā•idu lā
yuḥṣīhā ᶜaddun wa lā tudrik-hā bi-l-muqali

In each of his limbs were benefits beyond reckon
and beyond perception by the physical eye.

وَقَدْ أَحَاطَ كِتَابُ اللهِ مِنهَا بِمَا يُبْرِئُ كُلَّ سَقِيمِ القَلْبِ مِنْ عِلَلِ

Wa qad aḥāṭa kitābu-Llāhi minhā bi mā
Yubri•u kulla saqīmi-l-qalbi min ʿilali

From among them the Book of Allah has enclosed
that which cures every illness of the heart.

وَلَيْسَ يَقْدُرُ قَدْرَهُ الْعَظِيمَ فَتًى فَالعَجْزُ عَنْ مَدْحِهِ مِن أَحْسَنِ السُّبُلِ

Wa laysa yaqduru qadrahu-l-ʿaẓīma fatan
fa-l-ʿajzu ʿan madḥihi min aḥsani-s-subuli

Since none can reckon the immensity of his station
being unable to truly praise him is the best of paths.

وَقَدْ تَشَبَّهْتُ فِي مَدْحِي وَجِئْتُ إِلَى رُحْمَاكَ مُسْتَشْفِعًا لِلهِ تَشْفَعُ لِي

Wa qad tashabbahtu fī madḥī wa ji•tu ilā
ruḥmāka mustashfiʿan li-Llāhi tashfaʿu lī

In my praise I've copied [others] and to your mercy I have come
Seeking the intercession with Allah that you can grant.

يَا أَعْظَمَ الْخَلْقِ عِنْدَ اللهِ مَنْزِلَةً اِعْطِفْ عَلَيْنَا بِمَا نَرْجُوهُ يَا أَمَلِي

Yā aʿẓama-l-khalqi ʿinda-Llāhi manzilatan
iʿṭif ʿalaynā bi mā narjūhu yā amalī

O my hope, O you whose station is greatest with Allah!
Be kind to us in that for which we wish.

مَنْ يَحْتَمِي بِكَ يَضْحَى الكَوْنُ يَخْدُمُهُ   لِأَجْلِ جَاهِكَ يَا مُمِدَّ كُلِّ وَلِي

Man yaḥtamī bika yaḍḥa-l-kawnu yakhdumuhu
li ajli jāhika yā mumidda kulli walī

Creation serves the one who seeks shelter in you,
by your honor. You who are the aid of every saint!

بِكَ احْتَمَيْتُ فَلاَ تَكِلْنِي يَا سَنَدِي   لِلنَّفْسِ وَالجِنْسِ وَاجْبُرْنَا مِنَ الخَلَلِ

Bika-ḥtamaytu fa lā takilnī, yā sanadī
bi-n-nafsi wa-l-jinsi wa-jburnā mina-l-khalali

O my support! With you I seek shelter, so do not leave me
to the ego or the body, and heal us of our faults.

وَ لَيْسَ يُلْحَقُ عَبْدٌ أَنْتَ نَاصِرُهُ   فَأَنْتَ لِي عُمْدَةٌ فِي السَّهْلِ وَالجَبَلِ

Wa laysa yulḥaqu ʿabdun anta nāṣiruhu
fa anta lī ʿumdatun fi-s-sahli wa-l-jabali

A servant will not be overcome if you are his ally.
you are my staff in the flatlands and mountains.

وَقَدْ تَحَيَّرْتُ فِي أَمْرِي فَخُذْ بِيَدِي   فَلَا تَحَوُّلَ لِي عَنْ نُورِكَ الأَوَّلِ

Fa qad taḥayyartu fī amrī fa khudh bi yadī
fa lā taḥawwula lī ʿan nūrika-l-awwali

I am confused in my way so take me by the hand.
for me there is no turning from your principial light.

صَلَّى عَلَيْكَ إِلٰهُ الْعَرْشِ مَا ظَهَرَتْ   شَمْسُ الحَقِيقَةِ بِالأَسْمَاءِ وَالفِعَالِ

Ṣallā ʿalāyka Ilāhu-l-ʿarshi mā ẓahara
shamsu-l-ḥaqīqati bi-l-asmā•i wa-l-fiʿāli

May the God of the Throne send blessings upon you
as long as the sun of inner truth shines through the Names and Acts.

كَذَاكَ آلُكَ وَالأَصْحَابُ مَا نَبَتَتْ   عُشْبٌ وَمَا سَحَّتِ السَّمَاءُ مِن بَلَلِ

Kadhāka āluka wa-l-aṣ•ḥābu mā nabatat
ʿushbun wa mā saḥḥati-s-samā'u min balali

And upon your Family and Companions as long as new grass sprouts
and the sky pours down its moisture on the earth.

ثُمَّ الرِّضَى عَنْ رِجَالِ اللهِ كُلِّهِمِ   مَا سَبَّحَ الكَوْنُ مَنْ يُجَلُّ عَنْ مَثَلِ

Thumma-r-riḍā ʿan rijāli-Llāhi kullihimi
mā sabbaḥa-l-kawnu man yujallu ʿan mathali

And may divine contentment be with all the men of Allah
As long as creation glorifies the One beyond compare.

وَابْسُطْ لِإِخْوَانِنَا الْخَيْرَاتِ أَجْمَعَهَا   دُنْيَا وَأُخْرَى وَلَا تَكِلْنَا لِلْعَمَلِ

Wa-bsuṭ li ikhwānina-l-khayrāti ajmaʿahā
dunyā wa ukhrā wa lā takilnā li-l-ʿamali

Bestow upon our brethren goodness that includes
this world and the Next, and do not leave us to our deeds.

وَاغْفِرْ لِوَالِدِينَا الزَّلاَّتِ أَجْمَعَهَا   وَالمُسْلِمِينَ بِفَضْلٍ مِنْكَ يَا أَزَلِي

wa-ghfir li wālidīnā-z-zallāti ajmaʿahā
wa-l-muslimīna bi faḍlin minka yā Azalī

And O Allah, Eternal, forgive our parents their mistakes
and forgive all the Muslims by Your Infinite Grace.

-16-

الاستغفار

Asking Forgiveness

أَسْتَغْفِرُاللهَ إِنَّ اللهَ ذُوْ كَرَمٍ   وَرَحْمَةٍ لِلَّذِي قَدْ تابَ مِنْ زَلَلِ

Astaghfiru-Llāha inna-Llāha dhū karamin
wa raḥmatin li-ladhī qad tāba min zalali

I ask forgiveness from Allah. Truly, Allah is Most Generous
and Merciful to the one who turns from his errors in repentance.

أَسْتَغْفِرُاللهَ مِن ذَنْبٍ وَمِنْ زَلَلٍ   وَمِنْ خَطَايَا وَمِنْ وَهْمٍ وَمِنْ أَمَلِ

Astaghfiru-Llāha min dhanbin wa min zalali
wa min khaṭāyā wa min wahmin wa min amali

I ask forgiveness from Allah for my sins and errors
and for transgressions, illusions, and false hopes.

أَسْتَغْفِرُاللهَ مِن كِبْرٍ وَمِن حَسَدٍ   وَمِن رِيَاءٍ لِأَهْلِ المَالِ بِالعَمَلِ

Astaghfiru-Llāha min kibrin wa min ḥasadin
wa min riyā•in li ahli-l-māli bi-l-ʿamali

I ask forgiveness from Allah for my pride and envy,
and for pretentious actions done before the wealthy.

أَسْتَغْفِرُ اللهَ مِنْ ظَنٍّ قَبِيحٍ بَدَا   مِنْ رُؤْيَةِ النَّفْسِ عُجْباً مِنْهَا بِالحُلَلِ

Astaghfiru-Llāha min ẓannin qabīḥin badā
Min ru•yati-n-nafsi ʿujban minhā bi-l-ḥulali

I ask forgiveness from Allah for any ugly thought [I've had]
of another because of being impressed by myself.

أَسْتَغْفِرُ اللهَ مِنْ غِلٍّ وَحِقْدٍ وَمَا   أَضْمَرْتُ فِي سَالِفِ الأَعْمَارِ مِنْ عِلَلِ

Astaghfiru-Llāha min ghillin wa ḥiqdin wa mā
aḍmartu fī sālifi-l-aʿmāri min ʿilali

I ask forgiveness from Allah for rancor and envy
and for the flaws I concealed in my earlier days.

أَسْتَغْفِرُ اللهَ مِنْ نُطْقٍ بِفَاحِشَةٍ   وَمِنْ سُكُوتٍ عَنْ غِيْبَةٍ وَعَنْ خَلَلِ

Astaghfiru-Llāha min nuṭqin bi fāḥishatin
wa min sukūtin ʿan ghībatin wa ʿan khalali

I ask forgiveness from Allah for uttering base words
and for my silence in the presence of slander and hurt.

أَسْتَغْفِرُ اللهَ مِنْ زُورٍ وَمِنْ كَذِبٍ   وَمِنْ غُرُورٍ يَجُرُّ النَّفْسَ لِلْكَسَلِ

Astaghfiru-Llāha min zūrin wa min kadhibin
wa min ghurūrin yajurru-n-nafsa li-l-kasali

I ask forgiveness from Allah for fabrications and lies
and for self-deceptions which have let me be lazy.

أَسْتَغْفِرُ اللهَ مِنْ ذَنْبٍ بِجَارِحَةٍ   وَمِنْ حُقُوقٍ أَتَتْ لِلنَّاسِ مِنْ قِبَلِي

Astaghfiru-Llāha min dhanbin bi jāriḥatin
wa min ḥuqūqin atat li-n-nāsi min qibalī.

*I ask forgiveness from Allah for using my faculties for sin,
and for anything I've done that trespasses people's rights.*

أَسْتَغْفِرُ اللهَ مِنْ عِلْمٍ أَزِيغُ بِهِ   عَنِ الصِّرَاطِ القَوِيمِ الْمُفْضِي لِلْوَجَلِ

Astaghfiru-Llāha min ʿilmin azīghu bihi
ʿani-ṣ-ṣirāṭi-l-qawīmi-l-mufḍī li-l-wajali

*I ask forgiveness from Allah for any knowledge that makes me stray
from the straight path which requires the fear of Allah.*

أَسْتَغْفِرُ اللهَ مِنْ حَالٍ أَصُولُ بِهِ   وَمِنْ مَقَامٍ أَدَّى لِلْخَوفِ وَالْخَجَلِ

Astaghfiru-Llāha min ḥālin aṣūlu bihi
wa min maqāmin addā li-l-khawfi wa-l-khajali

*I ask forgiveness from Allah for any state in which I am overbearing
and for any station which leads to fear and shame.*

أَسْتَغْفِرُ اللهَ مِنْ فِعْلٍ بِلاَ نِيَّةٍ   وَمِنْ ذُهُولٍ أَتَى لِلْقَلْبِ عَنْ عَجَلِ

Astaghfiru-Llāha min fiʿlin bilā niyyatin
wa min dhuhūlin atā li-l-qalbi ʿan ʿajali

*I ask forgiveness from Allah for an action without intention
and for my heart's being distracted from the transience of this life.*

أَسْتَغْفِرُ اللهَ مِنْ دَعْوَى الحُلُولِ وَمِنْ   دَعْوَى اتِّحَادٍ أَدَّى لِلزَّيْغِ وَالْفَشَلِ

Astaghfiru-Llāha min daʿwā-l-ḥulūli wa min
daʿwā-ttiḥādin addā li-z-zayghi wa-l-fashali

I ask forgiveness from Allah for the claim of incarnation
and of "being joined into one" which bring deviation and failure.

أَسْتَغْفِرُ اللهَ مِن دَعْوَى الْوُجُودِ وَمِن   إِثْبَاتِ شَيءٍ سِوَى الْمَوجُودِ فِي الأزَلِ

Astaghfiru-Llāha min daʿwā-l-wujūdi wa min
ithbāti shay•in siwā-l-Mawjūdi fi-l-azali

I ask forgiveness of Allah for the claim of existence
and for affirming anything except the One Who eternally is.

أَسْتَغْفِرُ اللهَ مِنْ عَقَائِدٍ طَرَأَتْ   قَدْ خَالَفَتْ مِنْهَاجَ الْمُخْتَارِ وَالرُّسُلِ

Astaghfiru-Llāha min ʿaqā•idin ṭara•at
qad khālafat minhāja-l-mukhtāri wa-r-rusuli

I ask forgiveness from Allah for doctrines that are contrary
to the path of the Chosen Prophet and the Messengers

أَسْتَغْفِرُ اللهَ مِن جَهْلٍ وَمِنْ سَفَهٍ   وَمِنْ فُتُورٍ أَتَى لِلنَّفْسِ عَنْ مَلَلِ

Astaghfiru-Llāha min jahlin wa min safahin
Wa min futūrin atā li-n-nafsi ʿan malali

I ask forgiveness from Allah for ignorance and stupidity
and for apathy that arises from boredom in the soul.

أَسْتَغْفِرُ اللهَ مِنْ فِكْرٍ أَجُولُ بِهِ   بِلَا اعْتِبَارٍ جَرَى فِي الْعُلْوِي وَالسُّفُلِ

Astaghfiru-Llāha min fikrin ajūlu bihi
bilaʿtibārin jarā fi-l-ʿulwī wa-sufuli

I ask forgiveness from Allah for any idea I've followed—
whether exalted or mundane—without reflection.

أَسْتَغْفِرُ اللهَ مِقْدَارَ الْعَوَالِمِ مِنْ   عَرْشٍ وَلَوْحٍ وَعُمْرِ سَائِرِ الدُّوَلِ

Astaghfiru-Llāha miqdāra-l-ʿawālimi min
ʿarshin wa lawḥin wa ʿumri sā•iri-d-duwali

I ask forgiveness of Allah to the extent of all the worlds,
from the Throne and Tablet, as long as nations exist.

أَسْتَغْفِرُ اللهَ وَهَّابَ الْعَطَايَا لِمَنْ   قَدِ اتَّقَاهُ بِلَا حَوْلٍ وَلَا حِيَلِ

Astaghfiru-Llāha Wahhāba-l-ʿaṭāyā liman
qadi-ttaqāhu bilā ḥawlin wa lā ḥiyali

I ask forgiveness of Allah who grants every gift to one
who truly fears Him and abandons his own ruses and power.

أَسْتَغْفِرُ اللهَ مُعْطِى مَنْ يَلُوذُ بِهِ   مَعَارِفًا بِطُرُوْقِ العِلْمِ وَالنِّحَلِ

Astaghfiru-Llāha Muʿṭī man yalūdhu bihi
maʿārifan bi-ṭurūqi-l-ʿilmi wa-n-niḥali

I ask forgiveness of Allah who gives to the one who seeks shelter in Him
knowledge of the paths of sciences and doctrines.

أَسْتَغْفِرُاللهَ رَحْمَانَ الخَلاَئِقِ مِنْ جِنٍّ وَإِنْسٍ وَأَمْلاَكٍ وَكُلِّ عَالِي

Astaghfiru-Llāha Raḥmāna-l-khalā•iqi min
jinnin wa insin wa amlākin wa kulli ʿālī

I ask forgiveness of Allah, the Most Merciful to all creatures,
be they jinn, or humans, or angels, or any of the sublime

رَبِّ بِأَحْمَدَ كُنْ لِأَمْرِنَا وَلِيًّا وَمُرْشِداً لِإِتِّبَاعِ أَقْوَمِ السُّبُلِ

Rabbi bi Aḥmada kun li amrinā Waliyyan
wa murshidan li ittibāʿi aqwami-s-subuli

Dear Lord, by the honor of Ahmad, be our protector in all matters
and a guide to those who follow the straightest of paths.

عَلَيْهِ أَزْكَى صَلاَةِ اللهِ مَا هَطَلَتْ غَيْثٌ وَمَا قَدْ سَرَى فِي الأَرْضِ مِنْ بَلَلِ

ʿAlayhi azkā ṣalāti-Llāhi mā haṭalat
ghaythun wa mā qad sarā fi-l-arḍi min balali

Upon him be the purest of Allah's blessings as long as rains
pour down and moisture flows within the earth.

كَذَاكَ آلُكَ وَالْصَّحْبُ الْكِرَامُ وَمَنْ قَدِ اقْتَفَى إِثْرَهُمْ مِن مُتَّقٍ وَوَلِي

Kadhāka āluka wa-ṣ-ṣaḥbu-l-kirāmu wa man
qadi-qtafā ithrahum min muttaqin wa walī

And upon his Family as well, and the Noble Companions,
and every pious one and saint who walks in their footsteps.

-17-

الوهم
Illusion

كَانَ لِي وَهْمٌ فَلَمَّا أَنْ رَحَلْ   أَشْرَفَ القَلْبُ عَلَى نُورِ الأَزَلْ

Kāna lī wahmun falammā an raḥal
ashrafa-l-qalbu ʿalā nūri-l-azal

I had an illusion and when it departed
my heart looked out upon a Light from eternity.

رَكِبَ الشَّوْقَ الَّذِي طَارَ بِهِ   فَدَنَا مِنْ حِبِّهِ حَتَّى اتَّصَلْ

Rakiba-sh-shawqa-l-ladhī ṭāra bihi
fa danā min ḥibbihi ḥattā-ttaṣal

Then it mounted upon its yearning and flew forth to be near
to the One it loves until it arrived.

شَاهَدَ الْكَوْنَ خَيَالاً زَائِلاً   وَانْمَحَى رَسْمُ الوُجُودِ وَأَفَلْ

Shāhada-l-kawna khayālan zā•ilan
wa-nmaḥā rasmu-l-wujūdi wa afal

It beheld the cosmos as a fading chimera
and the forms of existence were effaced and disappeared.

ثُمَّ رُدَّ لِلْبَقَاءِ مُثْبِتًا   جَمِيعَ الكَوْنِ الَّذِي عَنْهُ انْعَزَلْ

Thumma rudda li-l-baqā•i muthbitan
jamīʿa-l-kawni-l-ladhī ʿanhu-nʿazal

Then was it returned to the state of subsistence,
and reaffirmed the cosmos from which it had withdrawn.

جَمَعَ الضِّدَّيْنِ فِي مَشْهَدِهِ   وَحَّدَ اللهَ وَقَامَ بِالعَمَلْ

Jamaʿa-ḍ-ḍiddayni fī mash•hadihi
waḥḥada-Llāha wa qāma bi-l-ʿamal

In this station it united all of the opposites
and affirmed Allah's Oneness inwardly through deeds.

حَازَ سِرًّا وَصِرَاطاً سَوِيًّا   قَلَّ مَنْ ذَاقَهُ مِنْ أَهْلِ الْكَمَالْ

Ḥāza sirran wa ṣirāṭan sawīyyan
qalla man dhāqahu min ahli-l-kamāl

It attained to a secret and a straight and level path
which only a few among the saintly taste.

رَبَّنَا صَلِّ عَلَى النُّورِ الَّذِي   كُلُّ عَبْدٍ أَمَّهُ حَازَ الأَمَلْ

Rabbanā ṣalli ʿalā-n-nūri-l-ladhī
kullu ʿabdin ammahu ḥāza-l-amal.

Our Lord, send blessings upon that Light—
he who takes him as imam attains his desire.

وَارْضَ عَنْ آلِهِ هُمْ أَهْلُ النُّهَى   وَصِحَابٍ مَعَ قُطْبٍ وَبَدَلْ

Wa-rḍa ʿan ālihi hum ahlu-n-nuhā
wa ṣiḥābin maʿa quṭbin wa badal.

And may You be well-pleased with his Family, the people of intellect, and the Companions, and the Pole, and the greatest of the saints.

-18-

الشهود والعيان

Seeing the Divine

يَا مَنْ يُرِدْ حَضْرَةَ العِيَانِ   إِرْقَ عَنِ الرُّوْحِ وَالأَوَانِي

Yā man yurid ḥaḍrata-l-ᶜiyāni
irqa ᶜani-r-rūḥi wa-l-awānī

O you who seek a vision of the Divine,
rise above both the spirit and the form.

وَالْعَدَمَ الأَصْلِيَّ الْزَمْنَهُ   وَكُنْ كَأَنْ لَمْ تَكُنْ يَا فَانِي

Wa-l-ᶜadama-l-aṣliyy-alzamnahu
wa kun ka•an lam takun yā fānī

And stay with primordial non-being:
be as if you are not – you who are effaced!

تَرَى بِسِرٍّ وُجُوْداً حَقًّا   سَرَتْ مَعَانِيْهِ فِي كُلِّ آنِ

Tarā bi sirrin wujūdan ḥaqqan
sarat maᶜānīhi fī kulli āni

You will see by a secret True Being,
its meanings flowing within every moment,

فَلَمْ يُعَدِّدْ ذَا الفِعْلِ شَيْءٌ مِنْ صُوَرِ الفِعْلِ وَالكِيَانِ

Fa lam yuʿaddid dha-l-fiʿli shay•un
min ṣuwari-l-fiʿli wa-l-kiyāni

And neither the forms of actions nor myriad creatures
will render that act multiple in any way.

فَمَنْ تَرَقَّى عَنْ كُلِّ فَانِ رَأَى وُجُودًا بِغَيْرِ ثَانِ

Fa man taraqqā ʿan kulli fāni
ra•ā wujūdan bi ghayri thāni

For the one who transcends all that is perishing,
sees no duality in existence.

يَا فَوْزَ مَنْ قَدْ غَدَا يُشَاهِدْ رَبًّا عَطُوفاً حَلِيماً دَانِي

Yā fawza man qad ghadā yushāhid
Rabban ʿaṭūfan ḥalīman dānī

And what a victory for the one who comes to witness
a Lord Who is Kind, Forebearing, and Near!

يَقْبَلُ مَنْ قَدْ أَتَى فَقِيراً قَدْ تَابَ مِنْ حَالِهِ الظُّلْمَانِي

Yaqbalu man qad atā faqīran
qad tāba min ḥālihi-ẓ-ẓulmānī

Who accepts anyone who comes in need
and has turned from his darkness in repentance.

فَتَوْبَةُ الْعَبْدِ تَصْطَفِيهِ   لِحَضْرَةِ الْحُبِّ وَالتَّدَانِي

Fa tawbatu-l-ᶜabdi taṣṭafīhi
li ḥadrati-l-ḥubbi-wa-t-tadānī

For repentance is the servant's being chosen
for the presence of love and approach.

وَذِكْرُهُ مَعْ شُهُودِ فَضْلٍ   يُحَصِّلُ الْوَارِدَ النُّورَانِي

Wa dhikruhu maᶜ shuhūdi faḍlin
yuḥaṣṣilu-l-wārida-n-nurānī

And his invocation, along with seeing Allah's grace,
will bring him luminous inspiration.

مَنْ كَانَ مِنْ نَفْسِهِ فِي أَمْنٍ   كَانَ مِنَ الْخَلْقِ فِي أَمَانِ

Man kāna min nafsihi fī amnin
kāna mina-l-khalqi fī amānī

Whoever is safe from his own ego,
is safe from everything in creation.

فَخَالِفِ النَّفْسَ فِي هَوَاهَا   وَصَاحِبَنْ عَارِفاً رَبَّانِي

Fa khālifi-n-nafsa fī hawāhā
wa ṣāḥiban ᶜārifan rabbānī

So oppose the ego in its cravings
and keep company with one of sacred knowledge.

يُرِيكَ مِنْ عَيْبِهَا الخَفِيِّ   يُعَالِجَنْ بِالدَّوَا الرُّوْحَانِي

Yurīka min ʿaybiha-l-khafiyyi
yuʿālijan bi-d-dawā-r-rūḥānī

He will show you the ego's hidden flaws
and treat your illness with a spiritual cure.

يَسْلُكُ بِالرِّفْقِ فِي الْمَسِيرِ   يَرْحَمُ أَهْلَ الْبَلاَ وَالْجَانِي

Yasluku bi-r-rifqi fi-l-masīri
yarḥamu ahla-l-balā wa-l-jānī

He will take you along the way with kindness
and compassion for those in trial and guilt.

يُفْنِيكَ بِالذِّكْرِ فِي الْحَقِيقَةْ   يُذَكِّرُ القَلْبَ بِالقُرآنِ

Yufnīka bi-dh-dhikri fi-l-ḥaqīqa
yudhakkiru-l-qalba bi-l-qurʾānī

He will efface you in the Real by the invocation,
and remind your heart by way of the Qur'ān,

يُرَوِّحُ الرُّوحَ بِالْإِشَارَةْ   فَتَنْجَلِي عِنْدَهَا الْمَعَانِي

Yurawwiḥu-r-rūḥa bi-l-ishāra
fa tanjalī ʿindahā-l-maʿānī

He will revive your spirits with allusions
whose meanings will be manifest and clear.

يَا رَبِّ صَلِّ عَلَى النَّبِيِّ مَا تُلِيَتْ سُورَةُ المَثَانِي

Yā Rabbi ṣallī ʿalā-n-Nabīyyi
mā tuliyat sūratu-l-mathānī

O Lord, shower blessings upon the Prophet
as long as the Oft-Repeated sūra is recited

وَآلِهِ وَالصِّحَابِ طُرّاً مَا رَبِحَ النَّاسُ بِالْإِيمَانِ

Wa ālihi wa-ṣ-ṣiḥābi ṭurran
mā rabiḥa-n-nāsu bi-l- īmāni

And upon his Family and Companions as well,
as long as people profit from faith.

وَأَطْلُبُ الْحَقَّ فِي السَّعَادَةْ لِكُلِّ مَنْ ضَمَّهُ زَمَانِي

Wa aṭlubu-l-ḥaqqa fi-s-saʿāda
li kulli man ḍammahu zamānī

I ask that Allah grant a portion of happiness
to all those who live in this my time.

-19-

سألت قلبي

وحدة الفعل والوجود

I asked my heart

(The Unity of Act and Being)

سَأَلْتُ قَلْبِي عَنْ قُرْبِ رَبِّي   فَقَالَ لاَ شَكَّ هُوَ حَاضِرْ

Sa•altu qalbī ʿan qurbi Rabbī
fa qāla lā shakka Huwa ḥāḍir

I asked my heart about the nearness of my Lord.
My heart's response: "Doubt not. He is Present."

فَقُلْتُ مَالِي لاَ أَرَاهُ   فَقَالَ لِي هُوَ فِيكَ ظَاهِرْ

Fa qultu māliya lā arāhu
fa qāla lī Huwa fīka ẓāhir

"But what is wrong with me, I wonder, for I do not see Him?"
My heart's response: "He is within you, clear as day."

فَقُلْتُ هَذَا الأَمْرُ عَجِيبٌ   فَكَيْفَ يَخْفَى وَالنُّوْرُ بَاهِرْ

Fa qultu hadhā-l-amru ʿajībun
fa kayfa yakhfā wa-n-nūru bāhir

"Surely this is an incredible affair," I reply,
"How can He hide when the Light is so bright?"

فَقَالَ وَهْمٌ هُوَ الحِجَابُ   وَهْوَ لِكُلِّ الأَنَامِ قَاهِرْ

Fa qāla wahmun huwa-l-ḥijābu
wa-hwa li kulli-l-anāmi qāhir

*My heart's response: "Delusion is the veil
and it is overpowering to all."*

لٰكِنَّ مَنْ كَانَ ذَا اجْتِبَاءٍ   غَابَ عَنِ الوَهْمِ بِالسَّرَائِرْ

Lākinna man kāna dha-jtibā•in
ghāba ʿani-l-wahmi bi-s-sarā•ir

*But any who is chosen may be freed
from delusion by his innermost being*

وَصَارَ رُوْحًا بِغَيْرِ جِسْمٍ   وَشَاهَدَ الرَّبَّ بِالْبَصَائِرْ

Fa ṣāra rūḥan bi ghayri jismin
wa shāhada-r-Rabba bi-l-baṣā•ir

*And become pure spirit unfettered by the body,
witnessing his Lord with inner vision.*

فَغَايَةُ الفَتْحِ فِي الْشُّهُودِ   لِحَضْرَةٍ مَالَهَا مِنْ سَاتِرْ

Fa ghāyatu-l-fatḥi fi-sh-shuhūdi
li ḥaḍratin mā lahā min sātir

*The ultimate opening resides in perceiving
a Presence with no veil before It.*

فَلَيْسَ فِعْلٌ وَلاَ وُجُودٌ   لِغَيْرِ رَبِّي عِنْدَ الأَكَابِرْ

Fa laysa fiᶜlun wa lā wujūdun
li ghayri Rabbī ᶜinda-l-akābir

For the greatest of Saints, there is neither action nor being
other than the Being and Action of their Lord.

فَكُلُّ مَنْ بَاحَ بِاخْتِيَارٍ   مِنْ غَيْرِ إِذْنٍ لَهُ الزَّوَاجِرْ

Fa kullu man bāḥa bi-khtiyārin
min ghayri idhnin lahu-z-zawājir

But anyone who willingly announces such matters
without permission causes turmoil and rebuke.

يَا رَبِّ افْتَحْ لَنَا الْبَصَائِرْ   وَنَوِّرِ الْقَلْبَ وَالسَّرَائِرْ

Yā Rabbi-ftaḥ lana-l-baṣa•ir
wa nawwiri-l-qalba wa-s-sarā•ir

O Lord, may our hearts and souls be enlightened
and may our inner sight, O Lord, be opened,

ثُمَّ الصَّلاَةُ عَلَى النَّبِيِّ   مَا جَدَّ حِبٌّ وَسَارَ سَائِرْ

Thumma-ṣ-ṣalātu ᶜala-n-Nabiyyi
mā jadda ḥibbun wa sāra sā•ir

And may Your blessings (in abundance) be upon the Prophet
as long a lover strives and a traveler journeys on.

وَءَالِهِ وَالصِّحَابِ جَمْعًا مَا طَارَ شَوْقاً لِلّٰهِ طَائِرْ

Wa ālihi wa-ṣ-ṣiḥābi jamʿan
mā ṭāra shawqan li-Llāhi ṭā•ir

And upon his Family as well and upon all his Companions
as long as birds soar aloft yearning for Allah.

-20-

النصح

Counsel

سَلَامٌ عَلَى الْإِخْوَانِ فِي كُلِّ مَوْضِعٍ   سَلَاماً يَعُمُّ الكُلَّ فِي كُلِّ مَجْمَعِ

Salāmun ʿala-l-ikhwāni fī kulli mawḍiʿin
salāman yaʿummu-l-kulla fī kulli majmaʿi

Greetings of peace to my brethren in every place,
greetings to each one in every gathering.

وَإِنِّي أُرِيدُ النُّصْحَ لِلْكُلِّ رَاجِياً   بُلُوغَ الْمُنَى وَالْعِزِّ وَالفَتْحِ الوُسْعِ

Wa innī urīdu-n-nuṣḥa li-l-kulli rājiyan
bulūgha-l-munā wa-l-ʿizzi wa-l-fatḥi-l-wusʿi

I wish to give counsel to all who hope to reach
the desired goal, honor, and a vast opening.

فَأَوَّلُ نُصْحِي لِلَّذِي حَرَّرَ التَّقْوَى   مُصَاحَبَةَ الأَخْيَارِ فِي الْجَلْبِ وَالدَّفْعِ

Fa awwalu nuṣ•ḥī li-l-ladhī ḥarrara-t-taqwā
muṣāḥabata-l-akhyāri fi-l-jalbi wa-d-dafʿi

The first advice to one who would make his piety sincere
is to keep company with the righteous in both difficulty and ease.

فَهَذَا أَسَاسُ الْخَيْرِ إِنْ كُنْتَ عَاقِلاً   فَعَوِّلْ عَلَيْهِ مَعْ مُرَاعَاةٍ لِلشَّرْعِ

Fa hādhā asāsu-l-khayri in kunta ʿāqilan
fa ʿawwil ʿalayhi maʿ murāʿātin li-sh-sharʿi

This is the basis of goodness if you are someone of sound mind,
so rely upon it and keep the Sacred Law.

وَكُلُّ الَّذِي قَدْ نَالَ عِلْماً وَسُؤْدَداً   فَمَا نَالَهُ إِلاَّ بِصُحْبَةِ خَاشِعِ

Wa kullu-l-ladhī qad nāla ʿilman wa su•dadan
fa mā nālahu illā bi ṣuḥbati khāshiʿi

All those who attain to knowledge and a place of honor
do so by being with one of humble reverence,

وَأَعْنِي بِهِ الشَّيْخَ الَّذِي فَاضَ نُورُهُ   وَجَاءَ بِأَسْرَارٍ وَخَيْرٍ مُتَابِعِ

Wa aʿnī bihi-sh-shaykha-l-ladhī fāḍa nūruhu
wa jā•a bi asrārin wa khayrin mutābiʿi

By which I mean a shaykh whose light is overflowing
and who brings with him mysteries and boundless good.

فَإِنْ شِئْتَ أَنْوَاراً وَفَتْحَ بَصِيرَةٍ   فَقَلِّدْهُ تَعْظِيماً وَعُجْ عَنْ مُنَازِعِ

Fa•in shi•ta anwāran wa fatḥa baṣīratin
fa qallid•hu taʿẓīman wa ʿuj ʿan munāziʿi

So if you wish for lights and the opening of inner vision
then follow him with respect and turn away from conflict.

وَوَاظِبْ عَلَى الذِّكْرِ المُلَقَّنِ بِالإِذْنِ وَلَا تَغْفُلَنْ فِي حَالَةِ الضَّيْقِ وَالوُسْعِ

Wa wāẓib ʿala-dh-dhikri-l-mulaqqani bi-l-idhni
Wa lā taghfulan fī ḥālati-ḍ-ḍayqi wa-l-wusʿi

Be regular in the invocation you've received with his permission –
do not neglect it in states of hardship or ease.

وَزِنْ وَارِدَاتِ الذِّكْرِ بِالشَّرْعِ حَاكِياً لِشَيْخِكَ كُلَّ مَا أَتَاكَ وَسَارِعِ

Wazin wāridāti-dh-dhikri bi-sh-sharʿi ḥākiyan
li shaykhika kulla mā atāka wa sāriʿi

Weigh by the Law what it might bring of inspirations
and hasten to recount them to your shaykh.

فَسَلْبُ اخْتِيَارٍ ثُمَّ كُلِّ إِرادَةٍ هُوَ المَوْرِدُ الأَصْفَى فَهَلْ أَنْتَ سَامِعِ

Fa salbu-khtiyārin thumma kulli irādatin
huwa-l-mawridu-l-aṣfā fa hal anta sāmiʿi

Giving up choice and the will's desires
is the purest spring to drink from, do you hear?

وَهَاكَ مَقَامَاتِ اليَقِينِ فَبَادِرَنْ بِتَوْبَةٍ زُهْدٍ ثُمَّ خَوْفٍ بِوَازِعِ

Wa hāka maqāmāti-l-yaqīni fa bādiran
bi tawbatin zuhdin thumma khawfin bi wāziʿi

And here are the stations of certitude: make efforts towards repentance
then detachment, and then fear that brings restraint.

رَجَاءٍ وَشُكْرٍ ثُمَّ صَبْرٍ تَوَكُّلٍ   كَذَاكَ الرِّضَى وَالحُبُّ لِلْكُلِّ جَامِعِ

Rajā•in wa shukrin thumma ṣabrin tawakkulin
kadhāka-r-riḍā wa-l-ḥubbu li-l-kulli jāmiʿi

Hope and gratitude, then patience and trust,
contentment and love, which combines them all.

وَأَسْبَابُهُ الْفِكْرُ الصَّفِيُّ فِي نِعْمَةٍ   وَحُسْنِ صِفَاتٍ ثُمَّ فِي النُّورِ اللَّامِعِ

Wa asbābuhu-l-fikru-ṣ-ṣafīyyu fī niʿmatin
wa ḥusni ṣifātin thumma fi-n-nūri-l-lāmiʿi

The means to reach them is pure reflection on Allah's bounty,
and the beauty of His Attributes, and then on a gleaming light,

وَ أَعْنِي بِهِ ذَاكَ الرَّسُولَ مُحَمَّداً   عَلَيهِ صَلاَةٌ عَدَّ وَتْرٍ مَعَ الشَّفْعِ

Wa aʿnī bihi dhāka-r-rasūla Muḥammadan
ʿalayhi ṣalātun ʿadda watrin maʿa-sh-shafʿi

And by this I mean the Messenger, Muḥammad,
upon whom be Allah's blessings as numerous as the even and odd,

وَ آلِهِ وَالْأَصْحَابِ مَعْ كُلِّ عَارِفٍ   دَعَا لِطَرِيقِ اللهِ فِي كُلِّ مَجْمَعِ

Wa ālihi wa-l-aṣḥābi maʿ kulli ʿārifin
daʿā li ṭarīqi-Llāhi fī kulli majmaʿi

And upon his Family and Companions and every single gnostic
who calls to Allah's Way in every gathering.

-21-

يا طالب الفنا في الله
O You who Seek Effacement in Allah

يَا طَالِبَ الفَنَا فِي اللهْ   قُلْ دَائِماً اللهْ اللهْ

Yā ṭāliba-l-fanā fi-Llāh
qul dā•iman Allāh, Allāh

O you who seek effacement in Allah,
be constant in saying – "Allāh, Allāh!"

وَغِبْ فِيهِ عَنْ سِوَاهُ   وَاشْهَدْ بِقَلْبِكَ اللهْ

Wa ghib fihi ʿan siwāhu
wa-sh•had bi qalbika Allāh

And pass away in Him from all else,
and witness with your heart... Allah!

وَاجْمَعْ هُمُومَكَ فِيهِ   تُكْفَى بِهِ عَنْ غَيْرِ اللهْ

Wa-jmaʿ humūmaka fīhi
tukfā bihi ʿan ghayri-Llāh

Gather all your cares into caring about Him
and you will be sufficed from all else but Allah.

وَكُنْ عَبْداً صِرْفاً لَهُ تَكُنْ حُرّاً عَنْ غَيْرِ اللهْ

Wa kun ʿabdan ṣirfan lahu,
takun ḥurran ʿan ghayri-Llāh

Be a servant who belongs to Him alone
and you'll be freed from belonging to other than Allah.

وَاخْضَعْ لَهُ وَتَذَلَّلْ تَفُزْ بِسِرٍّ مِنَ اللهْ

Wa-khḍaʿ lahu wa tadhallal
tafuz bi sirrin mina-Llāh

Submit to Him and be humble before Him,
and you'll be granted a secret that comes from Allah.

وَاذْكُرْ بِجِدٍّ وَصِدْقٍ بَيْنَ يَدَيْ عَبِيدِ اللهْ

Wa-dhkur bi jiddin wa ṣidqin
bayna yaday ʿabīdi-Llāh

And invoke with fervor and sincerity
along with the devoted servants of Allah.

وَاكْتُمْ إِذَا تَجَلَّى لَكْ بِأَنْوَارٍ مِنْ ذَاتِ اللهْ

Wa-ktum idhā tajallā lak
bi anwārin min dhāti-Llāh

Conceal it should He reveal Himself to you
through lights which come from the Essence of Allah.

فَالْغَيْرُ عِنْدَنَا مُحَالْ فَالْوُجُودُ الْحَقُّ لِلهْ

Fa-l-ghayru ʿindanā muḥāl
fa-l-wujūdu-l-ḥaqqu li-Llāh

*"The other," for us, is something that cannot be,
for existence is a right that belongs only to Allah.*

وَ وَهْمَكَ اقْطَعْ دَائِمًا بِتَوْحِيدٍ صِرْفٍ لِلهْ

Wa wahmaka-qṭaʿ dā•iman
bi tawḥīdin ṣirfin li-Llāh

*So constantly cut through your veil of illusion
by affirming the pure oneness of Allah.*

فَوَحْدَةُ الْفِعْلِ تَبْدُو فِي أَوَّلِ الذِّكْرِ لِلهْ

Fa waḥdatu-l-fiʿli tabdū
fī awwali-dh-dhikri li-Llāh

*The unity of the Acts appears
at the beginning of the invocation of Allah.*

وَوَحْدَةُ الْوَصْفِ لَهُ تَاتِي مِنَ الْحُبِّ فِي اللهْ

Wa waḥdatu-l-waṣfi lahu
tātī mina-l-ḥubbi fi-Llāh

*And the unity of His Attributes
will come [to you] from love in Allah*

وَ وَحْدَةُ الذَّاتِ لَهُ تُورِّثُ الْبَقَا بِاللهْ

Wa waḥdatu-dh-dhāti lahu
tuwarrithu-l-baqā bi-Llāh

And the unity of His Essence
will endow you with the state of subsisting by Allah.

فَهَنِيئًا لِمَنْ مَشَى فِي طَرِيقِ الذِّكْرِ لِلهْ

Fa hanī•an liman mashā
fī ṭarīqi-dh-dhikri li-Llāh

Happy is the one who walks the path
of invocation for the sake of Allah.

مُعْتَقِداً شَيْخاً حَيّاً يَكُونُ عَارِفاً بِاللهْ

Muʿtaqidan shaykhan ḥayyan
yakūnu ʿārifan bi-Llāh

Taking as his guide a living teacher
whose knowledge comes from knowing Allah.

وَلاَزَمَ الْحُبَّ لَهُ وَبَاعَ نَفْسَهُ لِلهْ

Wa lāzama-l-ḥubba lahu
wa bāʿa nafsahu li-Llāh

He loves him with an unflagging love
and sells his ego for the sake of Allah

وَقَامَ فِي اللَّيْلِ يَتْلُو كَلامَهُ شَوْقاً لِلهْ

Wa qāma fi-l-layli yatlū
kalāmahu shawqan li-Llāh

And rises for prayer in the night to recite
His Words with a yearning for Allah.

فَنَالَ مَا يَطْلُبُهُ مِن قُوَّةِ الْعِلْمِ بِاللهْ

Fa nāla mā yaṭlubuhu
min quwwati-l-ʿilmi bi-Llāh

And so attains what he is seeking:
the power of the knowledge of Allah.

وَفَيْضُنَا مِنْ نَبِيٍّ سَيِّدِ مَخْلُوقَاتِ اللهْ

Wa fayḍunā min Nabiyyin
Sayyidi makhlūqāti-Llāh

Our teaching flows from the stream of a Prophet:
the most honored of the creatures of Allah.

عَلَيْهِ أَزْكَى صَلاَةٍ عَدَدَ مَعْلُومَاتِ اللهْ

ʿAlayhi azkā ṣalātin
ʿadada maʿlūmāti-Llāh

Upon him be the purest blessings
as numerous as all that is known to Allah.

وَ آلِهِ وَصَحْبِهِ وَكُلِّ دَاعٍ إِلَى اِللهْ

Wa ālihi wa ṣaḥbihi
wa kulli dāʿin ʿila-Llāh

And upon his Family and his Companions,
and all of those who call to Allah.

-22-

روحي تحدثني
My Spirit Speaks to Me

رُوْحِي تُحَدِّثُنِي بِأَنَّ حَقِيْقَتِي نُوْرُ الْإِلٰهِ فَلَا تَرَى إِلَّاهُ

Rūḥī tuḥaddithunī bi anna ḥaqīqatī
nūru-l-Ilāhi fa lā tarā illāhu

My spirit speaks to me and says, My deepest nature
is Allah's light – so see no other.

لَوْ لَمْ أَكُنْ نُورًا لَكُنْتُ سِوَاءَهُ إِنَّ السِّوَا عَدَمٌ فَلَا تَرْضَاهُ

Law lam akun nūran la kuntu siwā•ahu
inna-s-siwā ʿadamun fa lā tarḍāhu

Were I not this light, I would be that "other":
and that "other" is nothingness – do not accept it!

وَإِذَا نَظَرْتَ بِعَيْنِ سِرِّكَ لَمْ تَجِدْ غَيْرَ الْإِلٰهِ فِي أَرْضِهِ وَسَمَاهُ

Wa idhā naẓarta bi ʿayni sirrika lam tajid
ghayra-l-ilāhi fī arḍihi wa samāhu

If you look with the eye of your soul, you will find
none other than Allah on His earth and in His sky

لٰكِنْ تَوَهُّمُ غَيْرِهِ يَخْفَى بِهِ فَانْبُذْ هَوَاكَ إِذَا أَرَدْتَ تَرَاهُ

Lākin tawahhumu ghayrihi yakhfā bihi
Fa-nbudh hawāka idhā aradta tarāhu

The illusion of another is what hides Him from you
be rid of your desires if you want to see Him

وَارْكَبْ سَفِينَةَ سُنَّةٍ تَنْجُو بِهَا وَاسْلُكْ سَبِيلَ رَئِيسِهَا فِي هَوَاهُ

Wa-rkab safīnata sunnatin tanjū bihā
wa-sluk sabīla ra•īsihā fī hawāhu

Board the ship of the Prophet's way to be saved
and follow in love its captain's course

وَصِلِ الشَّرَابَ بِكَأْسِهَا وَافْنَى بِهِ تَحُزِ الْبَقَاءَ بِسِرِّهِ وَعُلَاهُ

Wa ṣili-sh-sharāba bi ka•sihā wa-fnā bihi
taḥuzi-l-baqā•a bi sirrihi wa ʿulāhu

Join the wine to the cup and vanish therein
and you will reach [the station of] subsisting by His sublimity and secret

وَاشْهَدْ بِعَيْنِ بَصِيرَةٍ تَوْحِيدَهُ وَالْفَرْقُ شِرْعَتُهُ فَلَا تَنْسَاهُ

Wa-sh•had bi ʿayni baṣīratin tawḥīdahu
wa-l-farqu shirʿatuhu falā tansāhu

Witness His oneness with the eye of inward vision
but separation is His law – do not forget!

وَاجْعَلْ هُمُومَكَ وَاحِداً تُكْفَى بِهِ كُلَّ الْهُمُومِ وَتَدْخُلَنْ فِي حِمَاهُ

Wa-jᶜal humūmaka wāḥidan tukfā bihi
kulla-l-humūmi wa tadkhulan fī ḥimāhu

Make your cares a single care. He will suffice you
in all your cares and you will enter His shelter completely!

وَانْزِلْ أُمُورَكَ بِالَّذِي أَدْرَى بِهَا فَهْوَ الْخَبِيرُ بِقَلْبِنَا وَمُنَاهُ

Wa-nzil umūraka bi-l-ladhī adrā bihā
fa hwa-l-khabīru bi-qalbinā wa munāhu

Lay down your cares before the One Who best knows them:
He is the expert of our heart and its longings

يَا رَبِّ صَلِّ عَلَى النَّبِيِّ مُحَمَّدٍ سِرِّ الْوُجُودِ وَأَصْلِهِ وَسَنَاهُ

Yā Rabbi ṣalli ᶜalā-n-Nabiyyi Muḥammadin
sirri-l-wujūdi wa aṣlihi wa sanāhu

O Lord, shower blessing on the Prophet Muhammad,
the secret, the source, and the splendor of being.

-23-

التجلي

Unveiling

أَشَمْسٌ بَدَا مِنْ عَالَمِ الْغَيْبِ ضَوْؤُهَا أَمِ انْكَشَفَتْ عَنْ ذَاتِ لَيْلَى سُتُورُهَا

A shamsun badā min ʿālami-l-ghaybi ḍaw•uhā
ami-nkashafat ʿan dhāti Laylā sutūruhā

Is that a sun whose light has shone forth from the unseen world,
or were the veils that had hidden Layla lifted?

نَعَمْ تِلْكَ لَيْلَى قَدْ أَبَاحَتْ بِحُبِّهَا لِخِلٍّ لَهَا لَـمَّا تَزَايَدَ شَوْقُهَا

Naʿam tilka Laylā qad abāḥat bi ḥubbihā
li khillin lahā lammā tazāyada shawquhā

Yes, it is Layla and she's revealed her love
for her beloved when her yearning grew too great.

فَأَضْحَى أَسِيراً فِي مُرَادِ غَرَامِهَا وَنَادَتْ لَهُ الأَشْوَاقُ هٰذِي كُؤُوسُهَا

Fa aḍḥā asīran fī murādi gharāmihā
Wa nādat lahu-l-ashwāqu hādhī ku•ūsuhā

Then he become a captive of her ardent love,
and longing beckoned him to drink from her wine.

فَمَا بَرِحَتْ حَتَّى سَقَتْهُ بِكَأْسِهَا فَلا لَوْمَ فَاشْرَبْ فَالشَّرَابُ حَدِيثُهَا

Fa mā bariḥat ḥattā saqat•hu bi ka•sihā
Fa lā lawma fa-shrab fa-sh-sharābu ḥadīthuhā

And she did not depart until she had poured for him from her cup.
This is blameless, so drink, for her words are the wine.

وَمَا هِيَ إِلاَّ حَضْرَةُ الْحقِّ وَحْدَهَا تَجلَّتْ بِأَشْكَالٍ تَلَوَّنَ نُورُهَا

Wa mā hiya illā ḥaḍratu-l-ḥaqqi waḥdahā
tajallat bi ashkālin talawwana nūruhā

And she is naught but the presence of the Truth Alone
made manifest in form to which her light gives endless hues.

فَأَبْدَتْ بَدِيعَ الصُّنْعِ فِي طَيِّ كَوْنِهَا فَلاحِظْ صِفَاتِ الحِبِّ فِيكَ ظُهُورُهَا

Fa abdat badīʿa-ṣ-ṣunʿi fī ṭayyi kawnihā
fa lāḥiẓ ṣifāti-l-ḥibbi fīka ẓuhūruhā

She has shown the marvelous artistry contained within her,
so behold the Attributes of the Beloved that are manifest within you.

فَوَاللهِ مَا حَازَ السَّعَادَةَ كُلَّهَا سِوَى مَنْ بَدَا عَبْداً ذَلِيلاً يَؤُمُّهَا

Fa wa-Llāhi mā ḥāza-s-saʿādata kullahā
siwā man badā ʿabdan dhalīlan ya•ummuhā

By Allah, no one attains complete happiness
except the one who, as a lowly servant, turns in her direction.

فَغَطَّتْ قَبِيحَ الْوَصْفِ مِنْه بِوَصْفِهَا   ولاَحَتْ لَهُ الأَنْوَارُ يَبْدُو شُعَاعُهَا

Fa ghaṭṭat qabīḥa-l-waṣfi minhu bi waṣfihā
wa lāḥat lahu-l-anwāru yabdū shuʿāʿuhā

Then she covers his ugliness with her beauty
and lights appear for him and their rays shine forth.

فغَابَ عَنِ الْحِسِّ الَّذي كَانَ قَاطِعاً   وَعَانَقَ مَعْنًى لاَ يَحِلُّ فِرَاقُهَا

Fa ghāba ʿani-l-ḥissi-l-ladhī kāna qāṭiʿan
wa ʿānaqa maʿnan lā yaḥillu firāquhā

And he leaves this sensory world which had been an obstacle
and embraces an inner sense from which he may not part.

فحَرِّرْ أَخِي قَصْداً وأَعْرِضْ عَنِ السِّوَى   يَهُبُّ عَلَى الأَحْبَابِ مِنْكَ نَسِيمُهَا

Fa ḥarrir akhī qaṣdan wa aʿriḍ ʿani-s-siwā
yahubbu ʿala-l-aḥbābi minka nasīmuhā

So make sincere your intention, my brother, and turn from any other
and her breeze, from you, will waft over all the beloveds.

وتَفْتَحُ سَمْعاً لِلْفُؤَادِ مِنْ سَالِكٍ   لِأَنَّ لَطِيفَ الْعِلْمِ مِنْهَا دَلِيلُهَا

Wa taftaḥu samʿan li-l-fu•ādi min sālikin
li anna laṭīfa-l-ʿilmi minhā dalīluhā

And she will open the ears of the wayfarer's heart
for the very subtlety of her knowledge is her proof.

فَمُنَّ عَلَيْنَا دَائِماً بِوِصَالِهَا   وَغَيِّبْنَا عَنْ حِسِّ الْمَوْجُودَاتِ كُلِّهَا

Fa munna ʿalaynā dā•iman bi wiṣālihā
wa ghayyibnā ʿan ḥissi-l-mawjūdāti kullihā

Grace us always, O Allah, by being united with her
and efface us from the sensory world.

التطهير
Purification

فَإِنْ شِئْتَ تَطْهِيراً مِنَ الشِّرْكِ والدَّعْوَى   وَتَشْرَبَ مِن تَسْنِيمِ وَصْلٍ حَتَّى تَرْوَى

Fa in shi•ta taṭhīran mina-sh-shirki wa-d-daʿwā
wa tashraba min tasnīmi waṣlin ḥattā tarwā

If you desire to be purified from polytheism and pretense
and to drink from the spring of union 'til your thirst is quenched,

فَمَنْطِقْ بِصَبْرٍ ثُمَّ عَمِّمْ بِتَوبَةٍ   وَلَازِمْ قَمِيصَ الزُّهْدِ وابْذُلْ فِيهِ قُوَى

Fa manṭiq bi ṣabrin thumma ʿammim bi tawbatin
wa lāzim qamīṣa-z-zuhdi wa-bdhul fīhi quwā

Then don the mantle of patience, the turban of repentance,
the shirt of renunciation, and in it make effort.

وَلَا بُدَّ مِن نَعْلَيْنِ خَوْفٍ مَعَ الرَّجَا   وَعُكَّازِ إِيقَانٍ وَزَادٍ مِنَ التَّقْوَى

Wa lā budda min naʿlayni khawfin maʿa-r-rajā
wa ʿukkāzi īqānin wa zādin mina-t-taqwā

You must have both sandals, fear as well as hope,
the staff of certitude, piety as your provision,

وَقَائِدِ عِلْمٍ مَعْ مَطِيَّةِ هِمَّةٍ   وَصُحْبَةِ حِفْظٍ لِلْجَوَارِحِ مِنْ بَلْوَى

Wa qā•idi ʿilmin maʿ maṭiyyati himmatin
wa ṣuḥbati ḥifẓin li-l-jawāriḥi min balwā

The bridle of knowledge, the mount of aspiration,
and make protecting your limbs from trials your companion.

فَجُدَّ وَأَسْرِعْ فِي الْمَسِيرِ وَلَا تَقِفْ   بِفِكْرٍ عَلَى كَوْنٍ فَتُحْجَبَ عَنْ مَأْوَى

Fa judda wa asriʿ fi-l-masīri wa lā taqif
bi fikrin ʿalā kawnin fa tuḥjaba ʿan ma•wā

Then exert yourself and hasten in the way and do not stop
to ponder over creatures, for that will veil you from the shelter.

وَفَكِّرْ فِي إِحْسَانٍ وَأَخْلِصْ فِي شُكْرِهِ   وَقُمْ سَحَراً وَاخْضَعْ وَبُثَّ لَهُ الشَّكْوَى

Wa fakkir fī iḥsānin wa akhliṣ fī shukrihi
wa qum saḥaran wa-khḍaʿ wa buththa lahu-sh-shakwā

Reflect upon Allah's excellence and be truly grateful,
rise humbly before dawn and share with Him your cares.

وَصَلِّ عَلَى قُطْبِ الْوُجُودِ وَحِزْبِهِ   صَلَاةً تَعُمُّ السِّرَّ مِنَّا مَعَ النَّجْوَى

Wa ṣalli ʿalā quṭbi-l-wujūdi wa ḥizbihi
ṣalātan taʿummu-s-sirra minnā maʿa-l-najwā

May Allah bless the Pole of Being and his people
with a blessing that permeates the soul and its deepest center.

-25-

تزود أخي للموت

Make provision, my brother, for death

تَزَوَّدْ أخِي لِلْمَوتِ إنَّهُ نَازِلٌ   وَلاَ تُطِلِ الآمَالَ يَقْسُو لَكَ القَلْبُ

Tazawwad akhī li-l-mawti innahu nāzilun
wa lā tuṭili-l-āmāla yaqsū laka-l-qalbu

Make provision, my brother, for death that approaches
and let your hopes not be too lengthy lest your heart grow hard.

وَوَاظِبْ عَلَى الفِكْرِ الْمُعِينِ عَلَى الْجِدِّ   وَسَارِعْ إلى الأَعْمَالِ فَالْعُمْرُ يَذْهَبُ

Wa wāẓib ʿala-l-fikri-l-muʿīni ʿala-l-jiddi
wa sāriʿ ila-l-aʿmāli fa-l-ʿumru yadh•habu

Make a practice of reflection that aids you in diligence
and hasten toward good works, for life is passing on.

وَفَكِّرْ فِي أَحْوَالِ الْقِيَامَةِ دَائِماً   كَبَعْثٍ وَ نَشْرٍ وَالْمَوَازِينُ تُنْصَبُ

Wa fakkir fī aḥwāli-l-qiyāmati dā•iman
ka baʿthin wa nashrin wa-l-mawāzīnu tunṣabu

Always call to mind the states of the Day of Arising:
the Resurrection, the Gathering, the Scales to be set up,

وَكَالصِّرَاطِ الَّذِي لَهُ عَقَبَاتُهُ   تَطُولُ عَلَى الْعَاصِي وَمَشْيُهُ يَصْعُبُ

Wa ka-ṣ-ṣirāṭi-l-ladhī lahu ʿaqabātuhu
taṭūlu ʿala-l-ʿāṣī wa mashyuhu yaṣʿubu

The Traverse, which for the sinful will be long
and its crossing very hard,

وَ مَنْ كَانَ طَائِعاً وَلِلّهِ مُخْلِصاً   يَمُرُّ كَبَرْقٍ أَوْ كَرِيحٍ فَيَذْهَبُ

Wa man kāna ṭā•iʿan wa li-Llāhi mukhliṣan
yamurru ka-barqin aw ka-rīḥin fa yadh•habu

While the dutiful and sincere will pass over it
like lightning or like wind, and go on.

وَ إِنْ شِئْتَ أَنْ تُسْقَى مِنَ الْحَوْضِ فِي الْحَشْرِ   فَلَازِمْ حُبَّ النَّبِي وَمَنْ لَهُ يُنْسَبُ

Wa in shi•ta an tusqā mina-l-ḥawḍi fi-l-ḥashri
falāzim ḥubba-n-Nabī wa man lahu yunsabu

And if you wish, at the Gathering, to drink from the Pond
then be constant in love for the Prophet and his people.

وَصَلِّ عَلَى الْهَادِي الْمُشَفَّعِ فِي الْوَرَى   يَقُولُ أَنَا لَهَا إِذَا الْخَلْقُ يَرْهَبُ

Wa ṣalli ʿala-l-Hādi-l-Mushaffaʿi fi-l-warā
yaqūlu anā lahā idha-l-khalqu yarhabu.

May Allah bless the Guide, the Intercessor for mankind
who will say, "I have it," when all creatures are in fear.

عَلَيْهِ صَلَاةُ اللهِ فِي كُلِّ مَوْطِنٍ   وَآلٍ وَأَصْحَابٍ وَمَنْ يَتَحَبَّبُ

ʿAlayhi ṣalātu-Llāhi fī kulli mawṭinin
wa ālin wa aṣ•ḥābin wa man yataḥabbabu

Upon him be salutations of peace in every land,
and upon his Family and Companions and those who love them.

وَأَسْأَلُ رَبِّ اللهَ نَيْلَ سَعَادَةٍ   لِيَ وَلِلْأَحْبَابِ وَمَنْ يَتَقَرَّبُ

Wa as•alu Rabbi-Llāha nayla saʿādatin
liya wa li-l-aḥbābi wa man yataqarrabu

I ask Allah, my Lord, that happiness might come
to me, my beloveds, and all who draw near.

-26-

أهيم وحدي

I am alone, ecstatically in love

أَهِيمُ وَحْدِي بِذِكْرِ رَبِّي   فَذِكْرُ رَبِّي هُوَ الشِّفَاءُ

Ahīmu waḥdī bi dhikri Rabbī
fa dhikru Rabbī huwa-sh-shifā•u

I am alone, ecstatically in love with the remembrance of my Lord
for the remembrance of my Lord – that is the cure.

أَحْبَبْتُ رَباًّ هُوَ اعْتِمَادِي   لِكُلِّ شَيْءٍ هُوَ يَشَاءُ

Aḥbabtu Rabban Huwaʿtimādī
li kulli shay•in Huwa yashā•u

I love a Lord. He is the One on whom I depend
in all things, He is the One who wills.

وَكُلُّ حُبٍّ لِغَيْرِ رَبِّي   فِيهِ الْعَذَابُ فِيهِ الشَّقَاءُ

Wa kullu ḥubbin li ghayri Rabbī
fīhi-l-ʿadhābu fīhi-sh-shaqā•u

In every other love than the love of my Lord
there is torment and there is grief.

يَا فَوْزَ فَانٍ عَنِ الْفَنَاءِ   لَهُ الْحَيَاةُ لَهُ الْبَقَاءُ

Yā fawza fānin ʿani-l-fanā•i
lahu-l-ḥayātu lahu-l-baqā•u

Blessed be the one who is effaced from effacement.
His is life, his is subsistence.

يَا رَبِّ صَلِّ عَلَى مُحَمَّدٍ   مِنْ ذَاتِهِ النُّورُ وَالضِّيَاءُ

Yā Rabbi ṣalli ʿalā Muḥammad
min dhātihi-n-nūru wa-ḍ-ḍiyā•u

O Lord send blessings upon Muḥammad
from his essence is light, from his essence is splendor.

وَآلِهِ وَالصَّحْبِ الْكِرَامِ   لَهُم عُهُودٌ لَهُمْ وَفَاءُ

Wa ālihi wa-ṣ-ṣaḥbi-l-kirāmi
lahum ʿuhūdun lahum wafā•u

And upon his Family and noble Companions,
theirs is the covenant and theirs its fulfillment.

-27-

كم لك من

How many... ?

(Sung at the end of every majlis of the fuqarā')

كَمْ لَكَ مِنْ نِعْمَةٍ عَلَيَّ وَلَمْ تَزَلْ مُحْسِناً إِلَيَّ

Kam laka min niʿmatin ʿalayya
wa lam tazal muḥsinan ilayya

How many blessings You have bestowed upon me!
And You continue to be generous and kind towards me.

غَدَّيْتَنِي فِي الْحَشَا جَنِينَا وَكُنْتَ لِي قَبْلَ وَالِدَيَّ

Ghaddaytanī fi-l-ḥashā janīnā
wa kunta lī qabla wālidayya

You nourished me (while I was yet) a foetus in the womb.
You were with me before my two parents.

خَلَقْتَنِي مُسْلِماً وَلَوْلاَ فَضْلُكَ لَمْ أَعْرِفِ النَّبِيَّ

Khalaqtanī musliman wa law lā
faḍluka lam aʿrifi-n-Nabiyya

You created me a Muslim, and were it not
for Your grace, I would not know the Prophet.

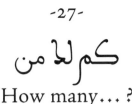

أَسْجُدُ حَقاًّ عَلَى جَبِينِي   نَعَمْ وَخَدِّي وَنَاظِرَيَّا

Asjudu ḥaqqan ʿalā jabīnī
naʿam, wa khaddī wa nāẓirayya

I prostrate, in truth, upon my forehead,
yes, and my cheeks and eyes

يَا رَبِّ صَلِّ عَلَى النَّبِيِّ   مَا تُلِيَتْ سُورَةُ الْمَثَانِي

Yā Rabbi ṣalli ʿalā-n-Nabiyyi
mā tuliyat Sūratu-l-Mathānī

O Lord, shower blessings upon the Prophet
as long as the Oft-Repeated Sūra is recited.

وَ آلِهِ وَالصِّحَابِ طُرًّا   مَا رَبِحَ النَّاسُ بِالْإِيمَانِ

Wa ālihi wa-ṣ-ṣiḥābi ṭurran
mā rabiḥa-n-nāsu bi-l-īmāni

And his Family and Companions as well
as long as people profit from faith

وَأَطْلُبُ الْحَقَّ فِي السَّعَادَةْ   لِكُلِّ مَنْ ضَمَّهُ زَمَانِي

Wa aṭlubu-l-Ḥaqqa fi-s-saʿāda
li kulli man ḍammahu zamānī

I ask Allah the Truth that happiness might
come to all those who live in this my time.

-28-

سلام على أهل الحمى

Greetings to the People of Protection

سَلَامٌ عَلَى أَهْلِ الْحِمَى حَيْثُمَا حَلُّوا   هَنِيئاً لَهُمْ يَا حَبَّذَا مَا بِهِ حُلُّوا

Salāmun ʿalā ahli-l-ḥimā ḥaythumā ḥallū
hanī•an lahum yā ḥabbadhā mā bihi ḥullū

Greetings to the people of protection wherever they may be.
Blessed be they and how excellent their abode!

لَهُمْ أَظْهَرَ الْمَولَى شُمُوسَ بَهَائِهِ   فَيَا لَيْتَ خَدِّي فِي التُّرَابِ لَهُمْ نَعْلُ

Lahum aẓhara-l-mawlā shumūsa bahā•ihi
fa yā layta khaddī fi-t-turābi lahum naʿlu

For them, the Guardian Lord has manifested suns of His splendor,
would that my cheek were their sandal in the dust!

مَتَى يَا عُرَيْبَ الْحَيِّ يَأْتِي بَشِيرُكُمْ   فَتَبْتَهِجَ الدُّنْيَا وَيَجْتَمِعَ الشَّمْلُ

Matā yā ʿurayba-l-ḥayyi ya•tī bashīrukum
fa tabtahija-d-dunyā wa yajtamiʿa-sh-shamlu

When, dear brothers, will one come with good news
of your arrival that we might rejoice and be united?

صِلُونِي عَلَى مَا بِي فَإِنِّي لِوَصْلِكُمْ   إِذَا لَمْ أَكُنْ أَهْلاً فَأَنْتُمْ لَهُ أَهْلُ

Ṣilūnī ʿalā mā bī fa•innī li waṣlikum
idhā lam akun ahlan fa antum lahu ahlu

Let me be among you even as I am,
for though I am not worthy of being among you, still you are worthy.

سَلَامٌ عَلَيْكُمْ شَرَّفَ اللهُ قَدْرَكُمْ   وَدَامَتْ عَلَيْكُمْ نِعْمَةٌ وَسُرُورُهَا

Salāmun ʿalaykum sharrafa-Llāhu qadrakum
wa dāmat ʿalaykum niʿmatun wa surūruhā

Peace be upon you and may Allah ennoble your rank
and may grace and joy always be yours.

فَمَا طَابَتِ الْأَيَّامُ إِلَّا بِذِكْرِكُمْ   فَأَنْتُمْ ضِيَاءُ الْعَيْنِ حَقًّا وَنُورُهَا

Fa mā ṭābati-l-ayyāmu illā bi dhikrikum
fa antum ḍiyā•u-l-ʿayni ḥaqqan wa nūruhā

Days are only sweet if they contain your mention;
you are the radiance of my eye and its light.

إِذَا نَظَرَتْ عَيْنِي وُجُوهَ أَحِبَّتِي   فَتِلْكَ صَلَاتِي فِي اللَّيَالِي الرَّغَائِبِ

Idhā naẓarat ʿaynī wujūha aḥibbatī
fa tilka ṣalātī fi-l-layāli-r-raghā•ibi

When my eye beholds the faces of my beloveds,
that is my prayer offered in the nights of yearning,

وُجُوهٌ إِذَا مَا أَسْفَرَتْ عَنْ جَمَالِهَا أَضَاءَتْ لَهَا الأَكْوَانُ مِنْ كُلِّ جَانِبِ

Wujūhun idhā mā asfarat ʿan jamālihā
aḍā•at laha-l-akwānu min kulli jānibi

Faces which, when their beauty is unveiled
illuminate the world in all directions.

أدعية دبر الصلوات

Supplications after the Five Prayers

A selection of supplications, any of which can be recited after the obligatory prayers.

أَسْتَغْفِرُ اللهَ الْعَظِيمَ الَّذِي لآ إِلٰهَ إِلَّا هُوَ الْحَيُّ الْقَيُّومُ وَأَتُوبُ إِلَيهِ (3)

Astaghfiru Llāha-l-ʿaẓīma-l-ladhī lā ilāha illā huwa'l-Ḥayyu'l-Qayyūm wa atūbu ilayhī

I seek forgiveness from Allāh Who is the One besides whom there is no god, the Living and Eternal, and I turn to Him in repentance

اللّٰهُمَّ مَغْفِرَتُكَ أَوْسَعُ مِنْ ذُنُوبِي وَرَحْمَتُكَ أَرْجَى عِنْدِي مِنْ عَمَلِي(3)

Allāhumma maghfiratuka awsaʿu min dhunūbī, wa raḥmatuka arjā ʿindī min ʿamalī

O Allah, Your forgiveness is vaster than my sins, and Your mercy gives me more hope than my deeds

اللّٰهُمَّ صلِّ عَلَى سَيِّدِنَا مُحَمَّدٍ عَبْدِكَ ونَبِيِّكَ وَرَسُولِكَ النَّبِيِّ الأُمِّيِّ وَعَلَى آلِهِ وَصَحبِهِ وَسَلِّمْ تسْليماً ، بِقَدْرِ عَظَمَةِ ذَاتِكَ فِي كُلِّ وَقْتٍ وَحِينٍ(3)

Allāhumma ṣalli ʿalā sayyidinā Muḥammadin, ʿabdika wa nabiyyika, wa rasūliki-n-nabiyyi-l-ummiyi, wa ʿalā a̱lihi wa ṣaḥbihi wa sallim taslīmā, bi qadri ʿaẓamati dhātika fī kulli waqtin wa ḥīn

O Allah! Send blessings to our master Muḥammad, Your servant, Prophet, and Envoy, the Unlettered Prophet, and send to his Family and Companions, salutations upon salutations of peace as infinite as the infinitude of Your Essence, at every time and place

سُبْحَانَ رَبِّكَ رَبِّ الْعِزَّةِ عَمَّا يَصِفُونَ ، وَسَلَامٌ عَلَى الْمُرْسَلِينَ،
وَالْحَمْدُ لِلَّهِ رَبِّ الْعَالَمِينَ

Subḥāna Rabbika Rabbi-l-ʿizzati ʿammā yaṣifūn, wa salāmun ʿala-l-mursalīn, wa-l-ḥamdu li-Llāhi Rabbi-l-ʿālamīn.

Glorified be your Lord, Lord of Honor, above all they attribute to Him, and Peace be upon all the Messengers, and Praise be to Allah, Lord of the Worlds

اللَّهُمَّ إِنَّا نَسْأَلُكَ فِعْلَ الْخَيْرَاتِ وَتَرْكَ الْمُنْكَرَاتِ وَحُبَّ الْمَسَاكِينِ،
وَإِذَا أَرَدْتَ بِعِبَادِكَ فِتْنَةً فَاقْبِضْنَا إِلَيْكَ غَيْرَ مَفْتُونِينَ . (3) آمين آمين آمين

Allāhumma innā nas•aluka fiʿl al-khayrāti wa tarka–l-munkarāti wa ḥubba–l-masākīn wa idhā aradta bi ʿibādika fitnatan, fa-qbiḍnā ilayka ghayra maftūnīn. (3) Āmīn Āmīn Āmīn

O Allah, we ask of You (that we might accomplish) what is good, and abandon what is reprehensible, and (that we might) love the poor, and that, if You will for servants tribulation, You take us unto You with our faith intact. Amen! Amen! Amen!

سُبْحَانَ رَبِّكَ رَبِّ الْعِزَّةِ عَمَّا يَصِفُونَ ، وَسَلَامٌ عَلَى الْمُرْسَلِينَ،
وَالْحَمْدُ لِلَّهِ رَبِّ الْعَالَمِينَ

Subḥāna Rabbika Rabbi-l-ʿizzati ʿammā yaṣifūn, wa salāmun ʿala-l-mursalīn, wa-l-ḥamdu li-Llāhi Rabbi-l-ʿālamīn.

Glorified be your Lord, Lord of Honor, above all they attribute to Him, and Peace be upon all the Messengers, and Praise be to Allah, Lord of the Worlds

سُبْحَانَ الله (33) الْحَمْدُ لِلهِ (33) اللهُ أَكْبَر (33)

Subḥān Allāh (33), al-ḥamdu li-Llāh (33), Allāhu akbar (33)

Glory to Allah, Praise to Allah, Allah is greater

لَا إِلَٰهَ إِلاَّ اللهُ وَحْدَهُ لَا شَرِيكَ لَهُ ، لَهُ الْمُلْكُ وَلَهُ الحَمْدُ ، وَهُوَ عَلَى كُلِّ شَيْءٍ قَدِيرٌ

Lā ilāha illa-Llāh, waḥdahu lā sharīka lah(u), lahu-l-mulku wa lahu-l-ḥamd, wa huwa ʿalā kulli shay•in qadīr

There is no god but Allah, One, without partner, His is sovereignty and His the Praise, and He, over all things, has power.

أَسْتَغْفِرُ اللهَ (٣) الْحَمْدُ لِلهِ وَالشُّكْرُ لِلهِ (٣) لَا حَوْلَ وَلَا قُوَّةَ إِلَّا بِاللهِ (3)

Astaghfiru Llāh (3), al-ḥamdu li-Llāh wa-sh-shukru li-Llāh (3), lā ḥawlā wa lā quwwata illā bi- l-Llāh

I ask forgiveness from Allah. Praise be to Allah and thanks be to Allah. There is no power nor strength but in Allah, the Sublime and All-Mighty

اللَّهُمَّ إِنَّا نَسْتَودِعُكَ دِينَنَا وَ إِيمَانَنَا فَاحْفَظْهُمَا عَلَينَا حِفظًا مُحَمَّدِيًا فِي حَيَاتِنَا وَعِنْدَ مَمَاتِنَا وَبَعْدَ وَفَاتِنَا ، وَارْزُقْنَا كَمَالَهُمَا بِمُتَابَعَتِهِ صَلَّى اللهُ عَلَيهِ وَسَلَّمَ فِي الأَقْوَالِ والأَفْعَالِ وَالأَخْلَاقِ واالأَحْوَالِ ، مُرِيدِينَ بِذَٰلِكَ وَجْهَكَ الْكَرِيمَ ، يَا أَكْرَمَ الأَكْرَمِين . آمين .

Allāhumma innā nastawdiʿuka dīnanā wa īmānanā faḥfaẓhumā ʿalaynā ḥifẓan muḥammadiyyan fī ḥayātinā wa ʿinda mamātinā wa baʿda wafātinā, wa-rzuqnā kamālahumā bi mutābaʿatihi ṣalla-Llāhu ʿalayhi wa sallam, fi-l-aqwāli wa-l-afʿāli wa-l-akhlāqi wa-l-aḥwāl, murīdīna bi dhālika wajhaka'l-karīm, ya akrama-l-akramīn. Āmīn.

O Allah, we place in Your care our religion and our faith. Protect them both for us with Muḥammadan protection during our lives and at the time of our deaths and after our passing away, and grant us their completion by following (the Prophet ﷺ) in our speech and our actions and our character and our states, aspiring in that way to Your Noble Face. O most noble of those who are noble. Amen.

﴿ بِسْمِ اللهِ الرَّحْمَٰنِ الرَّحِيمِ * الْحَمْدُ لِلهِ رَبِّ الْعَالَمِينَ ..الخ﴾ ..أمين

Bismi-Llāhi-r-Raḥmāni-r-Raḥīm ✶ Al-ḥamdu li-Llāhi Rabbi-l-ʿĀlamīn ✶ Ar-Raḥmāni-r-Raḥīm ✶ Maliki yawmi-d-dīn ✶ iyyāka naʿbudu wa iyyāka nastaʿīn ✶ Ihdina-ṣ-ṣirāṭa-l-mustaqīm ✶ ṣirāṭa-l-ladhīna anʿamta ʿalayhim, ghayri-l-maghḍūbi ʿalayhim wa la-ḍ-ḍāllīn ✶ Āmīn

Praise be to Allah, Lord of the worlds. The Merciful, the Compassionate. Sovereign of the Day of Judgment. You alone do we worship and You alone do we ask for help. Guide us along the straight path. The path of those whom You have graced, not those who have earned Your wrath nor those who go astray. Amen

﴿ اللهُ لاَ إِلَهَ إِلاَّ هُوَ ، الْحَيُّ الْقَيُّومُ . لاَ تَأْخُذُهُ سِنَةٌ وَلاَ نَوْمٌ . لَهُ مَا فِي السَّمَاوَاتِ وَمَا فِي الْأَرْضِ ، مَنْ ذَا الَّذِي يَشْفَعُ عِنْدَهُ إِلَّا بِإِذْنِهِ . يَعْلَمُ مَا بَيْنَ أَيْدِيهِمْ وَمَا خَلْفَهُمْ ، وَلَا يُحِيطُونَ بِشَيْءٍ مِنْ عِلْمِهِ إِلاَّ بِمَا شَاءَ . وَسِعَ كُرْسِيُّهُ السَّمَاوَاتِ وَالْأَرْضَ ، وَلَا يَئُودُهُ حِفْظُهُمَا ، وَهُوَ الْعَلِيُّ الْعَظِيمُ ﴾

Allāhu lā ilāha illā huwa l-ḥayyu l-qayyūm. Lā tākhudhuhu sinatun wa lā nawm. Lahu mā fī-s-samāwāti wa mā fī l-arḍ, Man dhā 'l-ladhī yashfaʿu ʿindahu illā bi-idhnihi. Yaʿlamu mā bayna aydīhim wamā khalfahum. Wa lā yuḥīṭūna bi shay'in min ʿilmihi illā bi mā shā'. Wasiʿa kursiyyuhu-s-samāwāti wa'l-arḍ, Wa lā ya'ūduhu ḥifẓuhumā, wa huwa l-ʿaliyyu l-ʿaẓīm

Allah, there is no god but He, the Living, the Self-Subsisting. Neither slumber overtakes Him nor sleep. To Him belongs whatsoever is in the heavens and whatsoever is on the earth. Who is there who may intercede with Him save by His leave? He knows that which is before them and that which is behind them. And they encompass nothing of His Knowledge, save what He wills. His Kursi embraces the heavens and the earth. Protecting them tires Him not, and He is the Exalted, the Mighty. (2:253-254)

﴿ آمَنَ الرَّسُولُ بِمَا أُنْزِلَ إِلَيْهِ مِنْ رَبِّهِ وَالْمُومِنُونَ . كُلٌّ آمَنَ بِاللهِ
وَمَلَائِكَتِهِ وَكُتُبِهِ وَرُسُلِهِ. لَا نُفَرِّقُ بَيْنَ أَحَدٍ مِنْ رُسُلِهِ . وَقَالُوا سَمِعْنَا
وَأَطَعْنَا غُفْرَانَكَ رَبَّنَا وَإِلَيْكَ الْمَصِيرُ . لَا يُكَلِّفُ اللهُ نَفْسًا إِلَّا وُسْعَهَا.
لَهَا مَا كَسَبَتْ وَعَلَيْهَا مَا اكْتَسَبَتْ. رَبَّنَا لَا تُؤَاخِذْنَا إِنْ نَسِينَا أَوْ أَخْطَأْنَا.
رَبَّنَا وَلَا تَحْمِلْ عَلَيْنَا إِصْرًا كَمَا حَمَلْتَهُ عَلَى الَّذِينَ مِنْ قَبْلِنَا. رَبَّنَا وَلَا
تُحَمِّلْنَا مَا لَا طَاقَةَ لَنَا بِهِ ، وَاعْفُ عَنَّا وَاغْفِرْ لَنَا وَارْحَمْنَا. أَنْتَ مَوْلَانَا ،
فَانْصُرْنَا عَلَى الْقَوْمِ الْكَافِرِينَ ﴾

A̲mana-r-rasūlu bimā unzila ilayhi min rabbihi wal-mūminūn. Kullun ā̲mana bi-l-Lāhi wa malā•ikatihi wa kutubihi wa rusulih(i). Lā nufarriqu bayna aḥadin min rusulih(i). Wa qālū: samiʿnā wa-aṭaʿnā ghufrānaka, Rabbanā, wa-ilayka l-maṣīr. Lā yukallifu l-Lāhu nafsan illā wusʿahā. Lahā mā kasabat waʿalayhā mā iktasabat. Rabbanā lā tu•ākhidhnā in nasīnā aw akhṭa'nā. Rabbanā walā taḥmil ʿalaynā iṣran kamā ḥamaltahu ʿalā alladhīna min qablinā. Rabbanā walā tuḥammilnā mā lā ṭāqata lanā bihi, waʿfu ʿannā, wa-ghfir lanā, wa-rḥamnā. Anta mawlānā fa-nṣurnā ʿalā l-qawmi l-kāfirīn

The Messenger believes in what was sent down to him from his Lord, as do the believers. Each believes in Allah, His angels, His Books, and His messengers. "We make no distinction between any of His messengers," And they say, "We hear and obey. Your forgiveness, our Lord! And to You is the journey's end." God does not burden a soul beyond its capacity. For it (is only) what it has earned, and against it (only) what it has deserved. "Our Lord, take us not to task if we forget or err! Lord, do not burden us as You burdened those before us. Lord, do not burden us with more than we have strength to bear. Pardon us, forgive us, and have mercy upon us. You are our Protector, so help us against disbelieving people."

(2:284-285)

﴿ شَهِدَ اللهُ أَنَّهُ لاَ إِلَهَ إِلاَّ هُوَ وَالْمَلاَئِكَةُ وَأُوْلُواْ الْعِلْمِ قَآئِماً بِالْقِسْطِ ، لاَ إِلَهَ إِلاَّ هُوَ ، الْعَزِيزُ الْحَكِيمُ . إِنَّ الدِّينَ عِندَ اللهِ الإِسْلاَمُ ﴾

Shahida-Llāhu annahu lā ilāha illā huwa, wa'l-malā•ikatu wa-ulū l-ʿilmi qā•iman bi'l-qisṭ(i). Lā ilāha illā huwa-l-ʿazīzu-l-ḥakīm. Inna d-dīna ʿinda-l-Lāhi'l-islām.

Allah bears witness that there is no god but He, as do the angels and the possessors of knowledge, upholding justice. There is no god but He, the Mighty, the Wise. Truly religion before Allah is submission (al-Islām). (3:18)

﴿ قُلِ اللَّهُمَّ مَالِكَ الْمُلْكِ تُوتِي الْمُلْكَ مَن تَشَاءُ وَتَنْزِعُ الْمُلْكَ مِمَّن تَشَاءُ ، وَتُعِزُّ مَن تَشَاءُ وَتُذِلُّ مَن تَشَاءُ ، بِيَدِكَ الْخَيْرُ ، إِنَّكَ عَلَى كُلِّ شَيْءٍ قَدِيرٌ. تُولِجُ اللَّيلَ فِي النَّهَارِ وَتُولِجُ النَّهَارَ فِي اللَّيلِ ، وَتُخْرِجُ الْحَيَّ مِنَ الْمَيِّتِ وَتُخْرِجُ الْمَيتَ مِنَ الْحَيِّ وَتَرْزُقُ مَن تَشَاءُ بِغَيْرِ حِسَاب ﴾

Quli-l-Lāhumma mālika l-mulki, tūtī -l-mulka man tashā•u wa tanziʿu l-mulka mimman tashā•u, wa tuʿizzu man tashā•u wa tudhillu man tashā•u, bi yadika -l-khayr(u). Innaka ʿalā kulli shay•in qadīr(u). Tūliju-l-layla fi-n-nahāri wa tūliju-n-nahāra fi-l-layl, wa tukhriju-l-ḥayya mina-l-mayyiti wa tukhriju-l-mayyita mina-l-ḥayy, wa tarzuqu man tashā•u bi ghayri ḥisāb.

Say, "O Allah, Owner of sovereignty, You give sovereignty to whom You will and You take sovereignty away from whom You will. You honor whom You will and You humble whom You will. In Your hand is [all] goodness, and indeed, You over all things have power. You cause the night to pass into the day and You cause the day to pass into the night, You bring forth the living from the dead and You bring forth the dead from the living, and You provide for whomsoever You will without measure." (3:26-27)

﴿ لَقَدْ جَآءَكُمْ رَسُولٌ مِنَ انْفُسِكُمْ عَزِيزٌ عَلَيهِ مَا عَنِتُّمْ ، حَـرِيصٌ عَلَيكُم ، بِالْمُومِنِينَ رَؤُوفٌ رَّحِيمٌ
فَإِنْ تَوَلَّوْا فَقُلْ حَسْبِيَ اللهُ ، لَآ إِلَٰهَ إِلَّا هُوَ ، عَلَيهِ تَوَكَّلْتُ ، وَهُوَ رَبُّ الْعَرْشِ الْعَظِيمِ ﴾

Laqad jā•akum rasūlun min anfusikum, ʿazīzun ʿalayhi mā ʿanittum, ḥarīṣun ʿalaykum, bi-l-mūminīna ra•ūfu-r-raḥīm. Fa in tawallaw, fa qul: ḥasbiya-Llāhu, lā ilāha illā Hu, ʿalayhi tawakkaltu, wa Huwa Rabbu-l-ʿArshi-l-ʿAẓīm

There has come to you a messenger from among yourselves, distressed if you suffer, anxious for your (welfare), full of compassion and mercy for the faithful But if they turn away, say, Allah is my sufficiency. There is no god but He. In Him I put my trust, and He is the Lord of the Mighty Throne. (9:129)

ثم تقرأ سورة الإخلاص (٣) ثم سورة الفلق (٣) و سورة الناس (٣)

[*Then recite sūrat al-Ikhlāṣ 3 times, sūrat al-Falaq 3 times, and sūrat al-Nās 3 times*]

اللّٰهُمَّ أَنْتَ رَبِّي ، لا إِلٰهَ إِلاَّ أَنْتَ خَلَقْتَنِي وَأَنَا عَبْدُكَ وَأَنَا عَلَى عَهْدِكَ وَوَعْدِكَ مَا اسْتَطَعْتُ ، أَعُوذُ بِكَ مِنْ شَرِّ مَا صَنَعْتُ ، أَبُوءُ لَكَ بِنِعْمَتِكَ عَلَيَّ وَأَبُوءُ بِذَنْبِي ، فَاغْفِرْ لِي ، فَإِنَّهُ لا يَغْفِرُ الذُّنُوبَ إِلاَّ أَنْتَ .
رَبِّ اغْفِرْلِي وَارْحَمْنِي وَتُبْ عَلَيَّ إِنَّكَ أَنْتَ التَّوَّابُ الرَّحِيمُ .

Allāhumma anta rabbī. Lā ilāha illā ant(a). Khalaqtanī wa ana ʿabduka wa ana ʿalā ʿahdika wa waʿdika ma-staṭaʿt (u). Aʿūdhu bika min sharri mā ṣanaʿt(u). Abū'u laka bi niʿamatika ʿalayya wa abū'u bi dhanbī, faghfirlī, fa innahu lā yaghfiru–dh-dhunūba illā ant(a) Rabbi-gh-firlī wa-r-ḥamnī wa tub ʿalayya, innaka Anta -t-Tawwābu -r-Raḥīm.

O Allah, You are my Lord. There is no god except You. You created me and I am your servant, and I am keeping Your covenant and Your promise as much as I can. I seek refuge in You from the wrong I have wrought. I acknowledge Your grace to me and I acknowledge my sin, so forgive me, for truly no one forgives sins except You. Lord forgive me and have mercy upon me and accept my repentance. You are truly the the Ever-Turning and the All-Merciful.

﴿بِسْمِ اللهِ الرَّحْمٰنِ الرَّحِيمِ . الْحَمْدُ لِلّٰهِ الَّذِي خَلَقَ السَّمَاوَاتِ
وَالْأَرْضَ وَجَعَلَ الظُّلُمَاتِ وَالنُّورَ، ثُمَّ الَّذِينَ كَفَرُوا بِرَبِّهِم
يَعْدِلُونَ، هُوَ الَّذِي خَلَقَكُم مِّنْ طِينٍ ثُمَّ قَضَى أَجَلاً، وَأَجَلٌ مُّسَمًّى
عِنْدَهُ، ثُمَّ أَنْتُمْ تَمْتَرُونَ . وَهُوَ اللهُ فِي السَّمَاوَاتِ وَفِي الْأَرْضِ يَعْلَمُ
سِرَّكُمْ وَجَهْرَكُمْ وَيَعْلَمُ مَا تَكْسِبُونَ﴾

Al-ḥamdu li-l-Lāhi-l-ladhī khalaqa s-samāwāti wa l-arḍa wa-jaʿala -ẓ-ẓulumāti wa-n-nūr. Thumma'l-ladhīna kafarū bi rabbihim yaʿdilūn. Huwa'l-ladhī khalaqakum min ṭīnin thumma qaḍā ajala(n), wa-ajalun musamman ʿindahu, thumma antum tamtarūn. Wa huwa-l-Lāhu, fī s-samāwāti wa fī l-arḍi, yaʿlamu sirrakum wa jahrakum wa yaʿlamu mā taksibūn.

Praise be to Allah, Who created the heavens and the earth, and made darkness and light. Yet those who do not believe ascribe equals to their Lord. He it is Who created you from clay, then decreed a term. A term is appointed with Him – yet still you doubt. He is Allah, in the heavens and on the earth: He knows your secret and that which you make public, and He knows that which you earn.

(6:1-4)

﴿ الْحَمْدُ لِلهِ الَّذِي هَدَانَا لِهَٰذَا وَمَا كُنَّا لِنَهْتَدِيَ لَوْلَا أَنْ هَدَانَا اللهُ لَقَدْ جَاءَتْ رُسُلُ رَبِّنَا بِالْحَقِّ ﴾ اللَّهُمَّ لَكَ الْحَمْدُ. اللَّهُمَّ لَكَ الْحَمْدُ. اللَّهُمَّ لَكَ الْحَمْدُ.

Al-ḥamdu li-l-Lāhi-l-ladhī hadānā li hādhā wa mā kunnā li nahtadiya law lā an hadānā l-Lāh(u). Laqad jā•at rusulu Rabbinā bi-l-ḥaqq.
Allāhumma laka'l-ḥamd (3)

"Praise be to Allah who guided us to this. We would never have been guided if Allah had not guided us. Truly, the messengers of our Lord had come with the truth." (7:42)

O Allah, Yours is all praise.

REPEAT THREE TIMES

اللَّهُمَّ مَآ أَنْعَمْتَ بِهِ فَمِنْكَ بِكَ لَكَ ، وَحْدَكَ لَا شَرِيكَ لَكَ لَآ أُحْصِي ثَنَاءً عَلَيْكَ أَنْتَ كَمَا أَثْنَيْتَ عَلَى نَفْسِكَ

Allāhumma, mā̲ anᶜmta bihi, fa minka bika lak, waḥdaka lā sharīka lak(a). Lā̲ uḥṣī thanā•an ᶜalayka anta kamā athnayta ᶜalā nafsik(a)

O Allāh, what You have given (us) by Your grace is from You, by You, and for You, You alone, You without partner. I cannot enumerate the praise due to You. You are as You have praised Yourself.

مَا شَاءَ اللهُ . لَا قُوَّةَ إِلَّا بِاللهِ (٣) الْحَمْدُ لِلهِ رَبِّ الْعَالَمِين

Mā shā' Allāh, lā quwwata illā bi-l-Lāh (3).
Al-ḥamdu li-l-Lāhi Rabbi-l-ᶜālamīn.

(This is what) Allah wills, there is no power except through Allah. Praise be to Allah Lord of the worlds.

[Then raise your hands invoking blessings upon the Prophet ﷺ and pray for his Family, all those near to Allah, your teachers in the way, and parents, brethren, friends, and all Muslims. Then say:]

اللّٰهُمَّ صَلِّ عَلَى سَيِّدِنَا مُحَمَّدٍ عَبدِكَ وَرَسُولِكَ النَّبِيِّ الأُمِّيِّ ، وَعَلَى آلِهِ وَصَحْبِهِ وَسَلِّمْ (3) وَ في الثالثة تقول (وَسَلِّمْ تَسْلِيمًا)

Allāhumma ṣalli ʿalā Sayyidinā Muḥammadin, ʿabdika wa rasūlika-n-nabiyyi-l-ummīyi, wa ʿalā ālihi wa ṣaḥbihi wa sallim (3) and to the third repetition you add *taslīmā,*

O Allah, send blessings to our master Muḥammad, Your servant and messenger, the unlettered prophet, and to his Family and Companions, and greetings upon greetings of peace.

اللّٰهُمَّ إِنَّا نَسْأَلُكَ إِيمَانًا دَائِمًا ، وَنَسْأَلُكَ قَلْبًا خَاشِعًا ، وَنَسْأَلُكَ عِلْمًا نَافِعًا، وَنَسْأَلُكَ يَقِينًا صَادِقًا ، وَنَسْأَلُكَ دِينًا قَيِّمًا ، وَنَسْأَلُكَ الْعَافِيَةَ مِنْ كُلِّ بَلِيَّةٍ ، وَنَسْأَلُكَ تَمَامَ الْعَافِيَةِ ، وَنَسْأَلُكَ دَوَامَ الْعَافِيَةِ ، وَنَسْأَلُكَ الشُّكْرَ عَلَى الْعَافِيَةِ ، وَنَسْأَلُكَ الْغِنَى عَنِ النَّاسِ .

Allāhumma innā nas'aluka īmānan dā'iman, wa nas'aluka qalban khāshiʿan, wa nas'aluka ʿilman nāfiʿan, wa nas'aluka yaqīnan ṣādiqan, wa nas'aluka dīnan qayyiman, wa nas'aluka-l-ʿāfiyata min kulli baliyyat(in), wa nas'aluka tamāma-l-ʿāfiya, wa nas'aluka dawāma-l-ʿāfiya, wa nas'aluka-sh-shukra ʿāla-l-ʿāfiya, wa nas'aluka-l-ghinā ʿani-n-nās.

O Allah, we truly ask You for constant faith, and we ask You for humble hearts, and we ask You for useful knowledge, and we ask You for genuine certitude, and we ask You for upright religion, and we ask You for well-being (that delivers us) from every trial, and we ask You for complete well-being, and we ask You for constant well-being, and we ask You for gratitude for well-being, and we ask You for independence from people.

اللّٰهُمَّ أَحْسِنْ عَاقِبَتَنَا فِي الْأُمُورِ كُلِّهَا وَأَجِرْنَا مِنْ خِزْيِ الدُّنْيَا
وَعَذَابِ الْآخِرَةِ

Allāhumma aḥsin ʿāqibatanā fi-l-umūri kullihā, wa ajirnā min
khizyi -d-dunyā wa ʿadhābi-l-ākhira.

*O Allah, make goodly the outcome of all our concerns and deliver us from disgrace
in this world and punishment in the Next.*

اللّٰهُمَّ يَا لَطِيفُ نَسْأَلُكَ اللُّطْفَ فِي مَا جَرَتْ بِهِ الْمَقَادِيرُ ﴿٣﴾

Allāhumma yā Laṭīfu nas'aluka-l-luṭfa fī mā jarat bihi-l-maqādīr. (3)

*O Allah, the Infinitely Kind, we ask for Your infinite kindness in however matters
that are destined unfold.*

﴿سُبْحَانَ رَبِّكَ رَبِّ الْعِزَّةِ عَمَّا يَصِفُونَ ۞ وَسَلَامٌ عَلَى الْمُرْسَلِينَ ۞
وَالْحَمْدُ لِلّٰهِ رَبِّ الْعَالَمِينَ﴾

Subḥāna Rabbika Rabbi-l-ʿizzati ʿammā yaṣifūn, wa salāmun
ʿala-l-mursalīn, wa-l-ḥamdu li-Llāhi Rabbi-l-ʿālamīn.

*Glorified be your Lord, Lord of Honor, above all they attribute to Him, and Peace
be upon all the Messengers, and Praise be to Allah,
Lord of the Worlds. (37: 180-182)*

Dhikr of Fajr

An aspirant should try not to miss some (supererogatory) rakaʿāt a little before the (call for the) Fajr prayer, and then should invoke blessings upon the Prophet ﷺ with the well-known Ṣalāt al-Mashīshiyya, followed by invocation of the Name Allāh 660 times. And after the call for the Fajr prayer is made and after having offered the supererogatory prayer of two bowings which is sunna before the Fajr prayer, an aspirant should invoke:

(يَا حَيُّ يَا قَيُّومُ ، لَا إِلٰهَ إِلاَّ أَنتَ) [إحدى وأربعين مرة]

Yā Ḥayy, Yā Qayyūm, Lā ilāha illā Ant (a)

O Living! O Eternal! There is no god but You. (x41)

(سُبْحَانَ اللهِ وبِحَمْدِهِ سُبْحَانَ اللهِ الْعَظِيمِ. أَسْتَغْفِرُ اللهَ) [عشراً]

Subḥān Allāhi wa bi ḥamdihi, subḥāna Allāhi-l-ʿAẓīm. Astaghfiru'Llāh.

Glory be to Allah and praise, glory be to Allah the All-Mighty.
I ask forgiveness of Allah. (x10)

اللهْ

Allāh (x7)

The pronunciation of the Name should be extended for as long as possible.

And then continue with the invocation of lā ilāha illa-Llāh and supplication until the call to stand for the Fajr prayer (al-iqāma) is made.

الصلاة المشيشية

Al-Ṣalāt al-Mashīshiyya

اللّٰهُمَّ صَلِّ عَلَىٰ مَنْ مِنْهُ انْشَقَّتِ الْأَسْرَارُ ، وَانْفَلَقَتِ الْأَنْوَارُ ، وَفِيهِ ارْتَقَتِ الْحَقَائِقُ ، وَتَنَزَّلَتْ عُلُومُ آدَمَ فَأَعْجَزَ الْخَلَائِقَ ، وَلَهُ تَضَاءَلَتِ الْفُهُومُ فَلَمْ يُدْرِكْهُ مِنَّا سَابِقٌ وَلَا لَاحِقٌ ، فَرِيَاضُ الْمَلَكُوتِ بِزَهْرِ جَمَالِهِ مُونِقَةٌ ، وَحِيَاضُ الْجَبَرُوتِ بِفَيْضِ أَنْوَارِهِ مُتَدَفِّقَةٌ ، وَلَا شَيْءَ إِلَّا وَهُوَ بِهِ مَنُوطٌ ، إِذْ لَوْلَا الْوَاسِطَةُ لَذَهَبَ كَمَا قِيلَ الْمَوْسُوطُ ، صَلَاةً تَلِيقُ بِكَ مِنْكَ إِلَيْهِ كَمَا هُوَ أَهْلُهُ ، اَللّٰهُمَّ إِنَّهُ سِرُّكَ الْجَامِعُ الدَّالُّ عَلَيْكَ ، وَحِجَابُكَ الْأَعْظَمُ الْقَائِمُ لَكَ بَيْنَ يَدَيْكَ ، اَللّٰهُمَّ أَلْحِقْنِي بِنَسَبِهِ ، وَحَقِّقْنِي بِحَسَبِهِ ، وَعَرِّفْنِي إِيَّاهُ مَعْرِفَةً أَسْلَمُ بِهَا مِنْ مَوَارِدِ الْجَهْلِ ، وَأَكْرَعُ بِهَا مِنْ مَوَارِدِ الْفَضْلِ ، وَاحْمِلْنِي عَلَىٰ سَبِيلِهِ إِلَىٰ حَضْرَتِكَ ، حَمْلًا مَحْفُوفًا بِنُصْرَتِكَ ، وَاقْذِفْ بِي عَلَى الْبَاطِلِ فَأَدْمَغَهُ ، وَزُجَّ بِي فِي بِحَارِ الْأَحَدِيَّةِ ، وَانْشُلْنِي مِنْ أَوْحَالِ التَّوْحِيدِ ، وَأَغْرِقْنِي فِي عَيْنِ بَحْرِ الْوَحْدَةِ ، حَتَّىٰ لَآ أَرَىٰ وَلَآ أَسْمَعَ وَلَآ أَجِدَ وَ لَآ أُحِسَّ إِلَّا بِهَا ، وَاجْعَلِ الْحِجَابَ الْأَعْظَمَ حَيَاةَ رُوحِي ، وَرُوحَهُ سِرَّ حَقِيقَتِي ، وَحَقِيقَتَهُ جَامِعَ عَوَالِمِي بِتَحْقِيقِ الْحَقِّ الْأَوَّلِ ، يَآ أَوَّلُ يَآ آخِرُ يَا ظَاهِرُ يَا بَاطِنُ ، اِسْمَعْ نِدَآئِي بِمَا سَمِعْتَ بِهِ نِدَآءَ عَبْدِكَ زَكَرِيَّا ، وَانْصُرْنِي بِكَ لَكَ ، وَأَيِّدْنِي بِكَ لَكَ ، وَاجْمَعْ بَيْنِي وَبَيْنَكَ ، وَحُلْ بَيْنِي وَبَيْنَ غَيْرِكَ ،

الله الله الله

The pronunciation of the Name should be extended for as long as possible.

إِنَّ الَّذِي فَرَضَ عَلَيْكَ الْقُرْآنَ لَرَادُّكَ إِلَىٰ مَعَادٍ

(رَبَّنَا آتِنَا مِن لَّدُنكَ رَحْمَةً وَهَيِّئْ لَنَا مِنْ أَمْرِنَا رَشَدًا) x3

إِنَّ اللَّهَ وَمَلَائِكَتَهُ يُصَلُّونَ عَلَى النَّبِيِّ يَا أَيُّهَا الَّذِينَ آمَنُوا صَلُّوا عَلَيْهِ
وَسَلِّمُوا تَسْلِيمًا

Allāhumma ṣalli ᶜalā man minhu-nshaqqati-l-asrār, wa-nfalaqati-l-anwār, wa fīhi-rtaqati-l-ḥaqā•iq, wa tanazzalat ᶜulūmu ā̱dama ᶜalayhi –s-salām, fa aᶜjaza-l-khalā•iq, wa lahu taḍā•alati-l-fuhūmu fa lam yudrikhu minnā sābiqun wa lā lāḥiq. Fa riyāḍu–l-malakūti bi zahri jamālihi mūniqa, wa ḥiyāḍu–l-jabarūti fi fayḍi anwārihi mutadaffiqa, Wa lā shay•a illā wa huwa bihi manūṭ, idh law lā-l-wāsiṭatu la dhahaba kamā qīla–l–mawsūṭ ṣalātan talīqu bika minka ilayhi kamā huwa ahlu. Allāhumma innahu sirruka–l-jāmiᶜu–d-dāllu ᶜalayk, wa ḥijābuka-l-aᶜẓamu-l-qā•imu laka bayna yadayk. Allāhumma alḥiqnī bi nasabih, wa ḥaqqiqnī bi ḥasabih, wa ᶜarrifnī iyyāhu maᶜrifatan aslamu bihā min mawāridi-l-jahl, wa akraᶜu bihā min mawāridi-l-faḍl, wa-ḥmilnī ᶜalā sabīlihi ilā ḥaḍratik, ḥamlan maḥfūfan bi nuṣratik, wa-qdhif bī ᶜala–l-bāṭili fa admaghu, wa zujja bī fī biḥāri-l-aḥadiyya, wa-nshulnī min awḥāli–t-tawḥīd, wa aghriqnī fī ᶜayni baḥri-l-waḥda, ḥattā lā̱ arā, wa lā̱ asmaᶜ, wa lā̱ ajida, wa lā̱ uḥissa illā bihā, wa-jᶜali-l-ḥijāba-l-aᶜẓama ḥayāta rūḥī, wa rūḥahu sirra ḥaqīqatī, wa ḥaqīqatahu jāmiᶜa ᶜawālimī, bi taḥqīqi–l-ḥaqqi–l-Awwali. Yā Awwalu, Yā Ākhiru, Yā Ẓāhiru, Yā Bāṭinu. Ismaᶜ nidā•ī bi mā samiᶜta bihi nidā' ᶜabdika Zakarīya ᶜalayhi as-salām. Wa-nṣurnī bika lak, wa ayyidnī bika lak, wa'jmaᶜ baynī wa baynak, wa ḥul baynī wa bayna ghayrik.

Allāh Allāh Allāh

(Inna-l-ladhī faraḍa ᶜalayka-l-Qur'ā̱na larādduka ilā maᶜād).

(Rabbanā ā̱tinā min ladunka raḥmatan wa hayyi' lanā
min amrinā rashadā.) x3

(Inna-Llāha wa malā•ikatahu yuṣallūna ᶜalā n-nabīy.
Yā ayyahu-l-ladhīna āmanū, ṣallū ᶜalayhi wa sallimū taslīma).

O Allah, bless the one from whom the Secrets dawned, and the Lights poured forth, and in whom arose the Truths, and (into whom) descended the sciences of Adam (upon whom be peace), so that he has rendered creatures powerless, and their understandings are diminished in his regard, so that none of us – neither predecessor nor successor – has truly known him. The meadows of the Malakūt are adorned with the blossoms of his beauty, and the pools of the Jabarūt overflow with the outpouring of his lights, and there exists nothing that is not linked to him: "Were it not for the mediator," as they say, "the one for whom he mediates would vanish." (Bless him) with a blessing befitting You, from You to him, as is his due. O Allah, he is Your Secret who unites and guides to You, and Your Supreme Veil raised up before You. O Allah, join me to his posterity and confirm me by his nobility, and cause me to know him with a knowledge by which I am delivered from the watering places of ignorance, and by which I may quench my thirst at the watering places of Favor. And bear me in his way to Your Presence with a bearing encompassed by Your aid, and hurl me against falsehood that I might strike at its brain, and plunge me into the Oceans of Oneness, and keep me back from the swamps of tawḥīd, and drown me in the center of the Ocean of Unity, so that I neither see nor hear nor am conscious nor feel except through it. And make of the Supreme Veil the life of my spirit, and of his spirit, the secret of my reality, and of his reality, the union of my worlds, by realization of the First Truth. O First, O Last, O Outward, O Inward! hear my call, as You heard the call of Your servant Zakariyya, upon whom be peace, and help me, by You, to You, and support me, by You, to You and unite me with You, and come between me and what is other than You.

Allah Allah Allah

Truly the One Who ordained the Qur'ān for you shall surely bring you back to the place of return. [28:85].

Our Lord, grant us mercy from Your Presence, and make of our plight right guidance [18:10].

Truly Allah and His angels invoke blessings upon the Prophet. O you who believe! Invoke blessings upon him, and greetings of peace! [33:56]